THE COMPLETE
PORK
COOK BOOK

THE COMPLETE
PORK
COOK BOOK

LOUISE SHERMAN SCHOON
& CORRINNE HARDESTY

5B

A SCARBOROUGH BOOK

STEIN AND DAY/*Publishers*/New York

To

Louis Who Tasted

and

Friends Who Advised

First Scarborough Books Edition 1979
The Complete Pork Cook Book was originally
published in hardcover by Stein and Day/*Publishers* in 1977
Copyright © 1977 by Louise Sherman Schoon and Corrinne Hardesty
All rights reserved.
Printed in the United States of America.
Stein and Day/*Publishers*/Scarborough House,
Briarcliff Manor, NY 10510

Library of Congress Cataloging in Publication Data

Schoon, Louise Sherman.
    The complete pork cook book.

    Includes index.
    1. Cookery (Pork)   I.   Hardesty, Corrinne, joint
author.   II.   Title.
TX749.S28   641.6'6'4   76-56672
ISBN 0-8128-6035-7

Contents

The Ancient and Honorable Pig

These recipes were collected in response to an acutely felt need. When Louise Sherman acquired a hog farm in Illinois, she took both a culinary and a financial interest in the use of pork. As both a practical and a gourmet cook, she set about looking for good recipes, more varied and imaginative than those the standard cook books yielded. The search was unrewarding. The business of originating, collecting, and testing recipes began. The idea of putting the results in book form was suggested by Corrinne Hardesty, reporter, war correspondent, and professional writer in other fields. This volume represents the joint efforts of the authors, who believe it will meet a need shared by others who cook for pleasure or because they must.

We seem to have lost sight of the fact that the pig is an ancient and honored animal, as well as a source of fine eating. The boar was sufficiently appreciated some forty thousand years ago to be represented in cave art on the walls of the Altamira caverns in Spain. He was also the emblem of the Roman Twentieth Legion. The sow was viewed respectfully by Greeks and Romans as the nourisher of Zeus. According to Darwin, the pig was domesticated in China around 5000 B.C., and ever since then the Chinese have recognized its value and delight as a food. Hogs came to the Western Hemisphere considerably ahead of the *Mayflower* passengers; Columbus brought eight on his second voyage.

The charm, good looks, and sagacity of pigs have been celebrated in fable, song, story, painting, and sculpture. Southey, Shelley, and Hood wrote poems of distinction about them; Rubens, Rembrandt, and Gainsborough, among others, included them in famous paintings. The hog's image decorates beautifully illuminated medieval manuscripts; his carved likeness adorns many famous cathedrals, on choir stalls, bench ends, pulpits, fonts, and altar screens.

The amiable temperament, talent, and playfulness of pigs are delightfully portrayed in pictures and images of pigs dancing, of pigs playing the fiddle, the harp (instrument of angels), and even bagpipes. A statue

of a sow and her farrow enlivens the Vatican Museum. Aesop wrote a
fable about a sow that cunningly outwitted a wolf, and the Chinese have
a story about a hog that warned his owner about a coming storm.

The pig's physical beauty was appreciated and recorded by Chesterton
in his essay "The Uses of Diversity," where he wrote that "the lines of
the pig . . . loveliest and most luxuriant in nature," and he declared the
hog has a "universal kind of shapeliness." Anyone can appreciate the
jauntiness of a little pig as it scampers about, tail tightly curled.

Better known to us, perhaps, than his contribution to the fine arts are
the hog's gifts to our language. Among the many enrichments we owe to
him are "in a pig's eye" (Chaucer used "pig's eye" as a term of
endearment), "a pig in a poke," "pig iron," "hogshead" and "pigtail"
(which meant a twist of tobacco before it meant a braid of human hair).

Reasons for the culinary neglect of pork are even harder to under-
stand. It is the most versatile of all meats: it may be cooked quickly or
slowly, indoors or out, by all standard cooking methods; it has many
different cuts, each unique, and almost nothing is wasted ("you can eat
all of the pig but the squeal"); it may be frozen, dried, smoked, or
canned; it can be the prime ingredient of casserole, stew, or salad,
making it useful and readily disguised as a leftover; it can be an elegant
entrée for dinners honoring distinguished guests.

Pork is high in nutritive value, and once it was somewhat less
expensive than other meats. This last may account in part for its fall
from social grace and thereby its disregard by some cooks and its skimpy
treatment by cook book writers. But it can no longer be considered "the
poor man's dish" (nor, alas, can any other meat!), and there is no
justification for its long neglect.

Pork deserves to be considered elegant party fare, worthy of the finest
menu and the best wine. We believe this book provides the recipes to
prove it. There are people who have always used pork because they like
it, other considerations notwithstanding; they will welcome these recipes.
Others who like pork have been discouraged by the paucity of interesting
ways to cook it; this is the book for them, too. Those who do not know
the merits of pork will be happily surprised.

Even though there are more than four hundred recipes in this
collection, we feel we have barely begun to explore the possibilities of
pork cookery. The field is far from exhausted. Any imaginative and
enterprising cook can devise and discover other appetizing pork dishes.
We hope every user of this book will try variations on our themes and
that they will enjoy the results.

HOW TO BUY PORK

The average consumption of pork in the United States is said to be about 56 pounds per person per year. For a family of four this comes to a sizable purchase. If you buy in the retail market, it behooves you to know what you are getting for your money.

This means, first of all, knowing the cut you are buying. In the past, naming of retail pork cuts seems to have been largely a matter of local preference of the butchers, and sometimes just whimsy. Now The National Live Stock and Meat Board, through its Meat Identification Standards Committee, is making a valiant effort to have retail cut names conform to an overall system of nomenclature. Compliance, which is voluntary, is increasing, and we have incorporated these standardized retail designations as far as possible in this book, believing the Board's standardization program will be a great help. Knowledge of the basic anatomical structure of the hog and the retail cuts that come from it will certainly assist you as both buyer and cook.

Wholesalers designate seven "primal" cuts. From these the retail buyer gets a wide choice of cuts, and knowing their source helps you judge quality, tenderness, flavor, and the best cooking method.

The primal cuts and the retail cuts that come from them are indicated in the accompanying diagrams.

If you are buying by eye alone, look for pink or grayish pink lean meat, white fat, and pink to red bone. Grayish pink indicates a younger animal. Flesh should be firm, not flabby, and its texture should appear fine. Pork in good condition is odorless.

You will take one of three approaches to determine the quantity you buy. You may buy for a specified number, for a given meal. If you are buying for family members, you will want to consider not only how many there are but the sizes of their appetites. A laboring husband will obviously eat more than his three-year-old daughter; his teen-age son may eat twice as much. When guests are included, consider how

1

generous you want to be about the size of servings and whether to offer "seconds." Generally, luncheon servings are smaller than those for dinner.

An economical way to buy pork is to consider planned leftovers. A number of cuts make excellent planned-over dishes. This approach to buying means taking the planned-over meal into account at the time you shop for the original meal.

A third possibility is to buy a large part of a side and have it cut up by the butcher. Although there can be savings, you will likely be concerned about the relatively heavy initial outlay, adequate storage space, and whether all the meat can be conveniently consumed before it begins to deteriorate in storage.

A modification of this kind of buying is to purchase a whole ham, for example, and have the butcher cut it into two roasts and then have him trim one or more slices from the center. A whole ham may seem to be expensive, but it can be an economical buy. A plump ham with a short, stumpy shank is best. The extreme shank end (the hock) may be removed and used separately in a number of ways. A whole loin may be bought and cut into roasts and chops.

Many of the recipes in this book clearly indicate, by the meat cut, how many servings they will provide. For example, we have assumed the chop buyer will decide how many chops per person are appropriate. Authorities differ somewhat as to just how many servings a given weight of a specified cut will provide. The accompanying chart is the most authoritative we can offer. Use it as a guide and supplement it with your own experience.

ANATOMICAL SOURCES OF FREQUENTLY USED RETAIL PORK CUTS

(CAPITAL LETTERS indicate ANATOMICAL LOCATIONS. Lower case indicate Retail cuts.)

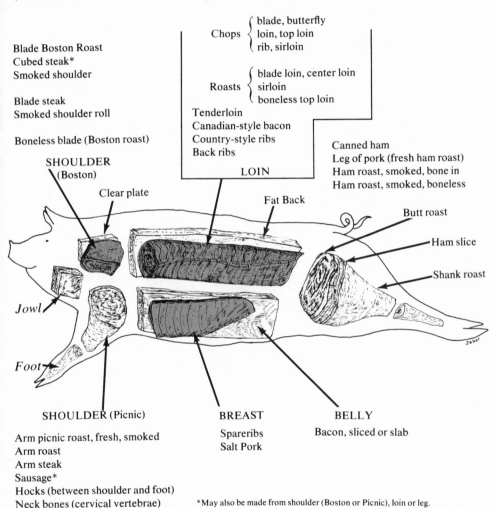

Chops
- blade, butterfly
- loin, top loin
- rib, sirloin

Roasts
- blade loin, center loin
- sirloin
- boneless top loin

Blade Boston Roast
Cubed steak*
Smoked shoulder

Blade steak
Smoked shoulder roll

Boneless blade (Boston roast)

SHOULDER (Boston)

Clear plate

Tenderloin
Canadian-style bacon
Country-style ribs
Back ribs

LOIN

Fat Back

Canned ham
Leg of pork (fresh ham roast)
Ham roast, smoked, bone in
Ham roast, smoked, boneless

Butt roast

Ham slice

Shank roast

Jowl

Foot

SHOULDER (Picnic)

Arm picnic roast, fresh, smoked
Arm roast
Arm steak
Sausage*
Hocks (between shoulder and foot)
Neck bones (cervical vertebrae)

BREAST

Spareribs
Salt Pork

BELLY

Bacon, sliced or slab

*May also be made from shoulder (Boston or Picnic), loin or leg.

Adapted from NATIONAL LIVE STOCK AND MEAT BOARD

RETAIL CUTS OF PORK

Courtesy American Meat Institute

SMOKED BONE-IN HAM

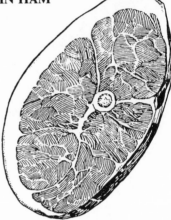

WHOLE HAM

HAM—CENTER SLICE

HAM SHANK

BONELESS HAM

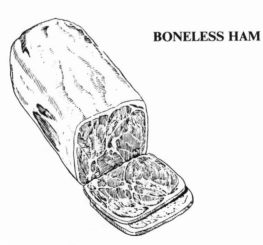

"BOILED" OR COOKED HAM

CANNED HAM (whole)

CUTS FROM THE PORK LOIN

LOIN ROASTS

LOIN PORK CHOP

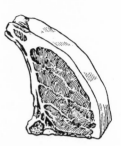

RIB PORK CHOP

CANADIAN-STYLE BACON

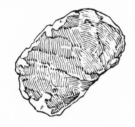

PORK TENDERLOIN FILLET

MISCELLANEOUS PORK CUTS

PORK HOCKS

SPARERIBS

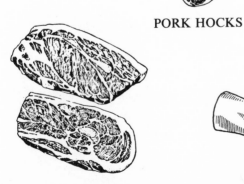

PORK SHOULDER STEAKS   PORK FEET

SHOULDER CUTS

SMOKED PICNIC   SHOULDER BUTT (fresh)

BONELESS SMOKED SHOULDER BUTT

BACON

SLAB BACON   SLICED BACON

SALT PORK

GUIDE TO SERVINGS PER POUND

CHOPS

Blade	3
Boneless	4
Loin	4
Rib	4

STEAKS

Ham, smoked (center slice)	5
Ham, fresh	4

ROASTS

Boneless leg (fresh ham)	3½
Bone-in leg (fresh ham)	3
Ham, smoked, bone-in	3–3½
Ham, smoked, boneless	5
Smoked shoulder roll	3
Blade loin	2
Top loin, rolled, boneless, fresh or smoked	2½–3½
Center loin	2½
Sirloin	2
Canned ham	5
Shoulder (Boston) boneless	3
Shoulder (picnic) bone-in, fresh, or smoked	2

OTHER CUTS

Country-style ribs	1½
Spareribs	1–1½
Tenderloin, whole	4
Bacon, sliced	6
Canadian-style bacon	5
Sausage	4
Hocks, fresh or smoked	1½
Cubes, fresh or smoked	4

For further guidance, write the Superintendent of Documents, U.S. Government Printing Office, Washington, D.C. 20402 for Department of Agriculture Home and Garden Bulletin No. 160, "Pork in Family Meals: A Guide for Consumers." You may also be able to obtain a copy from your local Home Economics Division, Food and Nutrition Service, of the U.S. Department of Agriculture.

HOW TO COOK
PORK

The proof of the pudding may be in the eating, but it is good cooking that ensures good eating. Cooking research has become a major undertaking. The old adages, the quaint methods, and the guessing and hoping have given way to the findings of university laboratories, cooking schools, nutrition authorities, and government and industry experiments. Cook book writers have taken note. In some instances past practices have present merit, but changes in food production and distribution call for reconsideration of old notions, and they frequently demand entirely new approaches.

Juices, flavor, aroma, and texture all enter into the proof of the eating. All are within the power of you, the cook, to modify. They respond to what you use and how you use it. You can wreck a prime cut; you can enhance a lesser one.

Time is of the essence. Cooking timetables for roasting are included with the roast recipes. The reliability and convenience of the meat thermometer cannot be overstressed. Cooking times, overall and for separate steps, have been specified in all recipes. Other general considerations with regard to timing are the size and shape of the cut; temperature of the meat when it goes into the cooking process (room, refrigerator, or frozen); proportion of bone to meat; amount and distribution of fat, and whether the meat is fresh or cured. The higher the heat the shorter the cooking time, the drier the meat, and the greater the shrinkage.

To a considerable extent you can control the tenderness of the meat you serve. The best tenderizer is correct cooking for the cut being served. While nearly any cut can be tenderized by boiling and stewing, these are not the methods of first choice for pork. Roasting preserves flavor and juices, thus making for tenderness. Simmering is recommended for certain cuts not suitable for roasting. The acids in marinades (vinegar,

8

wine, and lemon juice) act as tenderizing agents, helping to break down muscle fiber. White wine is usually preferable to red as it does not alter the delicate color of pork. Sour cream and tomatoes also act as tenderizers.

Seasoning is an art and a science. It has a long and honorable history, having been used by cooks since the beginning of cookery to enliven flavor and preserve food. We recommend in general a light touch here. A too-enthusiastic use of onion and garlic obliterates the delicacy of other spices used with them. In general salt and pepper are added to chops after they have been browned. If they are first coated with flour, they may be seasoned before browning.

Pork fat has long been a subject for controversy and misunderstanding. Better knowledge of the place of fat in the human diet has outmoded notions about its indigestibility. Pork no longer contains the high proportion of fat it once provided. Present breeding methods, the diet of hogs and their age at the time of marketing have erased the picture of the roly-poly pig. The modern hog goes to market younger and leaner than his forefathers. He is bred for meat, not for lard. Fat among the muscle fibers, called marbling, makes meat juicier and more tender. It is also a heat conductor and thus shortens cooking time.

Pork may be cooked by nearly every cooking method, although broiling is not generally recommended. As emphasized in other places in this book, pork must be thoroughly cooked. Broiling is not intended to do this. Our recipes specify which method to use.

The microwave oven's advantage is speed. It requires close attention. Crockery cookery is a long, slow process and requires only skilled inattention. Each method is limited to specialized recipes. This book concentrates on new, exciting, and imaginative ways to prepare an ancient delicacy by well-tested methods and with carefully considered ingredients. These should meet the needs of most cooks. We leave other methods to their special uses and further experimentation.

In looking toward the future, some metric equivalents of common cooking measurements are included.

HOW TO SERVE PORK

Skilled serving combines good looks and good cooking. It tempts the appetite and stimulates digestion. Planning ahead pays off at the moment of serving, as it does at every step of cookery. The basic plans include having adequate and appropriate serving dishes handy and hot. Make sure everything that will be served together finishes cooking together—no mean achievement. Garnishes should be ready and handily placed.

The meat sets the tone or style of the meal. A crown roast means a festive occasion, and the whole menu should reflect this. A chop for a hasty lunch deserves good but much simpler treatment. Other items on the menu are selected for their harmonizing or contrasting flavors, textures, and enhancing colors.

Don't overpower the taste buds. A meal too rich, too spicy, or too heavy is too much for discriminating eaters. On the other hand, one that is too bland, in either appearance or taste, causes a let-down feeling.

The ideal American diet—meat, vegetable, bread or other grain or starch, and fruit—provides a useful framework for menu making. Pork comes in a variety of cuts; it can be cooked by many methods, and is tastily served with almost every known vegetable. There is no excuse for monotony. The cook sometimes overlooks the fact that there are other foods to serve with pork besides applesauce and sweet potatoes, excellent as these are. Cauliflower and eggplant are two that enhance pork and are enhanced by it. The slightly bitter flavor of endive, the acid of tomatoes, and the subtle flavor of asparagus make them especially palatable with pork and are a special boon to variety meats. Butternut squash is a good companion to ham. A fruit or vegetable salad may supplement or take the place of a vegetable with this widely popular roast. Rice and noodles make good starch accompaniments. The flavors of stuffing and garnish should complement, not duplicate each other.

Fruit and pork make a happy couple. Spiced peaches and crab apples are old favorites. Prunes and plums make tasty additions to both chop and roast recipes. Apricots and figs provide a pleasingly delicate flavor. Pineapple, apples, tangerines, and oranges contribute welcome flavors and decorations. Cherries and grapes, with their tartness, and bananas, raisins, and currants, each with its distinctive flavor, continue but by no means exhaust the list of fruits to use with pork.

The charm of color is never wasted on food. It adds to the nutritive value of the meal by whetting the appetite and stimulating digestion. A plate of pale food gets a pale response. The contrast of green, yellow, and red vegetables, and the reds, pinks, and greens of garnishes make for a gay dish.

Well-cooked food deserves attractive serving, and the cook who takes the trouble to make what is good look good deserves and will reap a reward.

Wine with Pork

A great deal has been written about wines, but very little about the relationship of wines and pork. So, when you serve wine with any pork dish, you can be almost a pioneer. Certainly there is great latitude of choice. There are, of course, some helpful guidelines. First and foremost, remember that wine forms a partnership with the meal, a relationship in which each enhances and complements the other. However, wine has enemies, that is, foods that spoil its taste. These are vinegar, as in a tart, vinegary salad, and the kind of acid to be found in such citrus fruits as lemon, orange, and grapefruit. If your pork entrée has a preponderance of any of these, it would be wise to omit the wine. If you feel you absolutely must serve wine, then select one with enough flavor to stand up to any competition.

Of course it is perfectly true, and often stated, that with wines there is no substitute for experience. That doesn't mean we need to be experts. It does imply that experience will prevent our making choices that we regret. But if you select what you like and what is generally agreed is appropriate, your errors will be minimal. It is sometimes said that "when in doubt serve champagne." That sounds easy but obviously champagne is not always appropriate. For example, while it would be delightful with an elegant crown roast or a handsome fresh ham, it would be quite out of keeping with spareribs or a hominy casserole.

The old rule is that red wine should be served with red meat and white wine with white meat (pork and veal as well as such variety meats as sweetbreads). Nowadays, however, it is more honored in the breach than in the observance. As a matter of fact, there is some disagreement about classifying pork as a white or a red meat. Possibly, it is best to leave that argument aside and allow the determining factor to be how the meat is prepared and what is cooked with it. An extreme example of what not to do would be to serve a delicate white wine with pork hocks and sauerkraut. On the other hand, although you might otherwise prefer a dry dinner wine, chops cooked with pineapple could well be served with a slightly sweet white wine.

If you prefer red wine to white, or it seems more appropriate to the pork entrée you are serving, the authorities agree in recommending either a burgundy or a claret. If white is indicated then a white burgundy heads the preferred list. Rosé is between red and white and is, therefore, a compromise. But a compromise with much in its favor. Rosés range from dry to slightly sweet, but all are light-bodied and so should not be served with too hearty a dish. For that situation there is chianti, which goes well with dishes like Sausage-Sauced Spaghetti or Sausage Savory. Or perhaps you would like the Greek wine, retsina, for a strong-flavored casserole.

Ham is in a category by itself when it comes to wine. So here again it is wise to consider what goes into its preparation. For a beautiful big baked ham, either hot or cold, champagne or rosé might be indicated. However, a California zinfandel would be more unusual and consequently more interesting. If the ham is prepared with fruit, a lighter, sweeter wine would do it greater justice.

Wines and spirits are used in a number of the recipes in this book, and there are good reasons for this. Tenderizing is one of the special characteristics of wine. It helps to soften the fibers of meat and allows the flavors to penetrate. Dry wines are best for this purpose, and they can make a big difference in the final result, especially with inexpensive cuts. Remember, however, that red wine will discolor pork unless the meat is browned before the wine is added. Flavoring is the most usual purpose of wine in cooking. Where pork is concerned there are a few simple things to remember. Don't be too lavish in your use of wine in a recipe; the flavor of the pork itself might be drowned. If the recipe requires long cooking, add the wine partway through. That will prevent the flavor of the wine from being cooked out.

Note that even if you do not enjoy cooking with wine you need not pass by a recipe on that account. Simply substitute another liquid that will blend with the other ingredients—bouillon, tomato juice, fruit juice, or what you will.

Although wine is generally the preferred drink with a pork entrée at dinner, one should not overlook the fact that there are all sorts of delicious ways to serve pork at lunchtime. That is when beer, ale, or even stout is an excellent accompaniment. What could be nicer on a warm summer day than Pork and Macaroni Salad with a tall glass of chilled ale? Or, at a picnic, a Deviled Hamwich with your favorite beer? Stout is heavy, so it would be best with one of the sauerkraut-pork dishes or with Smoked Shoulder Roll with Mustard Sauce.

Whatever you decide to do, your own taste and pocketbook must be your guides in choosing from the vast array of imported and American wines. You will surely enjoy adventuring among these riches. Wine acts as a digestive. It accentuates the flavor of foods. It is both relaxing and stimulating and, above all, it is beautiful and festive.

Carving

All the world loves to watch a good carver. And if you can do your job with a special flourish, you can make even a humble cut of meat seem out of the ordinary. Furthermore, skilled carving is a practical accomplishment. It results in the least waste and the most usable leftovers.

To acquire the skill, two things are needed above all else: the proper tools and practice. A nine-inch knife with a curved blade, an eleven-inch knife with a narrow straight blade, and a good strong fork are most useful. And don't forget to keep the knives sharp. For the beginning or self-conscious carver, it is wise to do the work in the kitchen or at a side table in the dining room.

Prior planning and attention to a few rules are of great assistance. A roast should always "set" for fifteen to thirty minutes before being carved. It may be left in a turned-off oven or, what is really better, removed from the oven and covered loosely with foil. When the meat is put on the platter it should face the carver properly, as indicated by the diagrams on the following pages. An extra platter is a help. It may be used as a second carving surface or it may be used to pass individual servings, unless the portions are put directly onto the plates.

One of the cardinal rules of carving is to cut across the grain. Cutting in the same direction can make even the finest meat seem stringy. Thin slices help to enhance tenderness. Remember, too, to carve all the meat from one side of a roast before starting on the other side. Serving plates and platters should be warm, and since meat not only cools rapidly after it is cut, but also tends to dry out, do not attempt to do your carving far ahead of time. The quality of the meat will suffer.

Specific directions for carving the most generally served cuts of pork are given on the following pages. All of them are for right-handed carvers. The left-handed, as is usually the case, will have to make the necessary translations.

LOIN ROAST:

Courtesy National Livestock and Meat Board

1. Before bringing the roast to the table, remove the backbone. Cut it carefully so as to take off as little of the meat as possible. Place the roast on a platter with the rib side facing the carver so he can see the angle of the ribs and make his slices accordingly.

2. Insert a fork in the top of the roast. If thin slices are desired, cut close to the sides of the rib bones. One slice will contain a rib, the next will be boneless. For thicker slices simply cut halfway between the ribs so that each serving consists of one chop (bone in).

PICNIC SHOULDER:

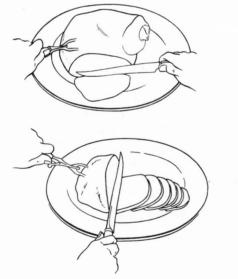
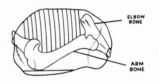
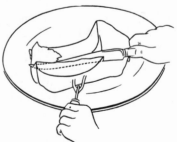

Courtesy National Livestock and Meat Board

1. Cut off a lengthwise slice, as shown in the illustration. Turn the roast so that it rests on this cut surface.

2. Cut down to the arm bone at a point near the elbow bone. Turn the knife and cut along the arm bone in order to remove this boneless section.

3. Place this portion on a cutting board or another platter and slice it perpendicularly.

4. Remove the meat from each side of the arm bone and slice these two pieces. To get more slices, cut lengthwise slices from the base, as shown.

WHOLE HAM:

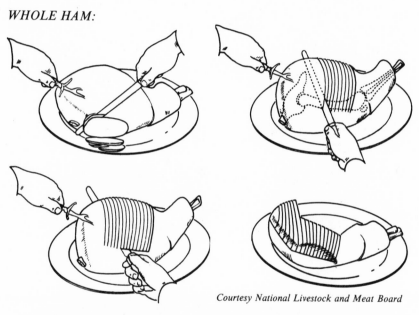

Courtesy National Livestock and Meat Board

1. Place the ham on the platter with the fat side up and the shank to the carver's right. In order to locate the bones, he must know whether it is a right or left ham. This may be done by locating the kneecap, which is on the thin side of the ham. Remove two or three slices from this side. Then turn the ham so that the thick side is up.

2. Make perpendicular slices through the thick side down to the bone.

3. Release the slices by cutting along the leg bone.

4. To serve the rest of the ham, slice as shown.

SHANK HALF OF HAM:

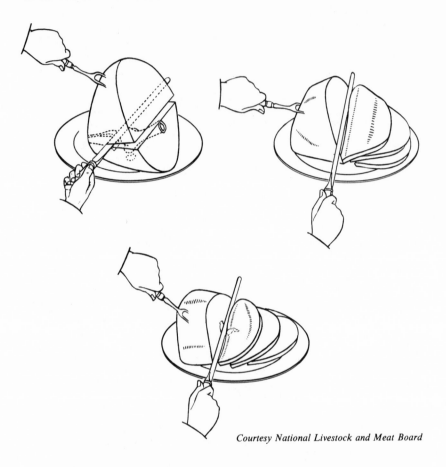

Courtesy National Livestock and Meat Board

1. With the shank at the carver's left (cut surface at right), turn the ham so that the thick cushion side is up. Cut from right to left along the leg and shank bones.

2. Lift off the boneless cushion and place it on a platter or cutting board. Slice perpendicularly, as illustrated.

3. For the other portion of the shank, cut around the leg bone with the tip of the knife in order to remove the meat from the bone. Then turn this meat so that the widest side is down and slice it in the same manner as the cushion piece.

BUTT HALF OF HAM:

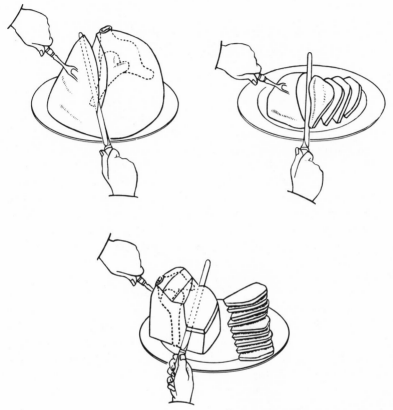

Courtesy National Livestock and Meat Board

1. Place the butt half on a platter with the "face" or cut side down. Cut along the aitch bone (see illustration) so as to remove a boneless piece from the side of the ham.

2. Place the boneless piece on a cutting board or platter with the freshly cut surface down. Slice it across the grain.

3. The meat remaining on the other side of the butt may be sliced by holding it firmly with a fork and cutting across the meat until the knife strikes the aitch bone. Each slice should be released from the bone by using the sharp point of the knife. Remove the slices as they are carved.

RECIPES

These recipes are grouped by cuts of pork and by use, for easy reference. As we said before, the nomenclature of cuts used by producers, processors, retailers, and professional cooks seems to have been more varied and imaginative than scientific. A shoulder can be a butt and a cutlet may be a steak, depending on where you live. And there's a smoked butt, which may be a ham. Some hams are calia (callie, calle, cala) hams, in some places, sometimes. There are blade and arm steaks and shoulder and butt roasts, and cottage rolls (made of the shoulder butt, boned and rolled). To the extent possible, we have made use of Meat Board suggestions in the naming of retail cuts. In chapter 1 you will find a chart of hog anatomy, showing the location of the cuts.

In some categories we have put recipes that might just as easily have been placed elsewhere. Cross-indexing is provided to make it as easy as possible for you to locate any recipe for any cut.

The number of pork recipes, about four hundred, indicates the whole point of this book—that pork is versatile and deserves the cook's best talent and that it should not be dismissed with the very limited and unimaginative treatment usually accorded it.

ORGANIZE

A little organizing before you actually use a recipe will help you keep your composure and avoid anxiety. Most of the recipe groups in this book are preceded by information and suggestions that apply to the cut of pork being prepared. What follows here is a recipe for general procedures. A cook with long experience almost automatically proceeds along these lines. Cooks still gaining experience will find these suggestions helpful.

First of all, read the recipe carefully. Be sure it suits your purpose: an elegant dinner, a hurry-up meal, or between-meal snack. Note which ingredients you have and which you will need to shop for. This will protect you from a rude shock in the midst of carrying out the recipe.

Consider the timing. Some recipes have several operations. This book presents recipes in such a way as to make the best use of overall preparation time. Check the preparation and cooking times and how they are distributed. Time for thawing must also be taken into account. Ideally, frozen meat should be thawed in the refrigerator and then brought to room temperature before cooking. Refrigerated meat also cooks better if brought to room temperature, a procedure that reduces cooking time and retains flavor for both frozen and refrigerated cuts.

Check your implements. If there is a device (e.g., blender, chopper) that you use infrequently and keep in a less accessible place, get it out and have it handy. Be sure to begin with bowls, saucepans, or other utensils of adequate size. Whenever possible use a combined cooking and serving dish.

All cooks profit by as much ahead-of-time preparation as the recipe allows. You will be especially well served if you remember that when you are a host or hostess. Many sauces, marinades, appetizers, sandwiches, and nearly all soups can be prepared well ahead of time. Some recipes have a natural break in their procedure. There is often a point in the preparation of a dish or in the cooking when nothing in flavor or appearance is lost by stopping, setting it aside, and completing the rest of the cooking just before serving. This advance work can save your nerves and increase your pleasure in the party.

Although this cook book is not especially designed as a shortcut guide, no time saver is scorned and all are welcome that do not damage the final result. Among these are canned or powdered soups, sauce and gravy mixes, and many frozen or prepared products.

Specific cooking directions, of course, accompany every recipe. Some general considerations apply to cooking nearly all cuts of pork by nearly all methods. Pork should usually be salted after the first cooking stage (e.g., brown chops in shortening, then sprinkle with salt and pepper), a procedure that does not apply to dredged meat. Salting before cooking tends to draw out juices, with consequent loss of flavor. Generally one teaspoon of salt seasons one pound of meat; one-fourth teaspoon of pepper does the same. Foil in the bottom of a baking pan helps avoid burning and incidentally makes the clean-up task easier. Fat should be siphoned off whenever possible in the cooking process, as it tends to speed up cooking because it gets hotter than the meat itself.

Meats wrapped by the butcher should be unwrapped as soon as possible. Keep them at an even temperature, loosely covered in the refrigerator.

Appetizers

Also answer to "hors d'oeuvres," "starters," "canapés."
Victorians called them "thumb bits." They have also been
referred to as "soakers," "splashers," and even "blotters"!

"Appetizer" is a home-grown American term, and it has come to mean
not only what it literally is, something to stimulate the appetite
immediately before a meal, but all sorts of tidbits served before a meal
or at a cocktail party.

A too-hearty appetizer can have the opposite effect. It can dull the
appetite for the best of meals. The best appetizer is the least filling. On
the other hand, canapés served at a cocktail party may be more
satisfying.

The form of the appetizer should suit the occasion. It is assumed that
guests having a drink and appetizers before dinner are sitting down. At a
cocktail party guests appreciate being served only what they can easily
eat (preferably in one bite) while standing up, talking, and balancing a
glass.

These recipes will help you make such fine distinctions and make your
guests glad they came.

HAM AND BLUE CHEESE STACK-UPS

1   cup ground, cooked ham
3   ounces (about ½ cup) blue cheese, finely crumbled
2   tablespoons pickle relish
2   tablespoons mayonnaise
1   tablespoon lemon juice
1   tablespoon prepared mustard
12 slices day-old bread

22

Combine all the ingredients except the bread. Mix well, then spread on the bread slices, making four sandwiches of three layers each. Trim off the crusts. Cut each sandwich into nine squares. Secure with wooden picks. Bake at 425° for 5 or 6 minutes. Serve hot.

Makes thirty-six

HAM PÂTÉ

1 cup diced, cooked ham
1 teaspoon unflavored gelatin
½ cup cold water
1 teaspoon prepared mustard

Chop or grind the ham very fine. Soften the gelatin in the cold water; place over hot water and stir until dissolved. Cool for 30 minutes. Combine the mustard and ham with the cooled gelatin. Pack into a mold, and chill until firm. Serve with crackers or rye Melba toast.

PEANUT BUTTER–HAM PUFFS

½ cup ground, cooked ham
½ cup peanut butter
1 egg, separated
1 teaspoon grated onion
¼ teaspoon salt
30 small rounds of toast or crackers

Beat the white of the egg until stiff and set aside. Beat the yolk until lemon colored. Then mix with the ham, peanut butter, onion, and salt. Fold into the egg white. Put small spoonfuls on the toast rounds and set on a baking sheet. Bake at 350° for about 10 minutes, or until puffed. Serve hot.

HAM SQUARES

6   **thin slices boiled ham**
½   **cup peanut butter**
2   **teaspoons grated onion**
1   **egg, beaten**
2   **tablespoons water**
½   **cup fine, dry bread crumbs**
1   **cup vegetable oil**

Mix the peanut butter and onion. Spread this mixture on half the ham slices and top with the remaining ham. Wrap in waxed paper and chill for about 1 hour. Then cut into 1-inch squares. Mix the egg and water. Dip the squares in the egg and then in the crumbs. Heat the oil and fry the squares for 2 minutes, or until brown. Insert a wooden pick in each square and serve hot.

Makes about fifty

HAM-MUSHROOM FANCIES

Thin slices of boiled ham
Sour cream or coffee cream
Blue cheese, at room temperature
Marinated (pickled) mushroom caps

Blend cream into cheese until it is of spreading consistency. Spread on the ham slices. Drain the mushroom caps and arrange a row of them, a little distance apart, across the center of each ham slice. Roll up. Stick a wooden pick through the ham and each mushroom and cut into tidbit portions between the mushroom caps. Chill before serving.

FRENCH CHEESE AND HAM SPREAD

¼   **cup ground, cooked ham**
½   **cup Camembert cheese**
½   **cup Roquefort cheese**
½   **cup ground walnut meats**
1   **teaspoon Worcestershire sauce**

1   **teaspoon catsup**
  Pinch of curry powder
  Salt
  Pepper

Cream together the cheeses and nut meats. Add the Worcestershire, catsup, ham, curry, salt and pepper to taste. Blend to smooth, even consistency. Pack into a glass jar and store in the refrigerator. The mixture will keep for several weeks.

Makes one and one-half cups

HAM IN PASTRY SHELLS

6 tablespoons finely chopped ham
2 eggs, lightly beaten
1 medium tomato, peeled, chopped, and thoroughly drained
1 tablespoon heavy cream or undiluted evaporated milk
1 package cocktail-size pastry shells
1 can (4 ounces) mushroom caps

Combine the ham, eggs, tomato, and cream in a heavy saucepan. Cook the mixture over medium heat, stirring constantly, until thick. Meantime, warm the pastry shells in the oven. Fill the shells with the ham mixture, using about ½ teaspoon to a shell. Place a mushroom cap on each and serve while still warm.

Makes about thirty

HOT HAM AND CHEESE CANAPÉS

6   tablespoons very finely chopped, cooked ham
2   scant tablespoons butter, softened to room temperature
12 bread rounds
3   tablespoons grated Cheddar cheese

Combine the ham with the softened butter. Spread on rounds of bread that have been toasted on one side (use the untoasted side for the top). Sprinkle the cheese over the ham. Put under the broiler long enough to melt the cheese, and serve hot.

Makes twelve

DEVILED HAM WITH CHUTNEY

1   can (4½ ounces) deviled ham
24 rounds of bread, 1¼ inches in diameter, toasted on one side
1   tablespoon finely chopped chutney
¼   cup Cheddar cheese
2   tablespoons butter, softened to room temperature
¼   teaspoon dry mustard
1   egg
    Paprika
    Salt

Mix the chutney with the deviled ham and place a small mound of this on the untoasted side of the bread rounds. With a small spoon make a depression in the center of each mound. Cream together the cheese, butter, mustard, salt, and paprika. When smooth, beat in the egg and fill the depressions in the ham mounds with the mixture. Bake at 400° for 10 to 15 minutes. Sprinkle with additional paprika and serve hot.

Makes twenty-four

DEVILED HAM AND HORSERADISH SPREAD

1   can (4½ ounces) deviled ham
3   tablespoons bottled horseradish, drained
2   tablespoons finely chopped fresh parsley

Blend all the ingredients until smooth. Use on crackers or small slices of pumpernickel.

Makes about three-fourths cup

COCKTAIL BISCUITS WITH HAM OR SAUSAGE

1   can (4½ ounces) deviled ham
        or
¼   pound pork sausage, crumbled, cooked, and drained
⅔   cup all-purpose flour
6   tablespoons grated Cheddar cheese

2 **tablespoons butter**
2 or 3 **tablespoons milk**
1 **egg, lightly beaten**
2 **tablespoons melted butter or margarine**
½ **teaspoon salt**

Mix the flour, cheese and salt. Cut in the butter with a pastry blending fork, then add enough milk to form a stiff dough. Roll out very thin on a floured surface and cut with a small, round biscuit cutter. Moisten the edges with lightly beaten egg. Spread half of the rounds with the deviled ham or sausage meat, cover with the remaining rounds, and press the edges together. Brush with melted butter and bake at 400° for 12 to 15 minutes, or until golden brown. Serve hot.

DEVILED HAM AND ONION SPREAD

1 **can (4½ ounces) deviled ham**
   Rounds or triangles of bread, toasted on one side,
        buttered on the other side
1 **teaspoon minced dried onion**
¼ **cup mayonnaise**

Spread the buttered side of the bread rounds or triangles with deviled ham. Combine the mayonnaise with the onion and spread over the ham. Just before serving, bake in a 450° oven until lightly browned.

HAM AND PEANUT SPREAD

1 **can (2¼ ounces) deviled ham**
1 **tablespoon chunky-style peanut butter**
   Mayonnaise
2 **dashes Tabasco sauce**

Combine the ham and peanut butter. Add enough mayonnaise to make a smooth spread. Add the Tabasco sauce, mix thoroughly, and chill before serving. Very easy, very delicious.

Makes about one-third cup

DEVILED HAM AND PIMIENTO

1   can (4½ ounces) deviled ham
1   jar (5 ounces) or 1 package (3 ounces) pimiento cheese
¼   teaspoon Worcestershire sauce
1   teaspoon chopped fresh parsley

Blend the ham and cheese until smooth, then add the Worcestershire sauce and mix thoroughly. Pack into a pretty serving bowl and allow to chill in the refrigerator for several hours before serving. Garnish with the chopped parsley.

PORK BALLS WITH WATER CHESTNUTS

1   pound ground pork
1   cup coarsely chopped water chestnuts
¼   cup finely chopped crystallized ginger
1   egg, lightly beaten
    Cornstarch
    Peanut oil for deep frying
    Salt

Combine all ingredients except the cornstarch and peanut oil and shape the mixture into bite-sized balls. Dust lightly with cornstarch. Heat peanut oil to 375°, then deep-fry the meat balls until cooked through. Serve hot, on wooden picks.

Makes twelve to sixteen balls

SPICED PORK SPREAD

2   pounds pork shoulder, boned
1   pound fatback, cut in 1-inch cubes
1   clove garlic
¼   teaspoon thyme
¼   teaspoon ground allspice
2   cups water
3   sprigs parsley

1   **bay leaf**
6   **peppercorns**
1   **tablespoon salt**

Mash together, in a mortar, the garlic, salt, thyme, and allspice. Place the meat in a deep dish and rub thoroughly with the garlic mixture. Cover and place in the refrigerator overnight.

The next day, cut the pork into 1½-inch pieces and put them in a casserole with the fatback. Add the water. Tie the parsley, bay leaf, and peppercorns in a small piece of cheesecloth and drop into the water. Bake, tightly covered, in a preheated 300° oven for 4 hours.

Place a colander over a bowl and pour the meat mixture into it. Transfer the meat and fatback to a plate, reserving the fat in the bowl. Shred the meat with two forks, then add salt and pepper to taste. Put the mixture into three 1-cup earthenware pots. Strain the reserved fat and pour a thin layer over the top of each pot. Allow to cool, then cover and refrigerate. The spread will keep for at least a month.

Makes three cups

COCKTAIL PASTRIES

1½   **pounds ground pork**
2   **tomatoes, chopped**
2   **medium onions, chopped fine**
2   **cloves garlic, crushed**
2   **large potatoes, peeled and cubed**
½   **tablespoon butter or margarine**
½   **teaspoon ground ginger**
½   **teaspoon ground cloves**
1   **teaspoon ground coriander**
2   **tablespoons vinegar**
    Pie crust mix
    Whole cloves
2   **teaspoons salt**
¼   **teaspoon freshly ground pepper**

Sauté the onion in the butter until transparent. Add the meat and brown slightly. Then add the tomatoes, garlic, potatoes, seasonings, and vinegar. Simmer until the meat and potatoes are done (about 45 minutes). Cool.

Prepare the pie crust mix and roll out to a thickness of 1/8 inch. Cut it into 3-inch squares and put a small portion of the mixture on each square. Fold the points to the center, moisten, and crimp to seal. Fasten with a whole clove. Bake on a cookie sheet at 450° for about 8 to 10 minutes, or until browned.

PORK AND CURRIED CHEESE CANAPÉS

1   cup ground, cooked pork
    Tomato paste
    Bread, cut into rounds or other shapes, toasted, and buttered
1   package (3 ounces) cream cheese
1 or 2 tablespoons sour cream
¼   teaspoon curry powder
    Paprika

Mix the ground pork with enough tomato paste to moisten it and spread on the toasted, buttered bread rounds. Allow the cheese to come to room temperature, then thin it with enough sour cream so it will spread easily. Blend in the curry powder. Cover the meat with a thin layer of the cheese and sprinkle with paprika.

ELEGANT PORK TERRINE

1¼ pounds ground lean pork
1¼ pounds ground pork fat
1½ pounds ground liver
 ½ pound ground beef
 ½ pound bacon
 7 tablespoons butter
 ⅓ cup chopped scallions
 2 cloves garlic, minced fine
 ½ pound chicken livers (whole, if possible)
 ¼ cup brandy
 3 tablespoons heavy cream

2   teaspoons lemon juice
2   tablespoons all-purpose flour
1   egg, lightly beaten
½   teaspoon ground allspice
1½ tablespoons salt
1   tablespoon freshly ground black pepper
¼   teaspoon cayenne pepper

Mix the ground meats in a large bowl. In a skillet melt 5 tablespoons of the butter and brown the scallions and garlic. Add to the meat and mix thoroughly.

In the same skillet melt the remaining 2 tablespoons butter and brown the chicken livers, turning them gently. Remove from the pan and set aside. Pour the brandy into the skillet, mix with the pan juices. Pour into the meat mixture. Combine the cream, lemon juice, flour, egg, and seasonings and add to the meat.

Lay thin strips of bacon in a terrine pan or 2-quart mold. Fill half full with the meat mixture. Lay the chicken livers on top, and cover with the remaining meat mixture. Cover the top with more strips of bacon, then cover the pan with aluminum foil and set in a larger pan containing ½ inch of hot water. Bake at 350° for 2 hours. Allow to cool, then refrigerate overnight. Remove from the pan and serve with Melba toast.

PORK CUBES WITH "POOR MAN'S BUTTER"

2   pounds lean pork, cut into 1- to 1½-inch cubes
2   ripe medium avocados, mashed
2   medium tomatoes, peeled, drained, and mashed
3   tablespoons red wine vinegar
1   tablespoon salad oil
    Salt
    Pepper

Put the pork cubes in a single layer in a shallow baking pan and sprinkle with salt and pepper. Allow to stand at room temperature for an hour or so, then bake in a 300° oven for 1½ to 2 hours, or until crisp. Every half hour during the baking stir the meat and pour off any fat. Remove from the oven and allow to cool.

Meanwhile, combine the avocados, tomatoes, vinegar, salad oil, and salt and pepper to taste. Stir until well mixed. This may be refrigerated until needed but must stand at room temperature for at least 30 minutes before serving.

When ready to serve, impale each meat cube on a wooden pick. Put the *mantequilla* ("poor man's butter" in Mexico) in a bowl in the center of a large plate. Surround with the meat cubes and serve.

Six to eight servings

CURRY TURNOVERS

¼ pound ground lean pork
1 tablespoon cooking oil or shortening
1 small onion, grated
1 clove garlic, chopped very fine
1 teaspoon curry powder
½ teaspoon turmeric
¼ teaspoon chili powder
1 tablespoon finely cut up chutney
Pastry for 1-crust pie

Heat the oil and sauté the onion and garlic for 5 minutes. Add the curry powder, turmeric, and chili powder. Mix well, then add the ground pork, mixing with a fork to prevent the meat from forming lumps. Brown the meat. Add the chutney and simmer for 5 minutes. Allow the mixture to cool.

Roll out the pastry approximately ⅛ inch thick and cut in rounds with a 2-inch round cookie cutter. Place a generous ½ teaspoon meat filling on each round of pastry, fold in half, and seal with cold water. Bake at 450° for 8 to 10 minutes, or until nicely browned, Serve hot.

Makes twenty to twenty-four

BACON NUT SPREAD

3 slices bacon, cooked until crisp
2 teaspoons tomato sauce or catsup
⅛ teaspoon prepared mustard
1 package (3 ounces) cream cheese
¼ teaspoon seasoned salt
3 tablespoons finely chopped pecans or almonds

Add the tomato sauce and mustard to the cream cheese. Blend until smooth. Chop the bacon. Add it, 2 tablespoons of the nuts, and the seasoned salt to the mixture. Mix gently until the ingredients are evenly blended. Put in a small bowl and sprinkle the remaining nuts over the top. This spread may be used at once or it will keep well in the refrigerator.

Makes about one and one-half cups

BACON AND STUFFED PRUNES

Thin-sliced bacon, at room temperature
Pitted, ready-to-eat prunes
Small green olives, pitted or stuffed

If stuffed olives are used, remove the stuffing. Fill the center of each prune with an olive. Wrap with ½ slice of bacon and fasten with a small skewer. Place the bacon-wrapped prunes on a rack in a shallow baking dish and bake at 375° for 10 to 15 minutes, until the bacon is crisp, then drain. Remove the skewer and replace with a serving pick. Serve hot.

HOT BACON AND CHEESE DIP

2   **slices bacon, cut up fine**
1   **cup cubed sharp Cheddar cheese**
½   **can (10½-ounce size) cream of mushroom soup**

Fry the bacon in a medium-sized heavy skillet until browned. Do not drain. Add the other ingredients to the skillet. Heat and stir until the cheese melts and the mixture is smooth. Serve in a chafing dish.

Makes about one cup

AVOCADO AND BACON SPREAD

6   **slices bacon**
1   **ripe avocado, mashed**
1   **teaspoon lemon juice**
    Salt
    Pepper

Fry the bacon until crisp. Drain it, crumble it fine, and mix into the avocado. Add the lemon juice and salt and pepper to taste. Serve with Melba toast or small slices of thin rye bread.

BACON AND CHICKEN LIVER SPREAD

6   slices bacon
6   chicken livers
    Brown sauce or softened butter

In a heavy skillet, slowly fry the bacon until it is very crisp. Remove from the skillet and chop fine. Pour off all except 1 tablespoon of the fat and sauté the chicken livers. Drain and chop very fine. Combine the bacon and liver and moisten to spreading consistency, using a small amount of brown sauce or softened butter.

CHEESE AND BACON SPREAD

2   slices bacon, fried crisp and chopped
1   package (3 ounces) cream cheese
1   tablespoon tomato juice

Mix the cheese and tomato juice until thoroughly blended. Add the bacon, mixing it evenly through the cheese. Use to fill tiny baking powder biscuits.

Makes twenty-four to thirty

BACON AND CHICKEN LIVERS

1   pound thin-sliced bacon
1   pound chicken livers, drained

Wrap each liver with a slice of bacon and fasten with a small metal skewer. Place on a rack set in a shallow baking dish and bake at 425° until the bacon is crisp and brown. Remove the skewers, insert wooden picks, and serve hot.

BACON AND CHEESE ROLLS

6   slices regular bacon (not thin sliced)
¼   cup grated American cheese or Cheddar spread
3   teaspoons finely chopped chutney

Cut each slice of bacon in half crosswise. Spread these pieces with the cheese and dot each one with ¼ teaspoon of the chopped chutney. Roll tightly and fasten with small metal skewers.

Heat the broiler. Place the bacon rolls on the broiler rack and set it in the lowest position. Turn the heat to medium and broil for about 3 minutes, then turn and broil the other side for about 2 minutes. Drain on paper towels. Replace the skewers with wooden picks and serve hot.

Makes one dozen

BACON-WRAPPED WATERMELON PICKLE

Thin-sliced bacon
Watermelon pickles

Cut the pickles into pieces about 1 inch square. Dry thoroughly. Wrap each square with a slice of bacon, overlapping well, and fasten with small metal skewers. Place on a rack in a shallow baking pan and bake at 425° until the bacon is done. Remove the skewers, replace with wooden picks, and serve hot.

BACON WITH PEANUT BUTTER

Bacon, cooked and chopped fine
Thin-sliced bread
Peanut butter
Chili sauce

Cut the bread into squares and toast one side. Spread the untoasted side with peanut butter mixed with chili sauce. Sprinkle with finely chopped, cooked bacon, and heat through in a 425° oven. Serve hot.

MUSHROOM CANADIAN BACON CANAPÉS

9   slices Canadian-style bacon, cut medium thin
1   pound small fresh mushrooms
1   tablespoon cream
3   tablespoons butter or margarine
18 rounds of white bread (1 inch in diameter), toasted on both sides
1   teaspoon salt
¼   teaspoon freshly ground pepper

Wash the mushrooms. Remove the caps and chop the stems fine. Mix with the cream, salt, and pepper and cook in 2 tablespoons of the butter for just a few minutes.

Cut 2 one-inch rounds from each slice of bacon (the trimmings may be added to scrambled eggs, green beans, or baked beans, or see the bacon section for ideas). In a separate skillet, brown the rounds in 1 tablespoon of butter and set aside. In the same pan cook the mushroom caps, adding more butter if needed.

For each canapé, place a bacon round on a toast round, add a small spoonful of chopped mushrooms, and top with a mushroom cap. Keep warm in the oven.

Makes eighteen

MOCK PÂTÉ DE FOIE GRAS

¾   pound liverwurst
1   package (3 ounces) cream cheese
¼   cup sour cream
3   tablespoons Cognac
⅛   teaspoon grated nutmeg

Remove the casing from the sausage. Allow it and the cheese to come to room temperature, then mix in the other ingredients and blend until completely smooth. Chill in the refrigerator for several hours or longer, as the pâté will keep well. Serve with small triangles or fingers of toast freshly made from thinly sliced bread.

LIVERWURST SPREAD

¼   pound liverwurst, casing removed
3   tablespoons mayonnaise
¼   cup cooked rice
½   teaspoon celery salt
20 rounds of toast or white bread, 1¼ inches in diameter
     India relish

Bring the liverwurst to room temperature and mash with a fork. Add the mayonnaise, rice, and celery salt. Place a small amount on each toast or bread round and make a shallow depression in the spread. Fill the depression with the relish.

Makes twenty

LIVER SAUSAGE PÂTÉ IN ASPIC

1   pound liver sausage
2   packages (3 ounces each) cream cheese
1   teaspoon minced onion
¼   cup brandy
1   tablespoon unflavored gelatin
1   cup canned consommé (with gelatin added)

Place a 3- to 3½-cup mold in the freezing compartment of the refrigerator to chill. Combine the liver sausage, cream cheese, onion, and brandy. Blend well and chill. Mix the gelatin with ¼ cup of the consommé and allow to stand until softened. Bring the remaining consommé to a boil and remove from the heat. Add the gelatin and stir until dissolved. Reserve ⅓ cup of the consommé and hold at room temperature.

Cool the remaining consommé until syrupy in consistency. Brush several thin coatings of syrupy consommé over the inside surface of the chilled mold. Chill until the coating is firm, then fill the mold with the liver sausage mixture and pour the reserved consommé over the sausage. Chill thoroughly. Unmold and chill again.

To serve, arrange the mold on a serving tray and surround with thinly sliced party rye bread, Melba toast, or crackers.

Makes three cups

VERY EASY SPREAD

3   slices bacon, cooked crisp and crumbled
1   can (4¾ ounces) liverwurst spread
     Rye toast rounds
     Pitted ripe olives

Mix the crumbled bacon with the liverwurst, spread on rounds of rye toast, and decorate with olives cut in halves.

Bacon

Bacon, both American and Canadian-style, is a fine dish in its own right and we consider it worthy of its own group of recipes. We especially recommend it for consideration at meals other than breakfast, where it traditionally makes its appearance, giving to the first meal of the day its appetizing early-morning aroma and taste.

Bacon is equally good fried, baked, or broiled. To broil, keep the slices 3 inches from the heat and keep a sharp eye on them. It takes only a few minutes. Baking, on a wire rack at 400°, takes from 10 to 15 minutes. The bacon may be baked the night before, kept in the refrigerator and taken out and reheated in the oven just as the coffee and toast are ready. However you cook it, first bring it to room temperature.

Bacon may be bought sliced or unsliced. To separate slices in the package, flex the package before opening it. Slices are also more easily separated when the bacon has come to room temperature.

Canadian-style bacon comes from the eye of the pork loin. It may be purchased in a roll suitable for baking. It may also be bought in slices, suitable for frying or broiling. Do not overcook it. It has very little fat and if it is cooked too fast or too long it becomes tough and stringy. Baking takes only about 20 minutes and frying only 3 or 4.

BACON AND EGGPLANT CASSEROLE

10 slices bacon, cut in halves
 2 eggplants (1 pound each)
¼ cup olive oil
½ cup melted butter or margarine
 1 cup milk
 1 cup freshly grated Parmesan cheese
    Salt

Peel the eggplants and cut them crosswise into ½-inch slices. Sprinkle on both sides with salt and allow them to drain for about 30 minutes. Pat them dry with paper towels.

Warm the olive oil in a skillet and sauté the eggplant slices, adding melted butter as needed. When the slices begin to get soft, remove them. Meanwhile, in another skillet, fry the bacon until it is partially cooked but not crisp. Drain on brown paper.

Grease a shallow baking dish and put in a layer of eggplant. Top this with part of the bacon, sprinkle on one-third of the cheese, and pour on ⅓ cup of the milk. Continue to make layers until all the ingredients are used, ending with a layer of cheese. Bake, uncovered, at 350° for 30 to 40 minutes, or until the eggplant is tender.

Six servings

BACON WITH HOMINY AND TOMATO SAUCE

6 slices bacon, cut in 1-inch pieces
2 cups canned hominy
1 cup tomato sauce
½ teaspoon salt
¼ teaspoon pepper

Drain the hominy. Let stand in cold water for 5 minutes, then drain again. Place the bacon in a skillet and cook over low heat until crisp. Remove and set aside, then cook the hominy in the bacon fat until browned. Add the bacon, tomato sauce, salt, and pepper, and cook until heated through.

Two to three servings

BACON, CORN AND TOMATO PIE

1 pound bacon, cut up
1 small onion, sliced thin
1 tablespoon all-purpose flour
1 can (8 ounces) tomatoes
1 can (11 ounces) whole-kernel corn
½ teaspoon marjoram
1½ pounds potatoes, cooked, mashed, and whipped with butter and cream

Salt
⅛ teaspoon pepper

Fry the bacon slowly. Add the onion and cook until tender (do not brown). Dust evenly with the flour, then stir in the tomatoes and corn, adding marjoram, salt and pepper. Turn into a shallow casserole and cover the top completely with potatoes put through a pastry bag. Place in a 450° oven or under the broiler for a few minutes to brown.

Four servings

BACON WITH LIMA BEANS AND MUSHROOMS

5   slices bacon, fried and crumbled
4   slices bacon, uncooked, each slice cut in half
2   packages (12 ounces each) frozen lima beans, thawed
1   can (10 ounces) sliced mushrooms, drained
2   medium onions, sliced thin
½   cup light cream
½   teaspoon sage
¼   teaspoon thyme
1½ teaspoons salt
½   teaspoon pepper

Put half the beans in a greased casserole. Sprinkle with half of the mushrooms, half of the onion slices, and half of the seasonings. Add the crumbled bacon, distributing it evenly. Then add the remaining beans. Sprinkle with the remaining mushrooms, onion, and seasonings, then pour cream over the mixture. Place the sliced bacon on top. Bake, uncovered, at 350° until the beans are bubbling and tender, then place under the broiler long enough to brown the bacon.

Six servings

BACON AND LEEK CASSEROLE

½   pound bacon   Salt
3   tablespoons butter or margarine   Pepper
3   tablespoons all-purpose flour
1½ cups milk
1   pound potatoes, cooked and sliced
¼   cup grated American cheese
1   pound leeks, cooked and sliced

Fry the bacon until crisp, then drain and break into small pieces. Melt the butter in a saucepan over low heat. Blend in the flour, then add the milk slowly, stirring constantly. Cook until thickened. Add salt and pepper to taste. Stir in the cheese and cook until melted.

Place the potato slices in a 1-quart casserole. Add the leeks. Pour the cheese over the potatoes and leeks, and sprinkle the bacon pieces on top. Bake, uncovered, at 375° for 20 minutes, or until heated through.

Four servings

SPAGHETTI WITH HAM AND BACON

6   ounces Canadian bacon, cut into narrow strips
6   ounces prosciutto ham, cut into narrow strips
1   package (16 ounces) thin spaghetti
4   tablespoons butter or margarine
¼   cup heavy cream
1   tablespoon A-1 sauce
3   tablespoons grated Parmesan cheese
½   teaspoon salt
⅛   teaspoon freshly ground black pepper

Cook the spaghetti according to the package directions. Drain and place in a heated bowl. Add 1 tablespoon of the butter or margarine and mix lightly. Then cover and keep warm. Melt the remaining butter in a skillet over medium heat. Add the bacon and ham and cook, stirring constantly, about 3 minutes. Add the cream and A-1 sauce and cook, stirring, until hot. Add the spaghetti and cheese. Remove the skillet from the heat, season with salt and pepper, and toss the mixture lightly. Serve at once.

Four servings

BACON AND CHEESE PIE

½   pound bacon, cut into bite-sized pieces
    Pastry for one 9-inch crust
2¼ cups grated sharp Cheddar cheese

2   **medium onions, sliced and separated i to rings**
¼   **cup all-purpose flour**
1   **cup milk**
3   **eggs**
¼   **teaspoon garlic salt**
¼   **teaspoon caraway seeds**
¼   **cup slivered ripe olives**
⅛   **teaspoon paprika**

Fry the bacon until crisp. Drain and set aside. Line a pie plate with the pastry. Sprinkle 1¼ cups of the cheese in the pastry shell. Add half the onion rings, and sprinkle evenly with bacon pieces. Add the remaining onions, then the remaining cheese. Combine the flour, milk, and eggs and beat with a rotary beater until smooth. Add the garlic salt and caraway seeds. Pour the sauce over the mixture in the pastry shell. Sprinkle with olives and paprika, and bake at 325° until the filling is brown and firm (about 55 minutes).

Six servings

PINEAPPLE FRENCH TOAST

8   **slices bacon**
2   **eggs**
1½   **tablespoons granulated sugar**
⅓   **teaspoon ground cinnamon**
½   **cup pineapple juice**
2   **tablespoons butter or margarine**
4   **slices day-old white bread**
½   **teaspoon salt**

Beat the eggs until light. Add the sugar, cinnamon, salt, and pineapple juice and beat until thoroughly mixed. Meanwhile, cook the bacon to the desired degree of crispness. Drain and keep warm. Wipe out the pan with a paper towel, then melt the butter in it. Soak the bread in the egg mixture and then brown it on both sides in the melted butter, adding more butter if needed.

To serve, make a cross of two bacon strips on each slice of toast.

Two servings

BACON ON FRENCH TOAST

18 slices bacon
 2 eggs
 1 cup milk
 6 slices day-old bread
    Butter or margarine
 3 tablespoons chopped fresh parsley
 ½ teaspoon lemon juice
 ⅛ teaspoon salt

Fry or bake the bacon until crisp. Drain on brown paper and keep hot until needed. Beat the eggs until white and yolk are blended, then add the salt and milk and beat together. Turn into a shallow dish. Dip the bread in the batter until fairly well soaked on both sides.

Melt about 1 or 2 tablespoons of butter or margarine in a heavy skillet. When hot, sauté the bread slowly on both sides until a delicate brown, adding butter as needed. In a separate pan, melt 4 tablespoons of butter. Add the parsley and lemon juice. Arrange 3 strips of bacon on each slice of toast and pour some of the parslied butter over each.

Six servings

BANANAS WITH BACON

12 slices bacon
 6 bananas, peeled and split lengthwise
    Salt
    Pepper

Arrange the bacon in a baking pan. Place half a banana, flat side down, on each slice. Sprinkle with salt and pepper and bake at 400° for 20 minutes, basting twice. Remove carefully to warm plates.

This combination makes an unusual and filling lunch when served with mashed potato cakes, nicely browned. Or it may be used as a garnish.

Six servings

BACON AND POTATO OMELET

4   strips bacon
2   tablespoons butter or margarine
1   cup diced, boiled potatoes
4   eggs
2   tablespoons cream
½   teaspoon salt
⅛   teaspoon pepper

Dice the bacon and fry in a skillet until crisp. Remove and drain. Pour off the fat and heat the butter in the same skillet. Add the diced potatoes and fry until golden brown. Return the bacon to the pan.

Combine the eggs, cream, salt, and pepper. Beat lightly, then pour into the skillet with the potatoes and bacon and mix vigorously. Turn the heat to low. Lift the edges with a pancake turner and tilt the skillet to permit the uncooked eggs to run to the bottom. When the mixture is of an even consistency, fold the omelet and serve at once.

Two servings

BACON RISOTTO WITH PEAS

¾   cup diced bacon
1   cup frozen green peas, thawed
1   cup raw short-grain Italian rice
3   cups hot beef stock or bouillon
3   tablespoons butter or margarine
1½ tablespoons grated Parmesan cheese

Cook the bacon in a large skillet for 4 minutes. Add the peas and cook until the bacon is lightly browned. Add the rice and stir until it is coated with the bacon drippings. Pour in 1 cup of the hot stock and cook over moderate heat until all the liquid is absorbed, adding more stock by cupfuls until the rice is tender. Using a fork, toss the rice with the butter and cheese and serve.

Four servings

RAGOÛT OF CANADIAN BACON

½ pound sliced Canadian bacon
1 pound round steak, cut in strips
   All-purpose flour for dredging
2 tablespoons cooking oil
4 medium potatoes, peeled and sliced
2 medium carrots, sliced
3 small onions, sliced
1 cup tomato juice
   Salt
   Pepper

Dredge the steak strips with flour and brown in hot oil. Remove and drain. Arrange the bacon, steak and vegetables (in the order shown above) in a skillet, seasoning the layers lightly. Add the tomato juice and cook over low heat for 35 to 40 minutes, or until all the ingredients are well done.

Four to six servings

CANADIAN BACON WITH GRAPES AND SWEET POTATOES

6 slices Canadian bacon, ½ inch thick
2 cans (1 pound 7 ounces each) sweet potatoes, drained
¾ cup milk
1 can (8¾ ounces) seedless grapes, drained
¼ cup brown sugar
½ cup chopped pecans
2 tablespoons melted butter or margarine
½ teaspoon salt

Mash the sweet potatoes and blend with the milk. Stir in the grapes, sugar, butter, pecans, and salt. Put in a 1½-quart casserole, arrange the bacon slices on top, and bake, uncovered, at 350° for 50 minutes.

Four to six servings

CANADIAN BACON AND BEAN CASSEROLE

4 slices Canadian bacon, ¼ inch thick
2 cans (16 ounces each) baked beans in molasses sauce
½ teaspoon dry mustard
2 tablespoons finely chopped fresh onion (or 2 teaspoons instant minced onion)
1 can (8¼ ounces) sliced pineapple, drained

Pour the sauce off the beans but do not drain them. Mix in the mustard and onion and put in a buttered casserole. Top with alternating slices of bacon and pineapple and bake, covered, at 350° for 30 minutes.

Four servings

CANADIAN BACON WITH CHEESE AND RICE

6 slices Canadian bacon, ¼ inch thick
1 cup shredded natural Cheddar cheese
¼ cup sliced scallions, tops included
2 tablespoons chopped parsley
4 cups hot, cooked rice
¼ teaspoon salt

Heat the bacon for a few minutes in a skillet or under the broiler. Mix the cheese, scallions, parsley, and salt with the rice. Toss together lightly, then arrange on a platter. Place the bacon slices attractively on top.

Six servings

Chops

To most people pork means chops. This point of view is not shared by the hog or the butcher. A 210-pound live hog yields only about 13 pounds of chops. The butcher gets 107 pounds in other cuts. The dressing process and fat claim the other 90 pounds.

The cook's view of pork as chops is understandable, and well supported by the many advantages of this excellent cut. The recipes here testify to the nearly endless ways chops may be cooked and served. They are appropriate for breakfast, lunch, and dinner for both family and guests. They can be purchased with reassuring exactness as to number of servings, one chop one serving, ten chops ten servings. Bone waste is minimal, and there are no leftovers to plague the cook who doesn't thrill to leftover cookery. They can be easily prepared for a hurry-up meal. A gourmet cook, on the other hand, can exercise her talents for half a day preparing an elaborate chop dish.

But chops take knowing. There are four basic cuts, and each has its special virtue. Center-loin or center-rib chops are the most desirable, from the standpoint of quality. Tender and of uniform size, they give more meat and less waste than any other unboned cut. Tell the butcher how thick you want yours. Butterfly chops are cut thick, split and flattened and may be with or without bone. The center-loin chop yields the bonus of a morsel of tenderloin. The center-cut rib chop is a match for the loin except for that tenderloin tidbit. The rib bone helps to conduct heat and thus reduces cooking time. The loin-end chop (sometimes called hip pork chop) contains more bone and less meat. Of course it is less expensive. The rib-end chop (sometimes called shoulder chop) is tender but has more fat and bone. Its advantage also is price.

These recipes specify the cut and thickness best suited to the procedure and the other ingredients.

48

CHOPS CHARCUTIÈRE

6   pork chops, ¾ inch thick
    Flour
5   tablespoons butter or margarine
2   tablespoons finely chopped onion
⅓   cup dry white wine
1   tablespoon vinegar
1   cup tomato purée
1   teaspoon beef extract
1   tablespoon prepared mustard
1   tablespoon chopped parsley
1   small sour pickle, chopped fine
1½   teaspoons salt
½   teaspoon pepper

Dredge the chops with flour, salt, and pepper. Sauté them in 3 tablespoons of the butter, over low heat, for 15 minutes on each side. Remove the chops and pour off any excess fat. Add the remaining butter to the skillet and sauté the onion until soft and golden. Add the wine and vinegar. Return the chops to the skillet. Cook for 30 minutes longer. Add the tomato purée and the beef extract. Cook over low heat for 10 minutes. Add the mustard, parsley, pickle, and remaining salt. Heat thoroughly, but do not allow the sauce to boil.

CHOPS TAHITIAN STYLE

8   pork chops, 1 inch thick
1½   tablespoons shortening
½   cup sherry
¼   cup soy sauce
¼   cup salad oil
¾   teaspoon ground ginger
¼   teaspoon oregano
1   tablespoon maple syrup

Brown the chops in the shortening in a heavy skillet. Remove them to a baking dish. Blend all the other ingredients until smooth. Pour over the chops. Bake, covered, at 325° for 1 hour. Turn the chops once during baking.

CHOPS IN CAPER SAUCE

6   loin pork chops, cut butterfly
2   tablespoons butter or margarine
1   tablespoon all-purpose flour
2   teaspoons prepared mustard
1   cup hot beef broth
¾   cup sour cream
2   teaspoons capers
2   teaspoons salt
¼   teaspoon pepper

In a large skillet, brown the chops on both sides in the butter. Remove and keep warm. Blend the flour, mustard, salt, and pepper in the skillet. Gradually add the broth, stirring constantly. Bring to a boil. Return the chops to the skillet. Baste several times. Simmer, covered, for about 20 minutes. Stir in the cream and add the capers. Heat but do not boil.

CHOPS IN CIDER

6   pork chops, ¾ inch thick
3   tablespoons butter or margarine
2   tablespoons olive oil
¼   teaspoon thyme
¼   teaspoon basil
¼   teaspoon marjoram
1   medium onion, chopped fine
⅔   cup cider
⅓   cup water
2   teaspoons salt
¼   teaspoon pepper

Sauté the chops in butter and oil until browned on both sides. Season with the salt and pepper. Place them in a shallow baking dish. Sprinkle with the thyme, basil, and marjoram. Cook the onion in the remaining fat until transparent. Add to the chops. Combine the cider and water and add to the chops. Bake, covered, at 350° for 50 minutes, or until tender.

CHOPS WITH SAUSAGES

 6 center-cut loin pork chops, 1 inch thick
12 pork sausage links
 6 apples, peeled, cored, and cubed
 6 medium potatoes, peeled and cubed
 2 medium onions, chopped
 2 cups beef stock
¼ cup cider
 1 teaspoon ground cinnamon
 2 tablespoons chopped fresh parsley
    Salt
    Pepper

Combine potatoes, apples, onions, cinnamon, salt, pepper, and beef stock in a saucepan. Bring to a boil. Reduce heat and cook slowly until the potatoes are tender and most of the liquid is absorbed, about 40 minutes. Remove the fat from chops and melt some in a skillet. Brown the chops in this, then add salt, pepper. Add cider and simmer, covered, for about 45 minutes. Meanwhile, cook the sausages until well done. Drain. Keep all ingredients hot.

To serve, place the potato mixture in the center of a platter. Sprinkle with parsley. Arrange the chops and sausage around the potato mixture.

CHOPS WITH GINGERSNAPS

 4 pork chops, ¾ inch thick
 2 tablespoons shortening
 2 celery stalks, sliced thin
⅔ cup cider vinegar or wine vinegar
 1 bay leaf
 4 peppercorns
 2 whole cloves
 1 cup water
 2 tablespoons tomato paste
 2 tablespoons granulated sugar
¼ cup crushed gingersnaps
 4 lemon slices
 1 teaspoon salt

Brown the chops in the shortening. Place in a 2-quart casserole and season with the salt. Sauté the celery in the chop pan until tender. Add the vinegar, bay leaf, peppercorns, and cloves. Bring the mixture to a boil and continue cooking until the liquid is reduced to about ½ cup. Remove the peppercorns and bay leaf. Add the water, tomato paste, and sugar and blend well. Add the gingersnaps, stirring constantly until the sauce thickens. Pour over the chops. Bake, covered, at 350° for 1 hour. Garnish with lemon slices.

BREADED CHOPS

- **6**   **pork chops, 1 inch thick**
      Juice of 1 lemon
- **½**   **cup olive oil**
- **1**   **egg, very lightly beaten**
- **1**   **tablespoon water**
- **1¼**   **cups dry bread crumbs**
- **⅓**   **cup grated Parmesan cheese**
- **2**   **tablespoons chopped parsley**
- **2**   **tablespoons olive oil**
- **2**   **tablespoons butter**
      Salt
      Pepper

Combine the lemon juice, ⅓ cup olive oil, salt, and pepper. Marinate the chops in this for about 2 hours. Drain the chops and pat dry on paper towels. Mix the egg and water. Dip the chops in this mixture. Combine the bread crumbs, cheese, and parsley. Coat both sides of the chops with this mixture. Brown the chops in 2 tablespoons each olive oil and butter, in a skillet. Bake, covered, at 350° for 45 minutes to 1 hour.

CHOPS WITH NOODLE SOUP

6 pork chops, ¾ inch thick
2 tablespoons butter or margarine
2 tablespoons all-purpose flour
1 teaspoon grated onion
1 cup chicken broth
1 cup canned chicken noodle soup
1 teaspoon salt
¼ teaspoon pepper

Brown the chops on both sides in the butter. Season with salt and pepper. Remove from the pan and set aside. Blend the flour and onion into the pan drippings. Add the chicken broth and cook, stirring constantly, until thick. Return the chops to the pan and cook, covered, over very low heat for 45 minutes. Add the noodle soup and heat through.

CHOPS BAKED WITH WHITE WINE

4 pork chops, about 1 inch thick
1 cup white wine
2 tablespoons shortening
⅛ teaspoon onion powder
1 teaspoon oregano
1 teaspoon minced parsley
¼ teaspoon rosemary
¼ teaspoon poultry seasoning
¼ teaspoon thyme
¼ teaspoon marjoram
1 teaspoon salt
¼ teaspoon pepper

Brown the chops on both sides in the shortening in a heavy skillet. Season with salt and pepper, and place in a casserole. Add all the other ingredients to the skillet. Mix well. Pour the mixture over the chops. Bake, covered, at 350° for 40 minutes. Lower the heat to 300° and bake 20 minutes longer, or until tender.

CHOPS IN MUSHROOM SAUCE

4   pork chops, center-cut, ½ inch thick, boned
2   tablespoons butter or margarine
1   medium onion, chopped
½   cup chopped mushrooms
1   tablespoon all-purpose flour
2   tablespoons cream
¼   cup apple juice, more if necessary
2   tablespoons water
2   tablespoons Worcestershire sauce
    Salt
    Pepper

Brown the chops in 1 tablespoon of the butter in a heavy skillet. Season with salt and pepper. Remove to a baking dish. Add the remaining tablespoon of butter to the skillet and fry the onion until golden. Stir in the mushrooms and fry lightly. Blend in the flour and cream. Slowly add the apple juice, water, and Worcestershire sauce. Stir over low heat until smooth. Pour over the chops. Bake, covered, at 350° for 1 hour, or until tender, adding apple juice if more liquid is needed.

WINE-MARINATED CHOPS

8   loin or rib pork chops, 1 inch thick
2   garlic cloves, sliced very thin
2   tablespoons cider vinegar
4   tablespoons olive oil
½   teaspoon thyme
1   cup white wine
1   cup pitted ripe olives, chopped medium fine
2   tablespoons Robert sauce
1½ teaspoons salt
¼   teaspoon pepper

Trim the fat from the chops and set it aside. Cut an opening in the side of each chop and insert a slice of garlic, then place the chops in a glass or enamel dish. Combine the vinegar, oil, salt, pepper, and thyme. Brush on both sides of the chops and pour any extra marinade around them. Allow the chops to marinate for 2 to 3 hours at room temperature, then remove and drain.

Cook the reserved pieces of fat in a heavy skillet over low heat until the bottom of the skillet is well coated with melted fat, then remove and discard the fat pieces. Brown the chops on both sides in the skillet, then place them in a baking dish. Add the wine and bake, covered, at 350° until tender (about 1¼ hours). Add the Robert sauce and the chopped olives to the juice in the baking dish and return to the oven just long enough to heat through (about 5 minutes).

OVEN-BARBECUED CHOPS

4 pork chops, 1 inch thick
1 large onion, sliced thin
1 tablespoon Worcestershire sauce
2 tablespoons vinegar
1 tablespoon granulated sugar
2 teaspoons chili powder
½ cup water
¾ cup catsup
   Salt
   Pepper

Trim most of the fat from the chops. Heat some of the fat in a heavy ovenproof skillet. Discard pieces of fat when the skillet is well greased. Brown the chops thoroughly in the skillet, then pour off all but 1 tablespoon of any remaining fat. Season the chops with salt and pepper and remove from the skillet.

Cook the onion in the skillet, stirring constantly, for about 3 minutes. Add the remaining ingredients. Blend thoroughly. Return the chops to the skillet, spooning some of the sauce over them. Bake, uncovered, at 325° for 1½ hours, or until tender. Baste occasionally with the sauce.

CORN-CRUSTED CHOPS

6 pork chops, 1 inch thick
1 egg, beaten
1 tablespoon milk
1 cup cornflakes, finely crushed
¼ teaspoon basil, crushed
3 tablespoons cooking oil
¼ cup water
1 teaspoon salt

Mix the egg and milk. Combine the cornflakes, basil, and salt. Dip the chops first in the egg mixture and then in the cornflakes, turning to coat all sides. In a skillet, brown the chops on both sides in the oil. Add the water. Simmer, covered, over low heat for 1 hour, lifting the chops occasionally to prevent sticking. Remove the cover for the last 15 minutes of cooking.

MOCK BOAR CHOPS

4 loin or rib pork chops, 1 inch thick
¾ cup bottled lemon juice
   Sprig of fresh rosemary or ½ teaspoon dried
½ cup flour
2 tablespoons cooking oil or fat
1 cup port wine
½ cup currant jelly
½ teaspoon salt
⅛ teaspoon pepper

Marinate the chops in the lemon juice, to which the rosemary has been added, for 2 or 3 hours or longer. Remove the chops from the marinade and drain them. Dredge the chops with the flour mixed with the salt and pepper. Brown in the oil over a low flame. Place in a casserole. Combine the wine and jelly by heating them in a small saucepan. Pour over the chops and bake, covered, at 350° for 1 hour.

TROPICAL CHOPS

6   loin or rib pork chops, ¾ inch thick
⅔   cup sherry
¼   cup soy sauce
6   canned pineapple slices, juice reserved
6   green pepper rings, parboiled until tender

Place the chops in a shallow baking pan. Combine the sherry, soy sauce, and reserved pineapple juice. Pour this over the chops and allow to stand at room temperature for at least 2 hours, turning the chops occasionally. Bake, uncovered, at 350° for 1 hour, turning and basting the chops three or four times.

To serve, top each chop with a slice of pineapple and a ring of pepper. Return to the oven to warm for a few minutes. This is especially good served with hot rice.

CHOPS WITH TOMATO SOUP

6   pork chops, 1 inch thick
    All-purpose flour
2   tablespoons shortening
6   slices onion
6   green pepper rings
1   can (10½ ounces) tomato soup
½   cup water
    Salt
    Pepper

Dredge the chops with the flour and season with salt and pepper. Brown quickly in the hot shortening, then place in a shallow baking dish. Put an onion slice and a green pepper ring on each chop. Dilute the soup with the water. Pour over the chops. Bake, covered, at 350° for 1 hour.

DEVILED CHOPS

4　pork chops, 1 inch thick
2　tablespoons butter or margarine
3　tablespoons chili sauce
1½　tablespoons lemon juice
1　tablespoon chopped onion
¼　teaspoon dry mustard
2　teaspoons Worcestershire sauce
⅛　teaspoon curry powder
½　cup water
¼　teaspoon paprika
½　teaspoon salt
⅛　teaspoon pepper

Brown the chops in the butter in a heavy skillet. Season with salt and pepper. Combine the chili sauce, lemon juice, and remaining ingredients. Pour the mixture over the chops. Simmer, covered, for 1 hour, or until the chops are tender. Serve over hot noodles or rice.

CHOPS AND PROSCIUTTO HAM

6　pork chops, 1 inch thick
2　ounces prosciutto ham, chopped fine
½　cup all-purpose flour
¼　cup olive oil
1　cup finely chopped onion
½　teaspoon finely chopped garlic
1　small bay leaf
1　cup drained, chopped canned tomatoes
½　cup dry white wine
1　cup water
1　hard-boiled egg, finely chopped
2　tablespoons chopped parsley
12　pitted black olives, cut in half lengthwise
¾　teaspoon salt
½　teaspoon freshly ground pepper

Dredge the chops with the flour and season with salt and pepper. Heat the oil in a heavy skillet and brown the chops in it, turning them frequently to brown evenly and to avoid burning. Remove the chops and keep them warm.

To the fat in the skillet add the onion, garlic, and bay leaf. Cook over moderate heat until the onion is soft and transparent. Add the tomatoes and ham and increase the heat. Cook until the pan juices are nearly evaporated. Slowly stir in the wine and the water. Add the egg, parsley, and olives. Bring to a boil. Return the chops to the skillet and baste them thoroughly with the sauce. Simmer, tightly covered, for 45 to 60 minutes, or until the chops are tender. Remove the chops to a warm platter and pour the sauce over them.

CHOPS PIQUANT

8   large pork chops, 1½ inches thick
2   tablespoons butter or margarine, more if necessary
1   large onion, grated, or 2 celery stalks, chopped
2   tablespoons all-purpose flour
1   teaspoon dry mustard
1   cup clear chicken stock
1   tablespoon capers
½   cup dry white wine
   Salt
   Pepper

Cut any excess fat from the chops. Cook them slowly, in the butter, on both sides in a large skillet until brown (about 30 minutes). Season with salt and pepper. Remove and keep warm. Sauté the onion or celery in the skillet until soft, adding more butter if necessary. Blend in the flour and mustard and slowly add the stock, stirring constantly. Return the chops to the skillet. Add the capers and wine, cover, and cook slowly for 40 minutes.

CHOPS WITH MUSHROOMS AND ONION SOUP

6   pork chops, ¾ inch thick
2   tablespoons butter or margarine
1¼ cups water
½   cup chopped celery
½   package dry onion soup mix
2   tablespoons all-purpose flour
1   tablespoon parsley flakes
1   can (6 ounces) evaporated milk
1   can (3 ounces) mushrooms, chopped
    Paprika
    Salt
    Pepper

Season the chops with salt, pepper, and paprika. Brown them on both sides in the butter, in a heavy skillet. Drain off the fat. Add 1 cup of the water, the celery, and the soup mix. Cook, covered, over low heat for 30 minutes. Turn the chops and cook for 30 minutes longer. Remove the chops from the skillet.

Combine the flour and ¼ cup of water and mix until smooth. Add the parsley and stir the mixture into the skillet juices. Add the milk and the mushrooms, then cook over low heat until thick and smooth. Just before serving, bring to a boil. Serve some of the sauce over the chops and the rest separately.

CHOPS AND APRICOTS IN CURRY SAUCE

8   pork chops, 1 inch thick
1   can (16 ounces) apricot halves
½   pound fresh mushrooms, sliced
2   medium onions, sliced
2   tablespoons butter or margarine
1   tablespoon curry powder
2   cans (10½ ounces each) cream of mushroom soup
½   cup dry white wine
    Salt
    Pepper

Place the chops in a shallow baking dish. Sprinkle lightly with salt and pepper. Drain the apricots, reserving ½ cup of juice. Place 2 apricot halves on each chop, cut side down, and set aside. Sauté the mushrooms and onions in the butter until the onions are soft. Stir in the curry powder, blending thoroughly. Then add the soup, wine, and apricot juice. Pour over the chops. Bake, uncovered, at 350° for 1 hour, or until tender.

DINNER PARTY CHOPS

4   thick pork chops, bones and fat removed
2   tablespoons all-purpose flour
½   teaspoon sage
2   tablespoons shortening
8   canned apricot halves, juice reserved
1½ tablespoons soy sauce
4   thin green pepper rings
1½ teaspoons salt
¼   teaspoon pepper

Put the flour, salt, pepper, and sage in a paper bag. Put one chop at a time in the bag and shake it until the meat is coated. Brown the chops in the shortening in a heavy skillet. Place 2 apricot halves on each chop. Add ½ cup of the reserved apricot juice and the soy sauce. Cover and simmer for 45 minutes to 1 hour, until the chops are tender. Put the pepper rings on top of the apricots 15 minutes before the meat is done.

APRICOT-GLAZED CHOPS

6   rib or loin pork chops, ¾ inch thick
1   cup dried apricots
1   tablespoon shortening
⅓   cup maple syrup
1   tablespoon lemon juice
    Salt
    Pepper

Soak the apricots for about 1 hour in water to cover. In a heavy skillet, brown the chops in the shortening. Pour off the excess fat. Season the chops with salt and pepper. Drain the apricots, reserving ⅓ cup of the liquid. Arrange the apricots on top of the chops. Combine the apricot liquid, syrup and lemon juice, mixing well. Pour this over the chops. Simmer, tightly covered, for 45 minutes to 1 hour, or until the chops are tender. Arrange the chops and apricots on a platter and spoon the sauce over them.

CHOPS WITH CURRY AND BANANAS

4   pork chops, ¾ inch thick
4   tablespoons butter
4   slices canned pineapple
4   cherry tomatoes
2   bananas
¼   teaspoon curry powder
1   teaspoon salt
    Pepper
    Hot, cooked rice

Sauce:

1   tablespoon minced onion
1½   tablespoons butter
1½   tablespoons all-purpose flour
1   cup beef bouillon
½   teaspoon curry powder
1   teaspoon tomato paste
¼   teaspoon salt
⅛   teaspoon pepper

Sauté the chops in 2 tablespoons of the butter until lightly browned. Transfer to a baking dish and season with salt and pepper. Bake, covered, at 350° for 50 minutes.

While the chops are baking, prepare the sauce as follows: sauté the onion in the butter. Blend in the flour. Add the bouillon, stirring constantly until smooth. Add the curry powder, tomato paste, salt, and pepper. Continue cooking until thick. Set aside until ready to serve.

Sauté the pineapple in the skillet in which the chops were browned. Remove the chops from the oven. Top each chop with a slice of pineapple and put a cherry tomato in the center of each slice. Return the chops to the oven for 5 to 10 minutes. While they finish cooking cut the bananas in half lengthwise. Blend the curry powder and 2 tablespoons of butter. Cook the bananas in this mixture until lightly browned.

Serve the chops on hot, cooked rice, surrounded with the banana halves and accompanied by the sauce.

CHOPS WITH PRUNES AND COGNAC

 6 **pork chops, 1 inch thick**
 ¼ **cup all-purpose flour**
 2 **tablespoons butter or margarine**
18 **unsweetened prunes**
 1 **cup port wine**
 2 **tablespoons Cognac**
 2 **tablespoons heavy cream**
1½ **teaspoons salt**
 ¼ **teaspoon freshly ground pepper**

Combine the flour, salt, and pepper. Coat the chops with this mixture by shaking together in a paper bag. In a heavy skillet, sauté the chops in the butter until brown, turning frequently. Remove to a baking dish and bake, uncovered, at 350° for 1 hour.

Soak the prunes in hot water for 15 minutes. Pour off the water, add the port, and cook for 15 minutes. Drain the prunes, reserving ½ cup of the liquid. Remove the pits. Warm the Cognac in a saucepan, pour it into the skillet in which you sautéed the chops, and set aflame. When the flame dies, add the prune liquid and the cream. Cook over high heat for 1 minute, scraping brown bits from the bottom of the skillet.

Place the chops on a serving platter and arrange the prunes around them. Pour the sauce over the chops.

FRUITED CHOPS

4   pork chops, ½ inch thick
1   tablespoon butter or margarine
1   cup prunes, pitted
1   cup dried apricots
1   cup orange juice, more if necessary
¼   teaspoon curry powder
2   tablespoons granulated sugar
1   teaspoon salt

Brown the chops in the butter in a heavy skillet. Remove to a shallow baking dish. Arrange the prunes and apricots around the chops. Blend the orange juice, curry powder, sugar, and salt. Pour this over the chops. Bake, covered, at 350° for 1 hour. During the baking, add more juice or water, if necessary, to keep the chops and fruit from sticking or drying out.

ORANGE CHOPS

4   loin pork chops, ¾ inch thick
1   tablespoon shortening
2   tablespoons chopped onion
½   cup fresh orange juice
2   tablespoons brown sugar
8   fresh orange sections
1   teaspoon salt
⅛   teaspoon pepper

Brown the chops on both sides in the shortening. Place in a shallow baking dish. Pour off all but 1 tablespoon of the shortening in the browning pan and use to brown the onion lightly. Stir in the orange juice, sugar, salt, and pepper and pour over the chops. Bake, covered, at 350° for 30 minutes. Arrange the orange sections over the chops. Bake for 15 minutes longer, or until the chops are tender.

CHOPS WITH ORANGE AND CHUTNEY

4 loin pork chops, ¾ inch thick
2 tablespoons cooking oil
½ cup water
¼ cup chopped chutney
¼ cup granulated sugar
2 tablespoons lemon juice
1 orange, peeled and cut in 4 slices, ½ inch thick

Brown the chops in the oil, on both sides, in a heavy skillet. Pour off excess fat and season the chops with salt and pepper. Add ¼ cup of the water. Simmer, covered, for about 45 minutes, or until tender.

Combine the chutney, sugar, lemon juice, and remaining ¼ cup of water. Place the orange slices on the chops. Pour the chutney mixture over chops. Continue cooking for 15 minutes, occasionally spooning the liquid over the chops, until it becomes syrupy. Arrange the chops on a serving dish. Stir the pan juices, pour over the chops.

CHOPS WITH ORANGE SLICES AND CATSUP

6 loin pork chops, ¾ inch thick
2 tablespoons cooking oil
6 tablespoons brown sugar
6 orange slices, including rind, ½ inch thick
6 slices sweet, red onion, same size as the orange slices
6 tablespoons catsup or chili sauce
½ cup warm water
2 teaspoons salt
⅛ teaspoon pepper

Brown the chops on both sides in the cooking oil. Place in a shallow baking dish. Season with salt and pepper. Top each chop with 1 tablespoon brown sugar, an orange slice, an onion slice, and 1 tablespoon catsup. Pour the water into the baking dish around the chops. Bake, uncovered, at 350° for 50 minutes, or until tender.

ORANGE GINGER CHOPS

6   pork chops
¼   cup orange juice
1   teaspoon ground ginger
1   large orange, peeled and cut into 6 slices
6   tablespoons sour cream
½   teaspoon salt

Trim the fat from the chops and place them in a shallow baking dish. Pour the orange juice over them. Bake, covered, at 350° for 30 minutes. Remove the dish from the oven, turn the chops, and sprinkle them with the salt and ginger. Place an orange slice on top of each chop, re-cover, and return to the oven for another 30 minutes.

When the meat is tender, put 1 tablespoon of sour cream on each chop and allow them to stand, covered, for 5 to 10 minutes before serving.

CHOPS CALCUTTA

2   large loin pork chops
1½ teaspoons shortening
¼   cup plum jam
¼   teaspoon grated orange peel
1   teaspoon mei yen seasoning
½   teaspoon curry powder
1¼ teaspoons instant minced dried onion
1   tablespoon lemon or lime juice
¾   cup water
½   teaspoon cornstarch
1   teaspoon salt
¼   teaspoon pepper

Brown the chops on both sides in the shortening. Season with salt and pepper and remove from the pan. Combine the plum jam, orange peel, mei yen seasoning, curry powder, and onion. Stir into the pan juices. Stir in the lemon juice and ½ cup of the water. Return the chops to the pan. Simmer, covered, for 1 hour. Turn chops occasionally to ensure an even glaze. Remove the chops to a platter and keep warm.

Skim the fat from the pan liquid. Combine the cornstarch with remaining ¼ cup water and stir into the pan liquid. Cook over low heat, stirring occasionally, until thick. Pour over the chops.

CHOPS IN PLUM SAUCE

4   loin pork chops, 1½ inches thick
2   tablespoons butter
1   cup plums with tapioca (junior food)
½   cup tawny port
1   teaspoon grated lemon rind
¼   teaspoon ground cinnamon
⅛   teaspoon ground cloves
    Dried sage
    All-purpose flour
    Salt
    Pepper

Season the chops on both sides with sage, salt, and pepper, then flour lightly and brown in the butter over medium heat. Place in a baking dish. Combine the remaining ingredients and pour over the chops. Bake, covered, at 325° for 1½ hours, basting occasionally.

PEACH-CROWNED CHOPS

4   loin pork chops, 1 inch thick
2   tablespoons brown sugar
2   tablespoons prepared mustard
1   tablespoon Worcestershire sauce
4   canned peach halves
½   teaspoon salt
¼   teaspoon pepper

Season the chops with the salt and pepper. Place in a shallow baking dish and bake, covered, at 350° for 30 minutes. Combine the sugar, mustard, and Worcestershire sauce. Uncover the chops and spread half of the mixture over them. Continue to bake, uncovered, for 20 minutes. Place a peach half, skin side down, on each chop and fasten with a wooden pick. Brush the chops and peaches with the remaining sugar mixture and continue to bake, uncovered, for 20 minutes, or until the chops are tender.

CHOP AND PEACH TOWERS

4   loin pork chops, 1 inch thick, with pockets
4   teaspoons chopped onion
2   tablespoons brown sugar
2   teaspoons prepared mustard
1   teaspoon Worcestershire sauce
4   canned peach halves
1   tomato, quartered
4   stuffed olives
  Salt
  Pepper

Sprinkle the chops with a little salt and pepper, including the insides of the pockets. Stuff each pocket with 1 teaspoon chopped onion. Place the chops in a shallow baking dish, cover with foil. Bake at 350° for 20 minutes.

Combine the sugar, mustard, and Worcestershire. Uncover the chops, spread with half of the sugar mixture, and return to the oven for 20 minutes longer. Remove from the oven and place a peach half, cut side up, on each chop, fastening with a wooden pick. Brush the chops and peach halves with the remaining sugar mixture and bake for 10 minutes longer.

Remove the chops to a serving platter. Fasten a tomato wedge and an olive to each peach.

CHOPS À LA BOURSE

6   pork chops, ¾ inch thick
2   tablespoons shortening
3   apples, peeled and sliced
4   potatoes, peeled and sliced
1   cup beef bouillon
¼   cup claret
6   drops Tabasco sauce
1   teaspoon Worcestershire sauce
6   slices bacon
2   onions, chopped fine
2   teaspoons salt
¼   teaspoon pepper

Brown the chops in the shortening in a hot skillet. Remove to a casserole, season with salt and pepper. Arrange the apples evenly over the chops. Place the potatoes over the chops and apples and sprinkle with salt. Combine the bouillon, wine, Tabasco, and Worcestershire. Pour over the contents of the casserole and set aside.

Fry the bacon to medium crispness. Remove from pan and pour off half the bacon fat. Add the onion and cook until soft. Spread over contents of the casserole. Arrange the bacon strips on top. Bake at 350° for 1 hour.

CHOPS BAKED WITH APPLES

4   pork chops, 1 inch thick, fat trimmed off
4   cups peeled, sliced tart apples
¼   cup raisins
¼   cup molasses
¼   cup water
1   tablespoon shortening
1   teaspoon grated lemon rind
    Salt
    Pepper

Brown the chops on both sides in the shortening. Sprinkle with salt and pepper. Combine the remaining ingredients and pour into a casserole. Put the chops on top. Bake at 350° for 1 hour, or until the chops are tender.

NORMANDIE CHOPS

6   pork chops, ¾ to 1 inch thick
2   tablespoons shortening
2   medium tart apples, cored and sliced
12   prunes, cooked and pitted
¼   cup granulated sugar
1   cup apple juice
1   teaspoon salt

Brown the chops in the shortening. Drain off excess fat and season with the salt. Arrange the apples and half the prunes in the bottom of a 2-quart greased casserole. Place the chops on the fruit. Place one of the remaining 6 prunes on each chop. Combine the sugar and apple juice. Pour over chops and fruit. Bake, covered, at 350° for 1 hour, or until tender.

CHOPS AND APPLE CASSEROLE

6   pork chops, ¾ inch thick
3   tablespoons shortening
3   apples, peeled, cored, and sliced in thirds
6   small white onions
2   teaspoons seedless raisins
1   tablespoon brown sugar
¼   teaspoon nutmeg
½   teaspoon thyme
¾   cup beef bouillon
1½   teaspoons salt
¼   teaspoon pepper

Brown the chops in the shortening, and season with salt and pepper. Place in a casserole. Cover with the apple slices. Add the onions and raisins and sprinkle with the sugar, nutmeg, and thyme. Carefully pour in the bouillon. Bake, covered, at 350° for 1 hour, or until the chops are tender.

FLEMISH CHOPS

4 loin or rib pork chops, 1¼ inches thick
4 tablespoons butter or margarine
2 apples, cored, peeled, and sliced ½ inch thick
¼ teaspoon cinnamon
1 tablespoon granulated sugar
¼ cup dark rum
   Salt
   Pepper

Brown the chops on both sides in 2 tablespoons of the butter, using an ovenproof skillet. Season with salt and pepper. Remove the chops and keep warm.

Sprinkle the apples with the cinnamon and sauté them on both sides in the skillet for about 4 minutes. Sprinkle them with the sugar and then with the rum. Place the chops on the apple rings. Dot each chop with ½ tablespoon of the remaining butter. Bake, covered, at 350° for 50 to 60 minutes, or until tender.

Transfer the apples and chops to a hot platter. Skim the fat from the skillet juice, and pour the juice over the chops.

CHOPS WITH PINEAPPLE AND PRUNES

6   pork chops, 1 inch thick
2   tablespoons shortening
3   large sweet potatoes
2   tablespoons lemon juice
6   slices canned pineapple, drained and juice reserved
12 large prunes
12 whole cloves
    Salt
    Pepper

Brown the chops in the shortening and sprinkle with salt and pepper. Peel the potatoes, cut lengthwise in 1-inch-thick slices, and rub with the lemon juice. Place on top of the meat. Top with the pineapple slices. Remove the pits from the prunes, insert one clove in each and place on the pineapple slices. Add the reserved pineapple juice. Cook, covered, over light heat until steaming. Turn the heat to very low and cook 45 minutes to 1 hour longer, or until tender.

HAWAIIAN CHOPS

8 pork chops, ¾ inch thick
2 tablespoons shortening
1 cup water
1 cup canned pineapple chunks, drained, juice reserved
¼ cup cider vinegar
½ cup brown sugar
2 tablespoons soy sauce
2 tablespoons cornstarch
1 green pepper, cut in strips
2 tomatoes, cut in wedges
1 cup canned, sliced bamboo shoots, drained
1 can (4 ounces) button mushrooms
1 cup canned water chestnuts, drained and sliced

Brown the chops in the shortening in a heavy skillet. Pour off excess fat. Add ¼ cup of the water. Cover tightly. Simmer for 45 minutes, until tender. Remove from the skillet and keep warm.

Meanwhile, combine ½ cup water, the reserved pineapple juice, vinegar, brown sugar, and soy sauce. Blend the cornstarch and the remaining ¼ cup water and stir into the mixture. Pour into the skillet and cook, stirring constantly, until thick. Add the remaining ingredients. Simmer for about 8 minutes. Pour over the chops and serve immediately.

ORIENTAL CHOPS

6   pork chops, 1 inch thick
2   tablespoons all-purpose flour
2   tablespoons butter or margarine
1   tablespoon cornstarch
1   can (13¼ ounces) pineapple chunks, drained, juice reserved
2   tablespoons sweet pickle relish
2   tablespoons soy sauce
1   tablespoon granulated sugar
1   can (11 ounces) mandarin oranges, drained
½   teaspoon paprika
1   teaspooon salt

Dredge the chops in the flour seasoned with the salt and paprika. Brown on both sides in the butter. Place in a shallow baking dish. Make a smooth paste of the cornstarch and 2 tablespoons of the reserved pineapple juice. Add the pineapple chunks and remaining juice, relish, soy sauce, sugar, and oranges. Mix thoroughly, and pour over the chops. Bake, covered with foil, at 350° for 1 hour, or until the chops are tender.

CHOPS CANTONESE

6   loin pork chops, ¾ inch thick
3   tablespoons shortening
¼   cup plus 2 tablespoons water
1   cup chicken broth
1   can (13¼ ounces) pineapple chunks, drained, juice reserved
2   teaspoons soy sauce
1   teaspoon ground ginger
2   tablespoons vinegar
1   tablespoon brown sugar
2   tomatoes, cubed
1   green pepper, cut in 1-inch squares
2   tablespoons cornstarch
1½   teaspoons salt
¼   teaspoon pepper

Brown the chops on both sides in the shortening. Season with salt and pepper, add the ¼ cup water, and cook, covered, over low heat for 40 minutes. Drain the chops and remove to a hot platter.

Add the chicken broth, reserved pineapple juice, soy sauce, ginger, vinegar, and brown sugar to the skillet in which the chops were cooked. Bring to a boil. Add the tomatoes, green pepper, and pineapple. Simmer for 5 minutes. Blend the cornstarch and the 2 tablespoons water. Add to the skillet mixture, stirring constantly until thick and clear. Pour over the chops.

CHOPS LIDDLE

5   pork chops
1   can (8 ounces) crushed pineapple
4   teaspoons honey
¼   teaspoon dry mustard
¾   teaspoon ground ginger
⅓   cup soy sauce

Marinate the chops in a mixture of the pineapple, honey, mustard, ginger, and soy sauce for at least 2 hours or as long as 8. Transfer the chops to a shallow baking pan and pour on the marinade. Bake, uncovered, at 350° for 30 minutes. Scrape the marinade from the tops of the chops and turn them. Replace the marinade on each chop and bake for another 30 minutes, or until the chops are tender.

To serve, leave the marinade that remains on top of each chop, but do not use the liquid in the pan.

CHOPS WITH CHESTNUTS AND RED CABBAGE

6   loin pork chops, ½ inch thick
1   egg, beaten with 1 tablespoon water
2   tablespoons butter
2   tablespoons all-purpose flour
1   cup chicken broth
1   teaspoon lemon juice

2   **teaspoons chopped fresh parsley**
1   **pound chestnuts, cooked and peeled**
3   **pounds red cabbage, shredded**
1   **cup dry red wine**
2   **teaspoons salt**
¼ **teaspoon pepper**

Dip the chops in the beaten egg. Brown in the butter for 5 minutes on each side. Cook, covered, over low heat for 30 minutes, turning twice. Remove and keep warm.

Combine the flour, salt, and pepper. Put into the pan in which the meat was cooked. Add the broth, stirring constantly until the mixture boils. Cook, covered, over very low heat for 10 minutes. Add the lemon juice and parsley. Combine the chestnuts, cabbage, and wine and add to the sauce. Cook, covered, over low heat for 15 minutes.

To serve, place the chops in the center of a platter and surround with the cabbage mixture.

BAKED CHOP DINNER

6   **loin pork chops, ¾ inch thick**
6   **medium potatoes, peeled and cut in half**
1   **package onion gravy mix**
2   **large tomatoes, each sliced in three crosswise, or 1 can (16 ounces) whole tomatoes**
1   **green pepper, diced**
2   **cups diced celery**
1   **can (4 ounces) mushrooms**
1   **teaspoon salt**
¼ **teaspoon pepper**

Arrange the chops and potatoes in a 13 × 9 × 2-inch baking dish and sprinkle with the salt, pepper, and gravy mix. Place a tomato slice on each chop. Combine the green pepper, celery, and mushrooms. Cover the chops and potatoes with the mixture. Bake, covered with foil, at 350° for 1 hour. Uncover and bake for 15 minutes longer.

CHOPS WITH KIDNEY BEANS

4   pork chops
2   tablespoons shortening
1   onion, sliced
1   can (8 ounces) red kidney beans, drained
2   tablespoons chili powder
1   can (10½ ounces) tomato soup
2   tablespoons water
4   green pepper rings
    Garlic powder to taste
    Salt
    Pepper

Brown the chops on both sides in the shortening, then add the onion and
sauté for a few minutes. Pour off the fat. Combine all the remaining
ingredients except the pepper rings and pour over the chops. Place a
pepper ring on each and simmer, covered, for 35 minutes, stirring
occasionally. Cook, uncovered, for 10 minutes longer to thicken the
sauce.

CHOPS WITH SWEET-SOUR CABBAGE

6   pork chops, trimmed
2   tablespoons cooking oil
1   cup tomato juice
1   onion, chopped fine
¼   cup vinegar
2   tablespoons soy sauce
1   tablespoon granulated sugar
5   cups coarsely cut cabbage
½   teaspoon salt
¼   teaspoon pepper

Brown the chops in the oil. Season. Combine all the other ingredients
except the cabbage and pour over the chops. Cover and cook at high
heat until steaming. Lower the heat and simmer for 35 minutes. Add the

cabbage, cover, and cook for 10 minutes. Remove the chops. Toss the cabbage in the sauce. Serve the chops and cabbage together.

CHOPS WITH SHREDDED CABBAGE

6 pork chops, 1 inch thick
2 tablespoons butter or margarine
¼ cup chopped onion
1 can (10½ ounces) mushroom soup
½ cup milk
3 medium potatoes, peeled and cut into ½-inch slices
1 quart shredded cabbage
¼ cup all-purpose flour
2½ teaspoons salt
½ teaspoon pepper

Brown the chops in the butter on both sides. Season and remove from the skillet. In the same skillet, combine the onion, soup, and milk. Place alternate layers of potatoes and cabbage in a 2-quart casserole. Sprinkle each layer with the flour, salt, and pepper. Pour some of the liquid mixture over each layer. Place the chops on top. Bake, covered with foil, at 350° for 1 hour 15 minutes.

SIMPLE CHOP CASSEROLE

4 lean pork chops or steaks
½ cup all-purpose flour
4 medium potatoes, peeled and sliced thin
  Butter
  Milk to cover
1 teaspoon salt
¼ teaspoon pepper

Combine the flour, salt, and pepper. Place a layer of potatoes in a baking dish. Sprinkle with the flour mixture and dot with butter. Repeat these layers until the baking dish is three-quarters full. Barely cover with warm milk and place the chops on top. Bake, covered, at 350° for 1 hour. Uncover and bake for 10 minutes longer to brown the chops.

SPANISH CHOPS

4 **pork chops**
1 **cup raw rice**
1 **onion, sliced**
2 **tablespoons chopped celery**
2 **cups tomato juice**
2 **tablespoons minced fresh parsley**
   Salt
   Pepper

Boil the rice in salted water for 10 minutes. Meanwhile, trim the fat off the chops, melt it in an ovenproof skillet and brown the chops in it. Season with salt and pepper. Remove the chops and brown the onion and celery in the same pan. Place the chops on top of the onion and celery mixture. Drain the rice and place a mound on each chop. Pour the tomato juice over and around the chops and rice and sprinkle with parsley. Bake, covered, at 350° for 45 minutes to 1 hour.

CHOPS WITH SAFFRON RICE

6 **pork chops, ½ to ¾ inch thick**
2 **tablespoons shortening**
1 **package (6 ounces) saffron rice mix**
1 **beef bouillon cube**
1¾ **cups hot water**
½ **cup sour cream**
½ **teaspoon salt**
   Pepper

Brown the chops in the shortening. Drain off excess fat and season with the salt and pepper. Add the rice mix. Dissolve the bouillon cube in the hot water and pour over the rice. Bring to a boil. Cover, reduce the heat, and cook as directed on the rice package. Remove the chops to a platter. Stir the sour cream into the rice mixture. Heat through, but do not allow to boil. Serve on the platter with the chops.

CHOPS WITH CHEESE

6 pork chops, 1 inch thick
2 tablespoons shortening
¾ cup raw rice
1 can (8 ounces) tomato sauce
1½ tablespoons taco seasoning
1½ cups water
½ cup grated Cheddar cheese
1 green pepper, cut into 6 rings, ½ inch thick
1 teaspoon salt

Brown the chops on both sides in the shortening, then season with the salt and place in a shallow baking pan. Sprinkle the rice around the chops. Combine the tomato sauce, taco seasoning, and water. Pour over the chops and rice. Bake, covered with foil, at 350° for 1 hour. Remove the cover, sprinkle with cheese, and top with the pepper rings. Then bake, covered, for 10 minutes longer.

CHOPS WITH RICE AND CHICKEN BROTH

4 pork chops, center-cut, ¾ inch thick
½ teaspoon ground ginger
1 tablespoon all-purpose flour
2 tablespoons shortening
¾ cup converted long-grain rice
4 green pepper rings
4 onion rings
4 tomato slices
1½ cups chicken broth
½ teaspoon salt

Mix the salt, ginger, and flour. Coat the chops with this mixture, then brown them in the shortening, on both sides, over moderate heat. Sprinkle the rice in a shallow casserole. Set the chops on the rice, then place a pepper ring, onion ring, and tomato slice on each chop. Pour the chicken broth over and bake, covered, at 350° for 50 to 60 minutes, checking occasionally to see if more broth is needed.

CHOPS À LA MADEIRA

 4 loin or rib pork chops, 1 inch thick
 2 tablespoons bacon drippings
 1 large onion, sliced thick
 4 green pepper rings
1½ cups raw rice
 2 cans (8 ounces each) tomato sauce
 ¾ cup Madeira or medium-dry sherry
 ½ teaspoon poultry seasoning
 ¼ cup boiling water, if necessary
 ¼ teaspoon salt
 ⅛ teaspoon pepper

Brown the chops slowly in the bacon drippings in a heavy skillet. Remove to a baking dish and place an onion slice and a pepper ring on each chop. Put the rice around the chops. Mix the tomato sauce and Madeira. Heat to the boiling point, and pour over the chops and rice. Bake, covered, at 350° for 30 minutes. Then check the liquid; if not sufficient, add ¼ cup boiling water. Continue baking another 30 minutes, or until the meat is tender.

CHOPS WITH SAUERKRAUT

 6 loin pork chops, 1 inch thick
3¼ cups drained sauerkraut
 2 teaspoons chopped chives
 ¼ teaspoon dill weed
 6 tablespoons butter or margarine
 1 cup chicken broth or bouillon
 6 medium baking apples
 ¼ cup firmly packed brown sugar
 ¼ cup dark, seedless raisins
    Salt
    Pepper

Combine the sauerkraut, chives, and dill and put in a large, shallow baking dish. Sauté the chops, in 3 tablespoons of the butter, in a heavy skillet until brown on both sides. Add salt and pepper. Remove the chops, reserving 2 tablespoons of drippings, and arrange them on the sauerkraut. Pour on the bouillon.

Core the apples and pare 1 inch of skin from the top. Combine the sugar, raisins, and 2 tablespoons of butter. Stuff the apples with the mixture. Place in the baking dish, around the chops. Melt the remaining butter and brush it over the apples. Cover only the chops with foil. Bake at 350° for 45 minutes, basting the apples occasionally with the skillet drippings. Remove the foil and continue baking 20 minutes longer, or until the apples are tender.

CHOPS WITH RICE AND ONION SOUP

4 loin pork chops, 1 inch thick
¾ cup raw rice
1 can (10½ ounces) onion soup
¼ cup dry white wine
½ cup water
1 package (¾ ounce) brown gravy mix, prepared as directed
   Salt
   Pepper

Mix the rice, soup, wine, and water and put in a casserole. Place the chops on top of the rice and season them with salt and pepper. Bake, covered, at 350° for 1 hour. Uncover, brush the chops with the gravy sauce, and bake for 30 minutes longer.

CHOPS WITH YAMS

8 loin pork chops, 1¼ inches thick
2 tablespoons shortening
½ cup molasses
½ teaspoon oregano
¼ teaspoon thyme
1 teaspoon soy sauce
2 tablespoons lemon juice
1 cup water
3 medium fresh yams, cooked and sliced, or
   ·canned yams, drained and sliced
½ teaspoon salt
¼ teaspoon freshly ground pepper

Brown the chops on both sides in the shortening, in an ovenproof skillet. Season with the salt and pepper. In a saucepan, thoroughly mix ⅓ cup of the molasses, the oregano, thyme, soy sauce, lemon juice, and water. Pour 1 cup of this sauce over the chops and bake, covered, at 325° for 1 hour. Remove the skillet from the oven and top each chop with a yam slice. Combine the remaining molasses with the remaining sauce and brush the yams with the mixture. Put under the broiler for a few minutes until the yams are browned.

CHOPS WITH MIXED VEGETABLES

6	pork chops, 1 inch thick
3	medium sweet potatoes or white potatoes, cut in half
1	package (10 ounces) frozen peas, thawed
2	medium carrots, cut in 1-inch slices
1	green pepper, chopped fine
1	tablespoon all-purpose flour
3	tablespoons butter or margarine
1	tablespoon cornstarch
1	cup hot water
1½	teaspoons salt
¼	teaspoon pepper

Place the potatoes, peas, carrots, and green pepper in a baking dish. Dredge the chops with flour, sprinkle with the pepper and ½ teaspoon of the salt, and brown in the butter. Remove from the skillet and place on top of the vegetables. Add the cornstarch to the skillet drippings, mixing carefully. Slowly add the hot water and stir until thick and smooth. Add 1 teaspoon salt, then pour the sauce over the meat and vegetables. Bake, covered, at 350° for 50 minutes. Uncover and bake 10 minutes longer.

CHOPS WITH RICE AND MUSHROOM SOUP

2	pork chops, 1 inch thick, with pockets
⅔	cup cooked rice
1	tablespoon finely chopped onion

1½   teaspoons chopped fresh parsley
½   teaspoon seasoned salt
1½   tablespoons shortening
 1   package (1½ ounces) dehydrated mushroom soup
 1   cup hot water
     Salt
     Pepper

Combine the rice, onion, parsley, and seasoned salt. Stuff the chops with
the mixture and secure with wooden picks. Brown in an ovenproof skillet
in the shortening, pouring off any excess fat. Season with salt and
pepper. Sprinkle the mushroom soup in the skillet. Add the water and
stir until the soup is dissolved. Bake, covered, at 350° for 1 hour.

CHOPS WITH CRANBERRY-WALNUT STUFFING

 4   pork chops, 1 inch thick, with pockets
 1   cup herb-seasoned stuffing mix
⅓   cup boiling water
 4   tablespoons butter
½   cup whole cranberry sauce
¼   cup chopped walnuts
¼   teaspoon grated orange rind
 1   can (10½ ounces) mushroom gravy
½   cup orange juice
⅛   teaspoon ground cloves
 4   orange slices
     Cinnamon
     Salt
     Pepper

Combine the stuffing mix, water, and half the butter. Add the cranberry
sauce, walnuts, and orange rind, mixing gently. Stuff the chops with the
mixture and brown them on both sides, in the remaining butter, in a
heavy skillet. Season with salt and pepper. Mix the gravy, orange juice,
and cloves and pour over the chops. Cook, covered, over very low heat
for 1 hour, or until tender. Before serving, top each chop with an orange
slice and sprinkle with cinnamon.

HAWAIIAN STUFFED CHOPS

8 rib pork chops, 1¼ inches thick, with pockets
2 tablespoons shortening
½ cup finely cut celery
1 tablespoon butter
1 can (8 ounces) crushed pineapple, drained and juice reserved
2 cups dry bread crumbs
½ plus ⅛ teaspoon ginger
   Water
   All-purpose flour
½ teaspoon salt
⅛ teaspoon pepper

Brown the chops on one side in the shortening. In another pan, cook the celery in the butter until tender. Combine the celery, drained pineapple, bread crumbs, salt, pepper and the ½ teaspoon ginger. Stuff the chops with this mixture, then place them, brown side up, in a baking dish. Sprinkle with the ⅛ teaspoon ginger and bake, covered, at 350° for 1½ hours. Combine the pan drippings with the reserved pineapple juice, and add water to make 1½ cups. Thicken with enough flour to make gravy and serve with the chops.

CHOPS WITH CRANBERRY-ORANGE STUFFING

4 pork chops, 1 inch thick, with pockets
2 tablespoons butter or margarine
1 cup chopped, peeled apple
½ cup diced celery
¾ cup cranberry-orange relish
⅓ cup granulated sugar
1 cup soft, coarse bread crumbs
1 teaspoon salt

Melt the butter in a small, heavy skillet. Add the apples and celery and cook slowly, covered, until the apples soften, stirring once or twice. Remove from the heat and add the relish, sugar, ½ teaspoon of the salt, and the bread crumbs. Toss lightly to blend. Stuff the pockets of the chops; fasten with wooden picks. Arrange in a baking dish, sprinkle with the remaining salt, and bake, uncovered, at 350° about 1½ hours, or until the chops are tender. Cover the baking dish after the chops have browned.

APPLE-STUFFED CHOPS

6   double-thick pork chops, with pockets
1   cup finely cut tart apples
2   tablespoons brown sugar
2   tablespoons lemon juice
1   can (8 ounces) tomato sauce
1   bottle (7 ounces) sparkling water
1½   teaspoons salt
⅛   teaspoon freshly ground pepper

Toss the apples with the brown sugar and lemon juice. Stuff the pork chop pockets with the mixture and sprinkle both sides of the chops with the salt and pepper. Place the chops in a shallow baking dish. Combine the tomato sauce and sparkling water, pour over the chops, and bake, uncovered, at 350° for 1½ hours, basting several times. Remove excess fat before serving.

CHOPS WITH GREEN OLIVES

12   pork chops, ½ inch thick
½   cup chopped celery
½   cup chopped onion
2   tablespoons butter
1   cup bread stuffing
1   cup sliced stuffed olives
2   cans (8 ounces each) tomato sauce

Cook the celery and half the onion in the butter until tender but not brown. Stir in the bread stuffing and ½ cup of the olives, mixing well. Place 6 chops in a shallow baking dish. Spoon some stuffing mixture on each chop, then place another chop on top. Fasten together with skewers or wooden picks and bake, covered with foil, at 350° for 45 minutes.

In a saucepan combine the tomato sauce and the remaining olives and onion. Heat through. Uncover the meat and spoon the olive mixture on the chops. Cook, uncovered, for about 20 minutes longer, or until the meat is tender.

CHOPS STUFFED WITH RICE

2 thick pork chops, with pockets
⅔ cup cooked rice
1 tablespoon finely chopped onion
1½ teaspoons chopped fresh parsley
½ teaspoon seasoned salt
1½ teaspoons shortening
1 package (1½ ounces) dehydrated mushroom soup mix
1 cup hot water
½ teaspoon salt
2 dashes freshly ground pepper

Combine the rice, onion, parsley, and seasoned salt. Stuff the chops with the mixture and secure with wood picks. Season the chops with the salt and pepper, then brown them in shortening in an ovenproof skillet. Pour off excess fat. Sprinkle the mushroom soup in the skillet and add the water, stirring to dissolve. Bake, covered, at 350° for 1 hour.

CHOPS STUFFED WITH PRETZELS

6 thick pork chops, with pockets
3 tablespoons shortening
¼ cup chopped onion
¼ cup chopped celery
¾ cup crushed pretzels
¼ teaspoon marjoram, crushed
3 tablespoons water
2 tablespoons all-purpose flour
1½ cups beef bouillon
1 teaspoon salt
⅛ teaspoon pepper

Brown the chops in the shortening in a heavy skillet. Season them with the salt and pepper, then remove and allow to cool. In the same skillet, cook the onion and celery until tender. Add the pretzels and marjoram, mixing well. Sprinkle with the water until evenly moist. Stuff the chops with the mixture and place in a baking dish. Bake, covered, at 350° for 45 minutes to 1 hour. Meanwhile, stir the flour into the skillet juices. Add the bouillon and cook, stirring constantly, until thick and smooth. Serve with the chops.

CHOPS STUFFED AND SKEWERED

8 rib pork chops, ½ to ¾ inch thick
2 tablespoons butter or margarine
1 cup water
1 package (7 ounces) herb-seasoned bread stuffing
1½ cups diced, unpeeled apples
½ cup seedless raisins
½ teaspoon sage
   Salt

Trim some of the fat from the chops and render it in a heavy skillet. Brown the chops in it. Remove the chops from the skillet and salt lightly and pour off the fat.

Melt the butter in the same skillet. Add the water and stir in the stuffing, apples, raisins, and sage. Make a stack, beginning with a chop, alternating with even amounts of the stuffing, and ending with a chop. Skewer together with long skewers. Place in a baking pan, turning over so the fat edges of the chops are up. Bake at 325° for 1 hour, or until tender.

CHOPS WITH PINEAPPLE STUFFING

6 rib pork chops, 1¼ inches thick, with pockets
½ cup finely cut celery
3 tablespoons butter or margarine
2 cups packaged stuffing, prepared as directed
1 can (8½ ounces) crushed pineapple, drained and juice reserved
¼ plus ⅛ teaspoon ground ginger
   All-purpose flour
1¾ teaspoons salt

Sauté the celery in 1 tablespoon of the butter until tender. Combine the celery, stuffing, pineapple, ¼ teaspoon of the salt and ¼ teaspoon ginger and stuff the chops with the mixture.

In a skillet, brown the chops on one side in the remaining 2 tablespoons butter. Remove the chops, leaving the drippings in the skillet, and place, brown side up, in a baking dish. Combine the salt and the ⅛ teaspoon ginger. Sprinkle over the chops, then bake, tightly covered, at 350° for 1¼ hours.

Measure the skillet drippings and add the pineapple juice and enough water to make 1½ cups. Thicken this with flour to make a gravy and serve with the chops.

CHOPS WITH WALNUT STUFFING

6   double rib pork chops, with pockets
¼   cup chopped walnuts
**½   package (8 ounces) herb-flavored stuffing, prepared as
       directed on the package**
3   teaspoons butter or margarine
¼   cup medium-dry sherry
¼   cup boiling water
     Salt
     Pepper

Add the walnuts to the prepared stuffing. Stuff the chops with the mixture, then brown, in the butter, on both sides in a skillet. Season with salt and pepper, then remove to a shallow baking dish. Pour the fat from the skillet. Add the sherry and water, stirring to mix in any brown bits in the pan. Pour this over the chops and bake, covered, at 350° for 1¼ hours, or until the chops are tender.

CHOPS STUFFED WITH CORN

8   double rib pork chops, with pockets
2   cups white bread crumbs
2   cups whole-kernel corn
1   teaspoon poultry seasoning
2   tablespoons chopped fresh parsley
1   tablespoon chopped onion
1   tablespoon butter or margarine, more if necessary
1   egg, beaten
1   cup chopped apple
¼   cup half-and-half
1   teaspoon salt
¼   teaspoon pepper

Mix the bread crumbs, corn, salt, pepper, and poultry seasoning. Sauté the parsley and onion in the butter and add to the corn mixture, then combine the beaten egg and the apple and add this as well. Lightly stir in the half-and-half. Stuff the chops with the mixture and fasten with wooden picks. Brown on both sides in the skillet, adding more shortening if needed. Sprinkle with the salt and pepper and bake, covered, at 350° for 1 hour, or until tender.

Glazes, Sauces, and Marinades

Too many cooks spoil not only the broth but sauces, glazes, and marinades by not giving enough attention to these delicacies, which are the distinctive mark of the gourmet cook and which have a special place in pork cookery. They are, for instance, the heart and soul of baked ham, giving it distinction and showing the originality and imagination of the cook. They heighten flavor and give a decorative color to many other dishes.

A non-metallic container is generally recommended for use with acid marinades, because it ensures safety and flavor.

A mixture of dry spices and herbs, to be rubbed into the meat (and sometimes erroneously referred to as "dry marinade") is not recommended. It is hard to spread on meat, and it draws out the juice instead of retaining and enhancing it.

PINEAPPLE SHERRY GLAZE

1   cup brown sugar
1   teaspoon dry mustard
¼   cup sherry
1   can (8 ounces) crushed pineapple, drained

Make a smooth paste of the sugar, mustard, and sherry, then blend in the pineapple. Spoon the mixture over a baked ham. Turn up the oven to 400° for about 10 minutes, basting once or twice.

RED CURRANT GLAZE

⅔ cup red currant jelly
1 teaspoon dry mustard
3 tablespoons port
2 teaspoons white wine vinegar

Combine all of the ingredients in a saucepan. Bring to a boil, stirring constantly, over moderate heat, then lower the heat and cook for 10 minutes, stirring occasionally. This may be used either as a glaze or a sauce.

HONEY GLAZE

1 cup honey, warmed
1 teaspoon dry mustard
½ teaspoon ground cloves

Combine all the ingredients until thoroughly blended. Spoon the mixture over the ham.

BEER AND MUSTARD GLAZE FOR HAM

1 cup granulated sugar
1 teaspoon dry mustard
   Beer to make a thick paste

Mix all the ingredients thoroughly and spread over the entire ham.

PAPRIKA CRUST

1 tablespoon dry mustard
2 tablespoons paprika
1¼ cups fine, dry bread crumbs
   Pan drippings

Mix the mustard, paprika, and bread crumbs with enough drippings from the roasting pan to bind the mixture together. Spread this over the top of a baked ham 20 minutes before it is due to be removed from the oven.

TOMATO AND RAISIN GLAZE

1   can (8 ounces) tomato sauce
¼   cup seedless raisins
½   cup orange marmalade
2   tablespoons soy sauce
2   tablespoons butter or margarine

Combine all the ingredients in a saucepan and simmer for about 10 minutes, stirring constantly. Use on a pork roast.

CATSUP GLAZE

⅔   cup catsup
½   cup orange marmalade
¼   cup soy sauce
¼   cup lemon juice
½   teaspoon marjoram
    Salt (if desired)
    Pepper

Combine all the ingredients in a saucepan and simmer for about 5 minutes. Use to baste a pork roast or a baked ham.

SPICED CRANBERRY GLAZE

1   can (16 ounces) cranberry sauce
2   tablespoons lemon juice
1   teaspoon prepared mustard
¼   teaspoon ground cloves

Combine all the ingredients in a saucepan and heat gently. Brush some of the glaze over a baked ham 30 minutes before the meat is done. Just before serving, spoon on the remaining hot glaze.

This glaze may also be used for barbecued pork or spareribs just a minute before removing the meat from the grill. If used earlier in the cooking process, it is likely to burn.

CRANBERRY ORANGE GLAZE

1   can (16 ounces) cranberry sauce
½   cup orange juice
½   cup brown sugar, tightly packed

Combine all the ingredients and heat until well blended. Brush half of this mixture onto a ham or pork roast 30 minutes before the meat is done. Spoon the remaining glaze (reheated, if necessary) over the meat just before serving.

HURRY-UP APRICOT GLAZE

1   jar (12 ounces) apricot jam

Put the jam through a fine sieve or a food mill to purée. Heat, stirring constantly, and spread over a baked ham.

MARMALADE–PEANUT BUTTER GLAZE AND SAUCE

½   cup orange marmalade
⅓   cup cider vinegar
¼   cup water
¾   cup brown sugar
3   tablespoons soy sauce
1¼   teaspoons ground ginger
2   tablespoons cornstarch
⅓   cup peanut butter

Combine all the ingredients except the peanut butter in a saucepan. Cook slowly over low heat, stirring constantly, until the mixture is clear and thick. Use ⅓ cup of this glaze for basting. Add the peanut butter to the remainder. Mix well, then heat thoroughly and serve separately with the meat.

Makes about two cups

PINEAPPLE-SOY SAUCE GLAZE

2   cans (8 ounces each) crushed pineapple
⅓   cup soy sauce
1   tablespoon cornstarch
2   tablespoons brown sugar
¼   teaspoon ground ginger
¼   teaspoon garlic salt

Combine all the ingredients in a saucepan. Cook over low to moderate heat for 5 minutes, stirring frequently. Use on a roast during the last 30 minutes it is on the rotisserie.

Makes about two and one-third cups

CHERRY-ALMOND SAUCE

1   can (16 ounces) pitted red sour cherries
2   tablespoons lemon juice
1   cup light corn syrup
3   tablespoons cornstarch
4   teaspoons grated orange rind
¼   teaspoon almond extract
¼   cup slivered almonds

Drain the cherries and set the fruit aside. Combine the cherry and lemon juices, stir in the corn syrup and the cornstarch, and blend well. Cook, stirring constantly, until thick and clear. Add the grated orange rind, the almond extract, almonds, and the reserved cherries. Heat through and serve hot.

Makes about three cups

MUSTARD SAUCE

1 cup mayonnaise
¼ cup prepared mustard
1 cup heavy cream, whipped

Blend the mayonnaise and the mustard. Fold this mixture into the whipped cream. Especially good with a ham loaf.

Makes about three and one-fourth cups

CINNAMON ORANGE SAUCE

1¼ cups granulated sugar
 1 cup orange juice (fresh or frozen)
 2 tablespoons cornstarch
 1 teaspoon ground cinnamon
 1 tablespoon whole cloves
2½ tablespoons grated orange rind
 1 teaspoon salt

In a saucepan, mix the cornstarch with 2 tablespoons of the orange juice. When smooth, add the remaining ingredients. Cook over medium heat, stirring constantly, until thick and clear. Strain to remove the cloves. Serve with chops or roast.

Makes about two cups

SHERRY AND ORANGE SAUCE

2 tablespoons granulated sugar
2 tablespoons cornstarch
1 cup fresh orange juice
1 cup beef bouillon
¼ cup dry sherry
2 tablespoons butter

Combine the sugar and cornstarch. Stir in the orange juice and bouillon, a little at a time, and simmer, stirring constantly, until thick and smooth.

Add the sherry and butter and continue to simmer until the butter is melted. Serve hot.

Makes about two and one-fourth cups

CHERRY SAUCE

1   jar (12 ounces) cherry preserves
¼   cup light corn syrup
¼   cup red wine vinegar
¼   teaspoon ground cloves
¼   teaspoon ground nutmeg
¼   teaspoon ground cinnamon
⅓   cup toasted, slivered almonds
¼   teaspoon salt

Combine all the ingredients except the almonds. Simmer for 5 minutes. Add the almonds and serve warm.

Makes about two cups

GINGER MARMALADE SAUCE

1   jar (16 ounces) ginger marmalade
2   tablespoons mustard sauce
3   drops red vegetable coloring

Blend the marmalade and mustard sauce. Add the coloring and mix thoroughly. If the sauce is used on hot ham, spread it over the ham and heat at 325° in the oven for 10 minutes. If it is used on cold ham, spread the sauce over the ham and heat at 375° in the oven for 15 to 20 minutes and then refrigerate for 1 hour before serving.

Makes about one and one-half cups

BARBECUE LOVERS' BARBECUE SAUCE

1   can (10½ ounces) onion soup
1   can (10½ ounces) tomato soup

2   **tablespoons cornstarch**
¼   **cup vinegar**
2   **large cloves garlic, minced**
3   **tablespoons brown sugar**
1   **tablespoon Worcestershire sauce**
⅛   **teaspoon Tabasco sauce**

Combine the cornstarch and the vinegar into a smooth paste. Stir into the soups. Combine this with all the other ingredients and mix thoroughly. Use for spareribs or ham.

Makes about two and one-half cups

GUAVA MUSTARD FOR HAM

1   **jar (16 ounces) guava jelly**
¼   **cup prepared mustard, more if desired**

Blend the jelly and mustard with a rotary beater until smooth. Taste the mixture. If desired, add more mustard and blend again. Serve with any plain ham.

Makes eight to ten servings

BRANDY MARINADE

¼   **cup brandy**
½   **cup salad oil**
2   **tablespoons lemon juice**
¼   **cup minced fresh parsley**
2   **bay leaves**
1   **teaspoon salt**
¼   **teaspoon freshly ground pepper**

Mix all the ingredients and allow to stand for several hours, or longer. When ready to use the marinade, remove and discard the bay leaves.

Makes three-fourths cup

SEASONED OIL MARINADE

1   cup salad oil
½   cup finely chopped onion
¼   cup lemon juice
2   teaspoons dry mustard
1   teaspoon garlic salt
1   teaspoon salt
¼   teaspoon freshly ground pepper

Mix and blend all the ingredients. Especially good for use with very lean meat, such as kebabs, this may also be used for basting during cooking.

Makes one and three-fourths cups

ORANGE MARINADE OR SAUCE

1   can (6 ounces) frozen orange juice, defrosted
½   cup honey
⅓   cup water
⅓   cup vinegar
1   teaspoon prepared mustard
1   teaspoon soy sauce
6   drops Tabasco sauce
4   teaspoons cornstarch (optional)
¼   cup orange liqueur (optional)
½   cup sour cream (optional)
¼   teaspoon salt

Combine all the ingredients except the optional ones and bring to a boil. Cool before using.

For use with a pork roast, marinate the roast in the refrigerator for 6 hours. For use as the basis for a sauce, combine 1 cup of the marinade with the cornstarch in a saucepan. Cook, stirring constantly, until thick and clear. Stir in the orange liqueur, then blend in the sour cream. Heat thoroughly but do not boil.

Makes about two cups marinade, or two and three-fourths cups sauce

MIKADO MARINADE

1   cup orange marmalade
1   cup soy sauce
2   cloves garlic, minced
1   teaspoon ground ginger
¼   teaspoon freshly ground pepper

Combine all the ingredients and blend thoroughly. Allow to mellow for several hours before using.

Makes two cups

BLENDER MARINADE

½   cup wine vinegar
⅓   cup lemon juice
¾   cup soy sauce
1½   cups salad oil
¼   cup Worcestershire sauce
1½   teaspoons parsley flakes
 2   tablespoons prepared mustard
2½   teaspoons salt
 2   teaspoons freshly ground pepper

Put all the ingredients in the jar of the blender and blend at low speed for about 45 seconds. Cover tightly and store in the refrigerator until ready to use.

Makes three and one-third cups

SAUTERNE MARINADE

½   cup sauterne
1   cup olive oil
1   tablespoon oregano
1   tablespoon rosemary, crushed
1   clove garlic

Combine all the ingredients and allow to mellow overnight in the refrigerator before using.

Makes one and one-half cups

HERB-FLAVORED WINE MARINADE

½ cup white wine
½ cup salad oil
1 clove garlic, crushed
1 medium onion, grated
¼ teaspoon rosemary
¼ teaspoon marjoram
¼ teaspoon thyme
½ teaspoon celery salt
½ teaspoon salt
¼ teaspoon freshly ground pepper

Combine all ingredients in a quart jar and shake thoroughly.

Makes one cup

FRENCH DRESSING MARINADE

1 cup French salad dressing
1 clove garlic, crushed
⅔ cup chopped onion
2 teaspoons barbecue spice
¼ teaspoon oregano
1 bay leaf, crushed
1 teaspoon salt

Combine the ingredients. May be used when an overnight marinade is called for. May also be used to brush over meat as it cooks.

Makes about one and one-third cups

Ham and Other Smoked Pork

The versatility of ham is almost staggering. It goes to parties as a delectable entrée or as an elegant hors d'oeuvre. It celebrates holidays, a tradition going back to the pre-Easter ham fairs in Nôtre Dame plaza in Paris. It graces a fancy luncheon or accommodates a hurried cook as a sandwich filling. It stays up for late parties and appears in good shape for breakfast. It goes to picnics and attends wedding buffets. It is a cosmopolite, being equally at home in areas as far apart as France and China. In early America it was a standby for pioneer and cowboy because it was easily preserved (by "jerking") and traveled well in wagon or saddlebag because it took up very little space. It remained safe and tasty through long winters and hot summers.

Ham is now available in many forms, and the first rule regarding it is "read the label." Then you take your choice and pay your money. Ham correctly means the hind leg of the hog, from pelvic bone to hock. However the term is also used to cover whole ham, with or without bone; butt and shank; smoked butt; and smoked shoulder. Picnic hams come from the shoulder; they are trimmed into shape and cured.

Hams come cooked, precooked, uncooked, partially cooked; with bone or boneless; skinned or unskinned; rolled and tied. Half a ham is an economical purchase. Have the butcher cut the whole ham in two for you; this assures that you get the entire half, including center-cut steaks that might otherwise be sliced off. The butt end is generally considered the preferable half.

"Country-style" hams, not easily obtainable unless especially ordered, are in a class by themselves. The diet of the hog and the wood used for smoking account for their distinctive features. The diet includes such mouth-watering items as peaches and clover. They are smoked with such pleasant woods as beechnut, hickory, and sassafras. Despite all these recommendations, you may be shaken when you unwrap your costly "Virginia" (or "Kentucky" or "Tennessee") ham and find it covered with an unappetizing greenish-gray mold. After that shock, brace yourself for a few hours of scraping and scrubbing, overnight soaking, boiling for part of a day and then skinning, and after all that, baking and glazing for varying periods of time.

For the opposite in preparation trouble, consider the many excellent domestic canned hams or the choices you can get from Denmark, England, Yugoslavia, Germany, Italy, or Poland. Read the label, open the can and serve an excellent meal.

Other smoked pork products are close or distant cousins to the ham, and some recipes for their use are included in this section. Others are found in other categories.

BAKED HAM WITH ORANGE-MINT GLAZE

1	ham, butt half
2	teaspoons cornstarch
1½	teaspoons rosemary
1	cup orange juice
⅓	cup chopped fresh mint
2	teaspoons salt
¼	teaspoon pepper

Place the ham on a rack in a shallow roasting pan, fat side up. Insert a meat thermometer and bake at 325° until the thermometer registers 140° to 145° (about 20 minutes per pound).

Meanwhile, in a heavy saucepan, combine the cornstarch, rosemary, salt, and pepper. Add the orange juice and cook, stirring constantly, until thick and clear. (This makes 1 cup of glaze.) About 20 minutes before the ham is done, remove it from the oven. Brush with ½ cup of the glaze. Return the ham to the oven to finish cooking. When done, remove, cover with the remaining glaze and sprinkle with the mint.

HAM BASTED WITH BEER

1   **ham (10 to 12 pounds)**
    Whole cloves
½   **cup brown sugar**
2   **teaspoons prepared mustard**
2   **tablespoons all-purpose flour**
2   **tablespoons cider vinegar**
2   **cups light beer**

Insert a meat thermometer and bake the ham, uncovered, at 300° until the thermometer registers 160° (18 to 20 minutes per pound). About 40 minutes before the meat is done, remove it from the pan; drain off and discard the drippings. Cut the skin off the ham and return the meat to the roasting pan. With a sharp knife, score the ham in a large diamond pattern. Put a clove in the center of each diamond.

Mix the brown sugar, mustard, flour, and vinegar into a smooth paste. Spread this over the top of the ham and return it to the oven to complete cooking. During this period, baste every 10 minutes, first with the beer and then with the drippings. For the last 15 minutes turn the temperature to 400°. Serve hot or cold.

GLAZED HAM WITH ORANGE CUPS

1   **precooked half ham**
    Brown sugar
3   **large oranges**
4   **medium sweet potatoes, cooked**
¼   **teaspoon nutmeg**
⅓   **cup milk**
3   **teaspoons butter**
½   **teaspoon salt**

Place the ham on a rack in an open roasting pan. Bake at 325° for 20 minutes per pound, or until a meat thermometer registers 140°. About 30 minutes before the ham is done, remove from the oven and score the fat in a diamond pattern. Rub into the fat as much brown sugar as it will absorb, then return it to the oven for another 30 minutes.

Cut the oranges into halves crosswise. Carefully remove the pulp, chop it, and set aside. Flute the edges of the orange halves with scissors. Peel and mash the potatoes. Add the nutmeg, salt, milk, and ⅓ cup of the orange pulp. Beat until fluffy, then pile the mixture lightly into the orange cups. Dot with butter and brown in the broiler or a hot oven for about 5 minutes.

Serve the ham on a platter, surrounded by the orange cups.

HONEY-GLAZED HAM

1 precooked ham (10 to 12 pounds)
¾ cup honey
¼ cup water
2 tablespoons steak sauce
2 tablespoons lemon juice
½ cup red cinnamon candies

Line a shallow roasting pan with foil. Place the ham on a rack in the pan, fat side up. In a saucepan, blend the honey, water, steak sauce, lemon juice, and candies. Bring to a boil, then reduce the heat and simmer until the candies are dissolved. Pour half of this mixture over the ham. Insert a meat thermometer and bake the ham at 325° until the thermometer registers 140° (15 to 18 minutes to the pound). Remove the ham from the oven, score the fat side in a diamond pattern, and spread on the remaining sauce. Return to the oven and increase the heat to 400°. Bake, basting frequently with the drippings, until the thermometer registers 140°.

STUFFED HAM

1 whole ham (12 to 14 pounds)
1 cup fine dry bread crumbs
1 cup finely chopped raisins
2 cups finely chopped pecans
¼ cup chopped orange peel
½ cup honey
¼ teaspoon ground cinnamon
¼ teaspoon ground ginger

¼   teaspoon ground nutmeg
¼   teaspoon ground cloves
1   cup brandy, approximately
     Granulated sugar

Ask the butcher to bone the ham down to the shank. Combine the
crumbs, raisins, nuts, orange peel, honey, spices, and enough brandy to
moisten. Stuff the ham with the mixture and tie it securely. Wrap it in
foil and put it in a roasting pan. Bake at 350° for 2 hours, then take the
ham from the oven and remove the foil. Sprinkle lightly with sugar, turn
up the oven temperature to 500°, and return the ham for a few minutes
to glaze.
   To serve, put the ham on a flameproof platter. Warm ⅓ cup of brandy,
light it and pour it, flaming, over the ham.

HAM SLICE WITH TOMATOES AND MUSHROOMS

1   ham slice, 1½ inches thick
2   teaspoons Dijon mustard
4   tablespoons brown sugar
1½   tablespoons all-purpose flour
1   teaspoon vinegar
2   cups canned tomatoes
1   cup sliced fresh mushrooms

Combine the mustard, sugar, and flour. Add the vinegar and tomatoes,
mixing until the liquid is smooth. Add the mushrooms. Put the ham slice
in a shallow baking dish and pour the tomato mixture over it. Bake,
uncovered, at 325° for 1¼ hours.

APPLE-HAM CASSEROLE

1   slice ham, 1 inch thick
5   tablespoons brown sugar
4   whole cloves
1   tablespoon onion juice
3   tart cooking apples
1   tablespoon butter
1   cup boiling water

Rub the ham slice with 1 tablespoon of the sugar and place it in a baking dish. Stick the cloves in the ham and sprinkle the onion juice over it. Peel and core the apples and slice them crossways. Place the slices on top of the ham. Sprinkle with the remaining brown sugar and dot with butter. Pour 1 cup of boiling water around the ham and bake, covered, at 325° until the meat and apples are tender.

HAM WITH CUCUMBERS

1 slice ham, ½ inch thick
2 medium cucumbers
1 tablespoon plus 1 teaspoon butter or margarine
1 teaspoon all-purpose flour
1 cup white wine

Peel the cucumbers, cut in half lengthwise, and remove the seeds. Drop them into boiling water for 3 minutes. Cut the ham into pieces the length and width of the cucumbers. Melt the tablespoon of butter in a skillet and fry the ham until browned. Remove from frying pan and keep the ham hot.

Add the wine to the skillet. Make a roux of 1 teaspoon butter and the flour and add to the wine. Heat and stir until thick and smooth, then add the cucumbers to the skillet. Cover and simmer until tender, reducing the sauce to a glaze. Turn the cucumbers over in it so they will be well flavored, then serve with half a cucumber laid on each piece of ham.

NUT-CRUSTED HAM SLICE

1 cooked ham slice (1½ pounds), ¾ inch thick
2 tablespoons honey, approximately
¼ cup finely chopped salted peanuts

Generously brush the ham slice with honey. Broil about 8 inches below heat for 5 to 10 minutes. Watch carefully; the honey burns easily. Turn the ham, brush the top side with more honey, and sprinkle with the chopped peanuts. Broil until the nut topping is lightly toasted (5 to 7 minutes).

SPANISH HAM

1 large slice ham, ¾ inch thick
3 tablespoons brown sugar
1 tablespoon all-purpose flour
2 teaspoons dry mustard
¾ cup boiling water, more if necessary
¼ cup milk

Spread the ham with a mixture of the sugar, flour, and mustard. Place in a heavy frying pan and pour the boiling water around it. Cover and simmer for 30 minutes, turning occasionally and adding water as needed. Ten minutes before serving, pour the milk over the ham and reheat.

HAM SLICE WITH SPICED CRANBERRIES

1 center-cut cooked ham slice, about 1 inch thick
1 cup fresh cranberries
¼ cup fresh orange juice
2 tablespoons granulated sugar
2 tablespoons honey
⅛ teaspoon ground cinnamon

Trim the fat from the ham, then place in a baking dish and bake at 325° for 15 minutes. Combine the remaining ingredients in a saucepan and bring to a boil. Reduce the heat and simmer for 5 to 10 minutes, or until the cranberries have stopped popping. Spread over the ham and return it to the oven for another 15 to 20 minutes.

Note: When fresh cranberries are not available, the following ingredients may be used:

¾ cup canned whole cranberries
2 tablespoons orange juice
1 tablespoon granulated sugar
1 tablespoon honey
½ teaspoon ground cinnamon

Combine these ingredients and heat thoroughly. Spread over the ham and proceed as directed above.

GYPSY HAM SLICE

1   ham slice, 1¼ to 1½ pounds
1   cup canned tomatoes
½   teaspoon finely crushed bay leaves
1   tablespoon butter or margarine
¼   cup brown sugar
2   small white onions, sliced thin
¼   teaspoon paprika
1   teaspoon salt
⅛   teaspoon freshly ground pepper

Heat together the tomatoes, bay leaves, seasonings and butter, breaking up the tomatoes with a fork. Sear the ham lightly on both sides in a hot, heavy skillet, then place it in an ovenproof dish and spread on the brown sugar. Moisten the sugar with a little of the juice from the tomatoes, then cover with onion slices. Pour the rest of the tomatoes around the edge of the ham and bake, covered, at 350° for 30 minutes, basting once. Remove the ham to a warm platter.

If necessary, boil the sauce briskly to cook it down a little, then pour over the meat and serve.

Six servings

HAM WITH SWEET-SOUR PEACHES

1   fully cooked center-cut ham slice (about 3 pounds), 2 inches thick
1   cup granulated sugar
2   tablespoons cornstarch
2   teaspoons seasoned salt
2   teaspoons dry mustard
½   teaspoon paprika
1   cup water
⅓   cup orange juice
¼   cup vinegar
2   egg yolks, lightly beaten
1   package (12 ounces) frozen sliced peaches, thawed and drained

Place the ham on a rack in a shallow baking pan. Bake at 325° for 45 minutes.

Meanwhile, in a saucepan, combine the sugar, cornstarch, seasoned salt, mustard, and paprika. Blend in the water, orange juice, and vinegar and cook over low heat, stirring constantly, until thick and smooth. Stir a small amount of this mixture into the beaten egg yolks, then pour quickly back into the saucepan. Continue to cook and stir until just boiling, about 1 minute. Add the peach slices.

Place the ham on a serving platter and spoon on a little of the sauce. Serve the remaining sauce separately.

Eight to ten servings

SKILLET HAM AND YAMS

1   ham slice, about ¾ inch thick
1   tablespoon cooking oil
¼   cup crumbled blue cheese
2   small onions, sliced thin
1   teaspoon Worcestershire sauce
½   cup sweet vermouth
4   medium yams, cooked, peeled, and sliced thick

Lightly brown the ham on both sides in the oil. Put the remaining ingredients except the yams on top of the ham. Cover and cook over low heat for 15 minutes, then add the yams, cover the skillet again, and cook for 15 minutes longer.

STUFFED HAM SLICES

2   smoked ham slices, ½ inch thick
1   package (10 ounces) frozen cranberry-orange relish, thawed
¼   cup chopped apple
¼   cup chopped celery
1   tablespoon butter or margarine
3   slices white bread, cubed and toasted
⅛   teaspoon ground cinnamon
¼   cup plus 2 tablespoons brown sugar
2   teaspoons cornstarch

Drain the cranberry-orange relish well, saving the liquid. Cook the apple and celery in the butter; add the relish, bread cubes, cinnamon, and the ¼ cup brown sugar. Mix well. Place one of the ham slices on a rack in an open roasting pan and spoon the cranberry stuffing over it. Top with the second ham slice and bake at 350° for 45 minutes.

Add enough water to the reserved cranberry liquid to make ¾ cup. Combine the 2 tablespoons of brown sugar and the cornstarch and add to the juice mixture. Cook, stirring constantly, until thickened. Serve the sauce over the ham.

TROPICAL HAM

1   center-cut ham slice
1   can (16 ounces) cling peach halves, drained but syrup reserved
1   large banana, peeled and quartered
¼   cup brown sugar, firmly packed
¼   cup shredded coconut
⅛   teaspoon ground nutmeg
1   tablespoon butter
2   tablespoons wine vinegar

Trim the fat from the ham, then brown it on both sides, using a small amount of the fat. Place in a shallow casserole. Drain the peaches and cut each half in two. Place the peaches and bananas on top of the ham. Sprinkle with the brown sugar, coconut, and nutmeg and dot with the butter. Combine the vinegar and ⅓ cup of the reserved peach syrup. Pour over the ham and fruit. Bake, uncovered, at 375° for 20 minutes. Especially good served with hominy grits.

GLAZED HAM LOAF WITH HORSERADISH SAUCE

2   pounds ground, cooked ham
1   pound ground pork
1   cup coarse cracker crumbs
2   eggs
1   cup milk

Horseradish Sauce:

1   **cup whipping cream**
2   **tablespoons horseradish**
2   **teaspoons granulated sugar**
1   **teaspoon lemon juice**

Mix thoroughly the ground meats, cracker crumbs, and eggs. Add the milk and mix, then pat into a 9-inch-square pan. Bake at 350° for 1 hour. Cut into squares and serve with the horseradish sauce, made by whipping the cream until stiff and folding in the remaining ingredients.

Ten to twelve servings

HAM LOAF WITH CORNFLAKES

1¼   **pounds ground smoked ham**
½   **pound ground pork**
1   **egg**
1   **cup finely crumbled cornflakes**
1   **tablespoon brown sugar**
¼   **teaspoon ground cloves**
½   **cup milk**
    Spiced peach halves (optional)

Beat the egg lightly in a bowl large enough to hold all the ingredients. Add the cornflakes, sugar, and cloves, mixing well. Add the milk and stir to an even consistency, then add the meat and work together thoroughly. Pack into a 5¼ x 9½-inch loaf pan and bake, uncovered, at 350° for 1 hour 15 minutes. May be served hot or cold, garnished with spiced peach halves.

Four to six servings

OLD RELIABLE HAM LOAF

1½   pounds ground uncooked ham
½   pound ground pork
1   egg
1   cup warm water
1   cup dry bread crumbs
1   teaspoon minced onion
½   cup minced green pepper
1   teaspoon dry mustard
½   teaspoon salt
½   teaspoon freshly ground pepper

Beat the egg lightly in a bowl large enough to hold all ingredients. Pour the water on the bread crumbs, mix well, and add to the beaten egg. Add the onion, green pepper, salt, pepper, and mustard. Mix well, then add the meat and mix thoroughly until of uniform consistency. Pack into a greased 5¼ x 9½-inch loaf pan. Bake, uncovered, at 350° for 1 hour 15 minutes.

Six or seven servings

MUSHROOM SOUP HAM LOAF

2   cups ground or chopped, cooked ham
2   tablespoons minced onion
2   tablespoons butter
1   tablespoon steak sauce
1   can (10½ ounces) cream of mushroom soup
¾   cup dry bread crumbs
    Dash of freshly ground pepper

In a skillet, sauté the onion in the butter until soft. Mix in the ham, steak sauce, soup, onion, and pepper, then add the bread crumbs. Mold into a loaf. Bake, uncovered, at 350° for 45 minutes.

Four servings

MANDARIN HAM LOAF

2   pounds ground smoked ham
1   cup rolled oats (quick or old-fashioned, uncooked)
¾   cup orange juice
2   eggs, beaten
¼   cup chopped onion
1   tablespoon Worcestershire sauce
1   teaspoon dry mustard
¼   teaspoon pepper
1   can (11 ounces) mandarin orange segments, drained
¼   cup brown sugar, firmly packed

Thoroughly combine the ham, oats, orange juice, eggs, onion, Worcestershire, mustard, and pepper. Firmly pack half of the mixture into a loaf pan 8½ x 4½ x 2½ inches. Arrange ½ cup orange segments over the ham mixture in a single layer. Sprinkle with half of the brown sugar, then pack the remaining ham mixture on top. Arrange the remaining orange segments in a row down the center of the loaf. Sprinkle the remaining brown sugar over the top and bake, uncovered, at 350° about 1 hour. Allow to stand about 5 minutes before slicing.

Four to six servings

BAKED CABBAGE ROLLS

2   cups ground, cooked ham
8   cabbage leaves
1   cup cooked rice
1   tablespoon minced onion
¼   cup chili sauce

Sauce:

3   tablespoons butter
3   tablespoons all-purpose flour
¼   teaspoon paprika
2   cups milk, scalded
½   cup freshly grated Parmesan cheese
¾   teaspoon salt
¼   teaspoon freshly ground pepper

Drop the cabbage leaves into boiling water for 2 minutes. Drain and cool. Combine the rice with ham, onion, and chili sauce. Place some of the mixture on each leaf, then roll and fasten with wooden picks. Arrange in a buttered baking dish.

Melt the butter in a saucepan and blend in the flour and seasonings. Add the milk and cook until thickened and smooth. Stir in the cheese. Pour the sauce over the cabbage rolls and bake at 350° for 30 minutes.

Eight servings

HAM SEMI-SOUFFLÉ

3   cups (about 1 pound) ground, cooked ham
2   tablespoons grated onion
2   tablespoons butter or margarine
2   cups soft bread crumbs
2   cups (½ pound) grated Cheddar cheese
3   eggs, separated
1⅓ cups milk, scalded
¼   teaspoon paprika
1   tablespoon minced fresh parsley, more if desired
½   teaspoon salt
¼   teaspoon pepper

Sauté the onion in the butter. Mix the bread crumbs, grated cheese, and egg yolks. Add the milk, salt, pepper, paprika, and onion. Blend, then stir in the parsley and ham. When thoroughly mixed, blend in the stiffly beaten egg whites. Turn into six buttered individual baking dishes. Bake, uncovered, at 350° for about 30 minutes, or until set. They may be garnished with more minced parsley.

Six servings

HAM AND RICE CROQUETTES

3   cups ground, cooked ham
1   can (10½ ounces) cream of celery soup
1   cup cooked rice
1   tablespoon finely chopped onion

 1   tablespoon finely chopped green pepper
1½   tablespoons prepared mustard
 1   egg, beaten
 1   cup fine bread crumbs
 2   packages (8 ounces each) frozen peas in cream sauce

Blend thoroughly the ham, soup, rice, onion, green pepper, and mustard. Chill. Shape the mixture into croquettes, using about ¼ cup per croquette. Dip each one in egg, then in crumbs. Allow to stand for a few minutes, then fry two or three at a time in deep hot fat (365°) for 3 to 5 minutes, or until brown, making sure the temperature of the fat remains at 365°. Drain the croquettes on paper towels.

Prepare the peas according to the package directions and serve over the croquettes.

Eight to ten servings

HAM ROLLS AU GRATIN

 8   thin slices boiled ham
 4   tablespoons butter
⅓   cup flour
1¾   cups milk
 1   cup grated Cheddar cheese
¼   cup sherry
 1   teaspoon Worcestershire sauce
 1   teaspoon horseradish
½   teaspoon prepared mustard
 1   cup macaroni, cooked, drained, and chopped fine
½   cup buttered bread crumbs
     Paprika
     Salt
     Pepper

Melt the butter and stir in flour. Add 1½ cups of the milk and cook, stirring constantly, until the mixture thickens. Stir in the cheese, wine, Worcestershire sauce, horseradish, mustard, and salt and pepper to taste. Mix ¾ cup of this sauce with the macaroni, then spread equal amounts of the mixture on each ham slice. Roll the slices up and place side by side in a greased, shallow baking dish. Add the remaining milk to the remaining sauce and blend. Pour over the ham, top with buttered crumbs, and sprinkle with paprika. Bake, uncovered, at 375° for about 25 minutes, or until heated through.

Four servings

INDIVIDUAL HAM LOAVES

1½　pounds uncooked ham and 1½ pounds lean pork, ground together
2　eggs
1　tablespoon prepared horseradish
1　cup uncooked oatmeal
1　cup soft bread crumbs
2　cups milk
　　Salt
　　Pepper

Glaze:

1　cup brown sugar
1　tablespoon dry mustard
½　cup vinegar
½　cup water

Horseradish sauce:

3　tablespoons horseradish
1　tablespoon granulated sugar
½　teaspoon prepared mustard
¼　cup heavy cream, whipped
½　teaspoon salt

Combine all the ingredients for the loaves and shape about 1 cup of the mixture into a small loaf. Repeat until all the mixture is used. Place the loaves side by side in a baking pan and bake, uncovered, at 325° for 30 minutes. Then baste with the glaze every 10 minutes while baking for another 30 minutes.

To make the glaze, combine the brown sugar and dry mustard in a saucepan. Gradually stir in the vinegar to make a smooth paste. Add the water and bring to a boil, stirring constantly.

Serve with horseradish sauce, made by combining the horseradish, sugar, mustard and salt, and folding the mixture into the whipped cream.

Eight to ten servings

CRÊPES WITH HAM AND CHEESE

8	thin slices boiled ham
8	thin crêpes
1	pound fresh mushrooms, sliced
4	tablespoons butter or margarine
2	teaspoons grated onion
2	tablespoons all-purpose flour
1	cup chicken broth
1	cup half-and-half
1½	cups grated Swiss cheese
1	teaspoon salt
⅛	teaspoon pepper

Prepare the crêpes ahead of time and have them ready. Sauté the mushrooms in the butter. Add the grated onion and cook a few minutes more, then blend in the flour, salt, and pepper. Add the chicken broth and the half-and-half, and cook, stirring constantly, until smooth and thick.

Sprinkle 1 cup of the grated cheese on the crêpes and top each with a slice of ham. Put 1 or 2 tablespoons of sauce on each crêpe, then roll and place in a shallow baking pan. Pour the remaining sauce over all; top with the remaining grated cheese. Bake at 375° for 10 minutes.

Four servings

HAM AND ENDIVE WITH CHEESE SAUCE

12	thin slices boiled ham	Salt
12	heads Belgian endive	Freshly ground pepper
2	tablespoons lemon juice	
3	tablespoons butter	
1	small onion, chopped fine	
3	tablespoons all-purpose flour	
2	cups light cream	
1	cup shredded Gruyère cheese	
	Freshly grated nutmeg to taste	
	Grated Parmesan cheese	

Trim the base of each endive and discard any withered leaves, then spread the heads apart and hold under running water to remove any dirt particles. Invert to drain. Place the endives in a large saucepan and cover with boiling water. Add the lemon juice and cook over low heat for 10 minutes. Remove the endives from the water and drain well. Roll a slice of ham around each endive and arrange in a buttered, shallow casserole with the seam of the ham down.

Melt the butter in a saucepan and sauté the onion until soft. Stir in the flour and blend well. Add the cream, a little at a time, and cook over low heat, stirring, until the sauce is thick and smooth. Add the Gruyère, salt, pepper, and nutmeg, and continue to cook over low heat, stirring occasionally, until the cheese is melted. Pour over the endive and ham rolls, and bake at 400° for about 30 minutes, or until tender. Sprinkle with grated Parmesan cheese and serve.

Six servings

HAM BISCUITS

¾ **cup ground Smithfield ham**
3 **cups all-purpose flour**
4 **teaspoons double-acting baking powder**
3 **tablespoons lard, cut into small bits**
¾ **cup plus 2 tablespoons milk**
½ **teaspoon salt**

Sift the flour, salt and baking powder together into a large bowl. Add the ham and lard and blend until the mixture is thoroughly combined. Then add the milk and toss until the milk is absorbed. Form the dough into a ball, transfer to a lightly floured surface and knead for 1 minute. Roll out ¼ inch thick. With a 2¼-inch cutter, cut the dough into rounds. Put them on a baking sheet and brush the tops with milk. Bake at 450° for 12 minutes, or until golden brown.

Makes about thirty

HAM AND SHRIMP JAMBALAYA

½   pound cooked ham, cut into 1-inch cubes (about 1½ cups)
1   pound cooked shrimp, peeled and deveined
1   small onion, finely chopped
2   tablespoons butter or margarine
1   tablespoon all-purpose flour
1   tablespoon Worcestershire sauce
1   small clove garlic, minced
1   can (16 ounces) tomatoes
1½ cups tomato juice
3   cups cooked rice
1   medium green pepper, chopped
½   cup grated cheese
2   tablespoons minced fresh parsley
    Dash of cayenne pepper
½   teaspoon salt

Sauté the onion in the butter for 5 minutes. Blend in the flour, then add all of the remaining ingredients except the cheese and parsley. Turn into a buttered casserole and bake at 350° for 25 minutes, or simmer in an electric skillet for 25 minutes. To serve, sprinkle with the cheese and parsley.

Six servings

FRIZZLED HAM

8   thin slices boiled ham
    Butter
8   sprigs fresh parsley

Coat the bottom of a heavy skillet with butter. Sauté the ham slices over moderate heat until the edges begin to curl and the meat darkens in color. Fold the slices into thirds and garnish with a parsley sprig.

Four servings

RED AND GREEN CASSEROLE

2   cups cubed, cooked ham
1   tablespoon bacon drippings
1   package (10 ounces) frozen cut green beans
1   can (4 ounces) water chestnuts
1   tablespoon butter
1   tablespoon all-purpose flour
½   cup milk
½   cup sour cream
1   tablespoon soy sauce
¼   cup fine bread crumbs, buttered

Melt the drippings in a large skillet and lightly brown the ham. After cooking the beans tender-crisp, according to package directions, add them to the skillet. Drain and slice the water chestnuts and add them to the skillet. Mix the ingredients gently and transfer to a casserole.

In another pan melt the tablespoon of butter, stir in the flour, and cook over low heat for 2 minutes. Add the milk and cook, stirring constantly, until the mixture is thick and smooth. Add the sour cream and soy sauce, blend thoroughly, then pour over the ham and vegetables. Sprinkle the buttered crumbs over the top and put in a 375° oven to heat through and brown the crumbs.

Four servings

HAM-CORNMEAL SOUFFLÉ

1   cup very finely cut up cooked ham
4   cups milk
⅔   cup white or yellow cornmeal
2   tablespoons butter or margarine
½   cup grated Cheddar cheese
6   eggs, separated
½   teaspoon paprika
2   teaspoons salt

Heat the milk to the boiling point. Stir in the cornmeal and butter, then reduce the heat and blend in the cheese. Cook these ingredients until thick, like mush. Add the paprika and salt. Beat the egg yolks and stir in. Cook, stirring, for a minute longer. Remove from the heat and cool.

When the mixture is cool, fold in the ham. Whip the whites of the eggs until stiff and fold them into the mixture. Turn into an ungreased baking dish and bake, uncovered, at 350° for about 45 minutes, or until the soufflé is slightly crusty.

Six servings

CURRIED PINEAPPLE HAM

2 cups cubed cooked ham
½ cup chopped onion
½ cup green pepper slivers
2½ tablespoons butter
3 tablespoons all-purpose flour
1 cup chicken broth
1 can (13¼ ounces) pineapple chunks, drained and juice reserved
2 tablespoons chopped chutney
2 teaspoons curry powder
¼ teaspoon granulated sugar
½ teaspoon salt
⅛ teaspoon pepper

In a skillet, cook the onion, along with the green pepper, in the butter until transparent, not brown. Stir in the flour, then add the broth and reserved pineapple juice. Stir in the chutney, curry, salt, pepper, and sugar and simmer for 10 minutes, or until thickened, stirring often. Add the pineapple and ham, then heat thoroughly and serve on hot rice.

Four servings

HAM À LA KING ON FRENCH FRIES

1½ **cups diced, cooked ham**
 4 **tablespoons butter or margarine**
 2 **tablespoons chopped green pepper**
 2 **cups half-and-half**
 ¼ **cup all-purpose flour**
 ¼ **cup pimientos, cut fine**
 1 **can (4 ounces) button mushrooms**
 ¼ **cup sliced celery**
 2 **packages (10 ounces each) frozen French-fried potatoes**
 ½ **teaspoon salt**
 ⅛ **teaspoon pepper**

Melt the butter in a saucepan or skillet. Sauté the green pepper and celery until tender, then mix in the flour and seasonings. Cook gently for 1 minute, then blend in the half-and-half. Cook, stirring constantly, until thick and smooth. Fold in the pimientos and mushrooms and heat through.

Just before serving, heat the potatoes in a small amount of fat in a skillet, turning to brown evenly. When crisp, drain on absorbent paper. Serve the ham à la king on the potatoes.

Four to six servings

SWISS HAM PIE

 1 **cup diced, cooked ham**
 1 **unbaked 9-inch pastry shell**
 2 **tablespoons butter or margarine**
 2 **tablespoons all-purpose flour**
 ⅛ **teaspoon freshly grated nutmeg**
1½ **cups milk**
 4 **ounces process Swiss cheese, shredded (1 cup)**
 3 **eggs, lightly beaten**

Bake the pastry shell at 450° for 7 minutes. In a medium-sized saucepan, melt the butter. Blend in the flour and nutmeg. Add the milk all at once and cook and stir until thickened. Add the cheese and stir until melted.

Cool slightly. Stir a small amount of the cheese sauce into the eggs, then stir the eggs into the cheese sauce. Add the ham, pour into the pie shell, and bake at 375° for 25 to 30 minutes. Let the pie cool for 10 minutes before serving.

Six servings

HAM IN CHEESE SAUCE

3   cups diced, cooked ham
½   cup all-purpose flour
½   cup melted butter or margarine
1   teaspoon Worcestershire sauce
3   cups milk, scalded
1   cup grated sharp Cheddar cheese
1   small green pepper, diced
1   teaspoon minced chives
1   cup sour cream
1   teaspoon salt
4   cups hot, cooked rice

Blend the flour and butter in a saucepan. Add the Worcestershire sauce and salt, then pour in the hot milk, stirring constantly, and cook until the mixture is thick and smooth. Add the cheese and stir constantly until it is melted. Stir in the ham, green pepper, and chives. Add the sour cream, continuing to heat gently but not allowing the mixture to boil. Serve over the rice.

Eight servings

HAM AND NOODLES

1   pound coarsely ground or minced ham
2   cups (4 ounces) noodles
1   small green pepper
1   egg, beaten
2   tablespoons melted butter or margarine
1   can (1 pound 1 ounce) cream-style corn
¾   cup shredded sharp process cheese
1½   cups cornflakes

Cook the noodles as directed on the package. Drain well. Cut 3 crosswise rings from the small end of the green pepper and reserve them for garnish. Chop the remaining pepper and combine ¼ cup of it with the ham, egg, butter, corn, cheese, and 1 cup of the cornflakes, mixing thoroughly. Stir into the drained noodles and pour the mixture into a casserole. Crush the remaining cornflakes, sprinkle them over the top, and bake, uncovered, at 350° for 45 to 50 minutes. Garnish with the pepper rings and serve.

Six servings

HAM–SWISS CHEESE CASSEROLE

2   cups (about ¾ pound) cubed, cooked ham
2   tablespoons butter
½   cup chopped onion
½   cup chopped green pepper
1   can (10½ ounces) cream of mushroom soup
1   cup sour cream
1   package (8 ounces) medium noodles, cooked and drained
2   cups (8 ounces) shredded Swiss cheese

Melt the butter in a 1-quart saucepan. Add the onion and green pepper and sauté. Remove from the heat and stir in the mushroom soup and sour cream. In a buttered 3-quart casserole, layer one-third of the noodles, one-third of the cheese, one-third of the ham, and pour over one half of the mushroom sauce. Repeat the layers, ending with the last third of the noodles, cheese, and ham. Bake at 350° for 30 to 45 minutes, or until heated through.

Six to eight servings

HAM AND NOODLES WITH CELERY SOUP

3   cups diced, cooked ham
1   package (8 ounces) medium noodles
2   tablespoons melted butter
1   teaspoon poppy seeds
1   can (10½ ounces) cream of celery soup
1   cup milk

¼ teaspoon basil
¼ teaspoon oregano
½ cup crushed cornflakes or fresh bread crumbs
½ cup grated cheese
½ teaspoon salt

Combine the noodles, 1 tablespoon of the melted butter, poppy seeds, ham, soup, milk, salt, and herbs. Turn into a buttered casserole. Combine the remaining butter, cornflakes, and cheese and sprinkle on the top. Bake, uncovered, at 350° for 20 to 30 minutes, or until heated through and top lightly browned.

Eight servings

HAM CASSEROLE WITH POTATOES

1 cup diced, cooked ham
3 cups diced, cooked potatoes
¼ cup pimientos, cut up
2 tablespoons all-purpose flour
8 ounces Cheddar cheese, grated
½ pint cream

Combine the ham, potatoes and pimientos. Put one-third of the mixture in a greased casserole. Sprinkle with some of the flour and cheese. Repeat the layers, ending with cheese. Pour the cream over all and bake, uncovered, at 350° for 30 minutes.

Four servings

HAM AND CHEESE SOUFFLÉS

2 cups minced, cooked ham
⅓ cup finely chopped onion
1 tablespoon butter
5 cups hot béchamel sauce
15 eggs, separated
4 cups grated Cheddar cheese
6 tablespoons coarsely chopped Cheddar cheese
¼ cup chopped fresh parsley
½ teaspoon salt

Sauté the onion in the butter until the onion is soft, then stir in the ham and set the mixture aside. Put the hot béchamel sauce in a large saucepan and slowly pour in the lightly beaten egg yolks, stirring constantly. Cover and let cool.

Meanwhile, generously butter six 2-cup soufflé dishes. Fit a 6-inch-wide band of double foil, buttered on the inside, around the top of each dish. The bands should extend 2 inches above the rims of the dishes.

Beat the egg whites in a large bowl, adding the salt, until they form stiff peaks. Fold one-quarter of the whites into the yolk mixture. Fold this mixture into the remaining whites, along with the grated cheese. Fill the soufflé dishes with alternating layers of the ham mixture and the egg mixture, ending with a layer of egg mixture. Sprinkle each dish with 1 tablespoon of the chopped cheese, then place the filled dishes in a baking pan. Put enough water into the pan to reach halfway up the sides of the dishes. Bake at 375° for 40 to 50 minutes, or until the soufflés are puffed and golden. Remove the foil collars, sprinkle with the parsley.

Six servings

CURRIED HAM WITH ORANGE

2   cups diced, cooked ham
1   tablespoon minced onion
2   tablespoons julienne-cut green pepper
2   tablespoons butter or margarine
2   tablespoons brown sugar, firmly packed
1   teaspoon curry powder
½   cup orange juice
¼   cup chopped orange sections
2   cups cooked rice
½   teaspoon salt

In a large skillet, sauté the onion and pepper in the butter for 5 minutes. Add the sugar and the ham and cook for 5 minutes, stirring to blend thoroughly. Blend in the curry powder, orange juice, chopped orange, and salt. When well blended, add the rice and toss to mix. Simmer just long enough to heat through.

Four to six servings

HAM, BEAN, AND RICE CASSEROLE

1½   cups cubed, cooked ham
 1   cup raw rice
½   cup Blue Lake beans, cut up
¼   cup white wine
 1   can (10½ ounces) cream of mushroom soup

Cook and drain the rice. Put half of it in the bottom of a greased 1- to
1½-quart casserole. Distribute the beans evenly on top of the rice, then
add the ham and cover with the remaining rice. Stir the wine into the
mushroom soup to make a smooth mixture. Pour over the top of the
casserole and bake at 325° for 30 minutes, or until thoroughly hot.

Four to six servings

HAM AND TURKEY ON CORNBREAD

 4   slices cooked ham
 4   pieces cornbread (about 1 inch thick and 3 inches square)
 4   slices cooked turkey
 3   cups mild Cheddar cheese sauce
½   cup or 1 can (3 ounces) button mushrooms, drained
     Salt

Place the cornbread in the bottoms of individual casseroles. Arrange the
slices of ham and turkey on top and sprinkle lightly with salt. Pour the
sauce over the meat, decorate with the mushroom caps, and bake at 350°
until the sauce is brown and bubbling. Serve at once.

HONEY-GLAZED HAM SLICES

 6   thick slices baked ham
 1   tablespoon butter
½   teaspoon Dijon mustard
½   cup honey

Melt the butter in a skillet. Blend in the mustard and then the honey. Lay the ham slices in the pan in a single layer, or do half at a time. Heat and turn the meat until it is glazed on both sides. This may be served for breakfast or brunch with poached eggs or for dinner with yams or stewed apples.

HAM AND CORN CASSEROLE

2   cups diced, cooked ham
1   egg
¾   cup milk
1   can (8 ounces) whole-kernel corn
1   tablespoon finely chopped green pepper
1   cup soft bread crumbs
½   teaspoon dried minced onion
½   cup crushed cornflakes
1½ tablespoons butter or margarine
½   teaspoon salt

Gently beat the egg into the milk, then combine with all the other ingredients except the cornflakes and butter. Turn into a well-buttered casserole and top with the cornflakes. Dot with the butter and bake, uncovered, at 350° for 45 minutes, or until the cornflakes are slightly browned.

Two or three servings

HAM POLYNESIAN

3   cups cut-up cooked ham
2   tablespoons butter
1   can (13½ ounces) pineapple chunks
2   medium green peppers, cut in strips
½   cup brown sugar
2   tablespoons cornstarch
½   cup vinegar
½   cup chicken bouillon
2   teaspoons soy sauce
3   cups hot, cooked rice

Brown the ham pieces lightly in the butter. Add the pineapple with its syrup and the green pepper strips, cover, and simmer for 15 minutes. Mix the brown sugar and cornstarch, then add the vinegar, bouillon, and soy sauce. Add this to the ham mixture and stir until thickened. Serve over the hot rice.

Six servings

HAM BRYN MAWR

6 slices baked or boiled ham
¼ cup milk
2 tablespoons sherry
1 can (10½ ounces) cheese soup or 1½ cups cheese sauce
3 English muffins
6 eggs

Stir the milk and sherry into the soup. Blend thoroughly, then heat carefully. Set aside and keep hot. Split and toast the muffins. Place a slice of ham on each. Poach the eggs and put one on each slice of ham. Pour the sauce over the eggs and serve at once.

Six servings

HAM AND SOUR CREAM CASSEROLE

½ pound baked ham, sliced
2 tablespoons butter or margarine
2 tablespoons all-purpose flour
1 pint sour cream
1 egg, lightly beaten
¼ teaspoon freshly grated nutmeg
¼ cup bread crumbs
2 cans (8 ounces each) sliced white potatoes
  Grated Parmesan cheese
¼ teaspoon salt

Blend the butter and flour in a saucepan over moderate heat. Slowly add the sour cream, stirring until smooth, then gradually stir in the egg, being careful to keep the mixture smooth. Add the salt and nutmeg. Continue to cook, stirring constantly, until the mixture is creamy and thick. Remove from the heat and allow to cool slightly.

Butter a casserole and sprinkle generously with bread crumbs. Put a layer of ham, cut into easily served pieces, in the casserole. Add a layer of potatoes and some of the sauce. Repeat the layers. Sprinkle the top with cheese and bake, covered, at 325° for 30 minutes.

Six servings

DIXIE YAM HAM SKILLET

1½ pounds fully cooked ham, cubed
2 tablespoons butter or margarine
3 tablespoons brown sugar, firmly packed
2 tablespoons cornstarch
¼ teaspoon ground cloves
¼ teaspoon ground cinnamon
2 cups apple juice
1 medium apple, cored and sliced
2 cans (16 ounces each) yams, drained, or 6 medium fresh yams,
      cooked, peeled, and quartered
¼ cup mixed salted nuts

In a skillet, brown the ham lightly in the butter. Combine the sugar, cornstarch, cloves, and cinnamon; stir in the apple juice and pour over the ham. Cook and stir until the sauce boils. Boil for 1 minute, then add the apple slices and cook over low heat until the apple is almost tender. Arrange the yams and apple slices around the skillet with the ham in the center. Sprinkle the nuts on top, cover, and heat through slowly.

Six servings

HAM AND VEGETABLE SOUFFLÉ

1 cup ham, cooked and diced
2 tablespoons chopped scallion
2 tablespoons butter
4 eggs, separated

½   cup sour cream
¼   cup all-purpose flour
3½ tablespoons grated Swiss cheese
3½ tablespoons freshly grated Parmesan cheese
⅛   teaspoon ground nutmeg
2   cups cooked cauliflower florets
1   cup cooked green peas
1   tablespoon softened butter
¾   teaspoon salt
¼   teaspoon white pepper

Sauté the ham and scallion in 2 tablespoons of the butter, in a skillet, for 5 minutes. Let cool. In a bowl beat the egg yolks and stir in the sour cream. Slowly stir in the flour, along with 1 tablespoon of the Swiss cheese, 1 tablespoon of the Parmesan cheese, the nutmeg, salt, and pepper. In another bowl beat the egg whites, with a pinch of salt, until stiff. Fold one-third of the whites into the egg-yolk mixture, then fold back into the remaining whites.

Spread half of this mixture in a buttered baking dish, 10 x 6 x 2 inches. Top with the cauliflower. Add the peas to the ham mixture and spoon half of this over the cauliflower. Sprinkle with 1 tablespoon Swiss cheese and 1 tablespoon Parmesan cheese. Spread with the remaining egg mixture. Top this with the remaining ham mixture. Sprinkle with the remaining 1½ tablespoons of each of the cheeses, and dot with the softened butter. Bake, uncovered, at 375° for 30 to 35 minutes, or until soufflé is puffed and golden.

Four servings

SMOKED CHOPS WITH RED CABBAGE À LA SACK

6   smoked chops
1   medium red cabbage, sliced
1   small onion, sliced
2 to 3 apples, peeled and cubed
4   whole cloves
3   tablespoons granulated sugar
2   tablespoons vinegar
    Salt

Combine all except the chops, sugar, vinegar, and salt in a heavy saucepan. Add a very small amount of water, then cover and simmer over low heat for at least 2 hours. Add the vinegar, sugar, and salt to taste and simmer 10 minutes longer. Meanwhile, put the chops in a lightly greased skillet. Cook, turning frequently, until lightly browned and cooked through (15 to 20 minutes).

To serve, place the cabbage in a deep platter and put the chops on top.

SMOKED CHOPS ON DRIED APPLES

4 smoked chops
½ pound dried apples
2 tablespoons brown sugar
¼ teaspoon ground cinnamon
⅛ teaspoon ground cloves

Soak the apples in enough water to cover, in a heavy saucepan for 1 to 2 hours. After the soaking period, check to make sure that the water is halfway up to the top of the apples. Add the brown sugar, cinnamon, and cloves and cook, tightly covered, over low heat until the apples are tender. Do not add water unless absolutely necessary to keep the apples from burning. Place in a buttered casserole, lay the chops on top, and bake, covered, at 325° for 30 minutes.

GLAZED SMOKED CHOPS WITH CHERRIES

4 smoked chops
2 tablespoons honey
½ cup water
½ cup dry white wine or apple juice
¼ cup granulated sugar
1 cup canned Bing cherries, pitted
    Juice of 1 orange

Place the chops in a heavy skillet. Add the honey and water, then place over low heat and simmer until the liquid has evaporated, turning the chops once. Transfer the chops to a greased ovenproof dish. Add the remaining ingredients and bake, covered, at 350° for 20 minutes, or until the cherries are hot.

SMOKED CHOPS, BACHELOR STYLE

4   **smoked chops**
½   **cup dark brown sugar**
2   **tablespoons prepared mustard**
2   **tablespoons butter or margarine**
¼   **cup port**

Rub the sugar into both sides of the chops, then coat them with mustard. Melt the butter in a heavy skillet, and when hot, put in the chops and brown on both sides. Cover, lower the heat, and cook for 15 minutes, turning once. Remove to a hot platter. Skim off any fat in the pan, pour in the port, and heat. When hot, pour over the chops.

SMOKED CHOPS WITH HAM AND VEGETABLES JULIENNE

4   **smoked chops**   **Salt**
1   **tablespoon butter or margarine**   **Pepper**
2   **tablespoons olive oil**
¾   **cup raw long-grain rice**
1   **cup thinly sliced onion**
½   **cup each fine julienne strips (fine matchsticks) of**
      ham, mushrooms, green pepper, and celery
1   **clove garlic, minced fine**
1   **tablespoon chopped parsley**
¼   **teaspoon thyme**
½   **cup dry white wine**
1   **cup chicken broth or bouillon**

Trim the fat from the chops. In an electric skillet or a 10-inch serving skillet, heat the butter and oil. Brown the chops slowly on both sides. Remove, then season with salt and pepper. Add the rice to skillet and cook and stir for 2 minutes. Return the chops to the pan and cover with the onion, ham, garlic, parsley, and thyme. Add the wine and simmer for 3 minutes. Add the chicken bouillon. Cover the skillet tightly and simmer for 10 minutes. Add the celery and green pepper and simmer for 10 minutes longer, until the vegetables are cooked but still slightly crisp. Serve from the skillet.

GERMAN-STYLE SMOKED CHOPS

6   smoked chops
1   large onion, sliced
4   tablespoons butter or margarine
1   can (16 ounces) sauerkraut, rinsed and drained
1   medium apple, peeled, cored, and sliced thin
1   tablespoon caraway seeds
1   clove garlic, crushed
½   cup dry white wine
½   cup water
1   teaspoon salt
⅛   teaspoon freshly ground pepper

In a large skillet, sauté the chops and onion in the butter. Cook the chops for 5 minutes on each side, then remove from the pan and set aside. Add all the other ingredients to the skillet and mix thoroughly. Place the mixture in a 1½-quart casserole and top with the chops. Bake, covered, at 350° for 30 minutes.

SMOKED SHOULDER BUTT WITH APPLESAUCE

8   slices smoked butt
1   cup unsweetened applesauce
2   teaspoons Brownulated sugar
¼   teaspoon ground cloves
¼   teaspoon ground cinnamon

Mix the applesauce with the sugar and spices. Place the meat slices in a shallow baking dish. Top each with 2 tablespoons of applesauce. Bake, uncovered, at 325° for 30 minutes.

Four servings

SMOKED SHOULDER ROLL WITH MUSTARD SAUCE

1   smoked shoulder roll (2 to 3 pounds)
2   tablespoons pickling spice

1   stalk celery or 1 teaspoon celery seed
1   medium onion, cut in half
1   tablespoon butter or margarine
½   tablespoon flour
⅓   cup boiling water
½   tablespoon cider vinegar
2   tablespoons prepared mustard
1   teaspoon prepared horseradish
1   tablespoon sugar
⅛   teaspoon salt

Cover the meat with the water and add the pickling spice, celery, and onion. Simmer, covered, until the meat is tender, allowing about 45 minutes to the pound.

Meanwhile, melt the butter in a saucepan and add the flour and salt. Gradually add the boiling water, stirring until thick and smooth. Add the vinegar, mustard, horseradish, and sugar. Simmer for about 5 minutes, stirring constantly. If a thinner sauce is desired add 1 or 2 more tablespoons of boiling water. Stir to blend. Serve with the meat.

Four to six servings

PICNIC SHOULDER WITH APRICOTS

1   smoked picnic shoulder (6 pounds), boneless
½   cup brown sugar
¼   cup cider vinegar
1   tablespoon prepared mustard
1   can (16 ounces) apricot halves, drained and juice reserved
    Whole cloves

Place the meat in a Dutch oven with water to cover. Simmer, covered, until tender (about 45 minutes per pound). Remove to a baking pan. In a saucepan blend the sugar, vinegar, mustard, and apricot juice. Stud the apricot halves with a few cloves and simmer them in the vinegar mixture for 5 minutes. Drain them and pour this sauce over the meat. Pin a few apricot halves to the meat with small skewers or wooden picks. Bake, uncovered, at 400° for 15 minutes or until the glaze is browned. Use the remaining apricot halves for garnish.

Eight to ten servings

COTTAGE ROLL WITH SPICE SAUCE

1	cottage roll (2 pounds)
4	cups water
12	small onions
6	whole cloves
1	bay leaf
4	potatoes, peeled and quartered
6	carrots, sliced
⅓	cup brown sugar
1	tablespoon cornstarch
¼	teaspoon ground cinnamon
¼	teaspoon ground allspice
2	cans (8 ounces each) tomato sauce
½	cup seedless raisins
2	teaspoons salt

Place the pork, water, onions, cloves, bay leaf, and salt in a kettle. Simmer, covered, for 1 hour, then add the potatoes and carrots and simmer, covered, for 25 minutes. Combine the sugar, cornstarch, and spices, then stir in the tomato sauce and raisins. Cook, stirring constantly, until thick and shiny (approximately 3 minutes). Place the meat and vegetables on a platter. Spoon some of the sauce over and serve the remainder separately.

Six servings

Leftovers

There is no good reason for failing to completely utilize all cuts of pork. The leftover or "planned-over" dish can be as tempting as the original. The imagination of cooks for generations has been inexhaustible in the service of second performances; indeed, improvisation has been piled on improvisation. Here we have tried to take the hazards out of imaginative treatment by specifying more precisely the ingredients and procedures likely to enhance the leftover and still leave the imaginative touches intact.

Initial purchases of good-quality meat and skilled original treatment ensure better leftover results. This changes "leftover" into "planned-over." Planned-over is not only more inspiring than the tired leftover connotation, it is far less likely to conjure up the vision of a bored, harried cook in front of an overcrowded refrigerator, with the dinner hour bearing down on her.

The planned-over approach also means there is enough left over with which to do something special. Thus the discouragement of a lot of ill-related or altogether incompatible dabs is avoided. This planning also carries the bonus of being sure of enough of the original dish to satisfy an extra-hungry family member or to extend an invitation to an unexpected guest (or one thought of after the original list).

You might consult the appetizer section for possible use of some meager quantities. Some cooks will throw anything into the soup pot, although we are not among them, considering that approach the last dying gasp. Some meat scraps and bones yield excellent soup stocks, and this is a worthy end in itself.

The common denominator of these recipes is that all the meats have been cooked before. After that the field is open, wide, and fertile. Ham and roasts, of course, provide the best basis for planned-over pork dishes. Smoked meats come through the recycling recipe retaining both flavor and texture.

137

Take a little time and thought to give your planned-over some style. Dress it smartly in garniture. On the other hand, some meats can go to the next meal just as they are. See, for example, a cold pork sandwich recipe in that section. Others are easily made presentable in an attractively concocted new sauce.

SOUTH AFRICAN BOBOTIE

2	heaping cups ground, cooked pork
5	slices "very thin," or Melba, white bread
4	eggs
1	cup half-and-half
1	onion, chopped
2	tablespoons butter
1	tablespoon curry powder
½	lemon
	Salt

In a large bowl crumble the bread into coarse crumbs. Beat the eggs with the half-and-half. Fry the onion in 1 tablespoon of the butter. Stir in the remaining tablespoon of butter and the curry powder. Add to the bread crumbs, along with the pork, mixing thoroughly. Put in a casserole. Squeeze the lemon over the top. Bake at 325° for 45 minutes. Serve with hot rice and chutney.

Four servings

PORK WITH ORANGES AND BANANAS

2	cups cubed, cooked pork
½	cup chopped onion
2	tablespoons cooking oil
1	can (8 ounces) tomato sauce
	Tabasco sauce to taste
1	tablespoon cornstarch
1	cup pineapple juice
1	green pepper, sliced in thin rings
2	oranges, peeled and sliced
2	bananas, peeled and sliced diagonally
3	cups hot, cooked rice
½	cup seedless raisins, plumped in hot water and drained

Brown the meat and onion, in the oil, in a large skillet. Stir in the tomato sauce and Tabasco. Blend the cornstarch with 1 tablespoon of the pineapple juice and stir this into the remaining juice. Add to the meat mixture. Bring to a boil. Reduce the heat and simmer until thick and smooth, about 10 minutes. Add the green pepper rings and cook for 10 minutes longer. Add the oranges and bananas and allow to heat gently. Toss the rice with the raisins and serve with the meat mixture.

Four or five servings

PORK WITH FRIED RICE

½   cup cooked pork, cut in slivers
¼   cup cooked, crumbled bacon
2   eggs, beaten
3   tablespoons cooking oil
½   cup chopped scallions, including tops
1½ cups cooked rice, cooled
2   tablespoons soy sauce
½   teaspoon granulated sugar
½   teaspoon salt

Scramble the eggs in 1½ tablespoons of the oil and remove from the pan. Add the remaining oil, the bacon, pork, and scallions. Cook a few minutes, stirring constantly. Add the cooked rice and continue to stir. Break up the scrambled eggs and add to the rice mixture. Add the soy sauce, sugar, and salt. Heat through and serve.

Four servings

PORK PIE

3   cups thin strips of lean, cooked pork
2   tablespoons butter or margarine
2   tablespoons cornstarch
1½ cups milk
½   cup finely chopped celery
1   tablespoon finely chopped onion
¾   teaspoon paprika
¾   teaspoon salt
¼   teaspoon pepper
    Pastry for double-crust pie

Melt the butter and blend in the cornstarch, then add the milk. Cook and stir to a smooth sauce. Add the celery, onion, and seasonings. Then add the meat.

Roll out half the pastry and line a shallow 1½-quart casserole. Fill with the meat mixture, roll the second half of the pastry to fit the top. Fold the top edge of the pastry under the bottom edge and crimp to seal, cut two gashes for steam to escape, then bake the pie at 375° for 45 minutes.

Six servings

FRIED RICE WITH PORK AND BEAN SPROUTS

1½ cups cubed, cooked pork
 1 tablespoon butter or margarine
 1 egg
 ¼ cup finely chopped onion
 1 can (8 ounces) bean sprouts, drained
 3 cups cooked rice, cooled
 1 teaspoon soy sauce
 ¼ teaspoon salt
 ⅛ teaspoon pepper

Melt the butter in a heavy skillet. Add the salt and heat until very hot. Add the egg and scramble it. Mix in the pork, onion, bean sprouts, and rice. Add the soy sauce and pepper. Cook, stirring constantly, for 1 minute longer. Serve with additional soy sauce.

Four servings

RISOTTO

1¾ cups cubed, cooked pork
 1 tablespoon butter or margarine
 1 small onion, chopped
 4 medium tomatoes, peeled and cubed, or
       ½ cup canned, sliced baby tomatoes, drained
 ¾ cup raw rice
1½ cups beef bouillon
 1 green pepper
 1 teaspoon salt
 ⅛ teaspoon pepper

Melt the butter in a large skillet. Sauté the onion without browning, then add the tomatoes, rice, bouillon, salt and pepper. Bring slowly to a boil. Lay aside 4 pepper rings. Cut up the rest in small pieces and add them to the rice mixture. Add the meat and transfer to a casserole. Bake, covered, at 350° for 30 to 45 minutes, or until most of the liquid has been absorbed and the rice is tender.

Meanwhile, cook the pepper rings in hot, salted water for 3 minutes. Use them to garnish the casserole.

Four servings

EASY CHOP SUEY

1½   **cups julienne strips of cooked pork**
2   **tablespoons butter or margarine**
1   **cup diagonally sliced celery**
1   **can (16 ounces) bean sprouts, drained**
1   **can (8 ounces) water chestnuts, sliced**
1   **can (8 ounces) bamboo shoots**
1   **can (10 to 12 ounces) mushroom gravy**
2   **teaspoons soy sauce**

Melt the butter in a heavy skillet and sauté the celery until crisp-tender. Add the pork and brown lightly. Add the bean sprouts, water chestnuts, and bamboo shoots. Stir in the gravy and soy sauce. Serve with hot, cooked rice and additional soy sauce.

Four servings

HASH TAIWAN

1½   **cups cubed, cooked pork**
2   **tablespoons cooking oil**
   Dash of garlic powder
2   **cups cooked rice**
3   **tablespoons soy sauce**
2   **eggs, well beaten**
2   **cups shredded lettuce**

Brown the meat in the cooking oil in a frying pan or electric skillet. Sprinkle on the garlic powder. Add the rice and soy sauce. Cook for 5 minutes, stirring frequently. Mix in the beaten eggs and cook for 1 minute longer, stirring constantly. Remove from the heat. Add the lettuce, and toss lightly. Serve immediately.

Four servings

STUFFED EGGPLANT SUPREME

1   cup ground leftover pork
1   large eggplant
½   green pepper, chopped fine
1   medium onion, chopped fine
½   cup cooked rice
2   ripe tomatoes, peeled and chopped
½   cup chicken broth
⅓   cup buttered bread crumbs
    Salt
    Pepper

Cut the eggplant in half lengthwise. Scoop out the inside, leaving a shell ½ inch thick. Cook the pulp in boiling salted water until tender. Drain well and mash. Using the same water, cook the green pepper for 5 minutes. Drain. Mix the pork, mashed eggplant, pepper, onion, rice, and tomatoes. Season with salt and pepper, add enough chicken broth to bind. Fill the eggplant shell. Place in a shallow baking dish. Top with the buttered crumbs. Bake at 350° for 30 minutes.

Four servings

JOY'S TASTY CASSEROLE

4   cups cooked pork, cut into bite-size cubes
¼   cup finely chopped onion
4   tablespoons butter or margarine
4   cups diced, cooked potatoes
½   cup heavy cream
½   cup red wine or sherry
1   tablespoon soy sauce
    Paprika
    Salt
    Pepper

Sauté the onion in butter until tender. Put it and all the other ingredients except the seasonings in a 2½- to 3-quart casserole. Mix thoroughly but gently. Add salt and pepper to taste and sprinkle the top with paprika. Bake, covered, at 350° for 15 minutes and uncovered for 15 minutes longer.

Six servings

LOU'S PORK AND SAUSAGE CASSEROLE

1 cup diced, cooked pork
2 dinner sausages, cooked and sliced
1 can (16 ounces) sliced white potatoes, drained
2 tablespoons chopped green pepper
½ cup tomato juice
4 tablespoons grated Parmesan cheese
   Salt
   Pepper

Put half the potatoes in the bottom of a well-buttered casserole. Season lightly with salt and pepper. Next make a layer of the pork and sausage. Sprinkle on the green pepper, cover with the remaining potatoes, and pour on the tomato juice. Sprinkle with salt and pepper and then the cheese. Bake, uncovered, at 325° for 30 minutes, or until heated through.

Three servings

PORK BALLS IN TANGERINE SAUCE

2 cups diced, cooked pork
½ cup chopped celery
2 teaspoons soy sauce
½ cup finely chopped scallions
¼ teaspoon ground ginger
¼ cup fine, dry bread crumbs
2 eggs, lightly beaten
   Salt
   Pepper
2 cups hot, cooked rice

Mix all the ingredients except the rice in a large bowl. Form into balls, using about ¼ cup of the mixture for each ball. Place the balls in a lightly greased shallow baking dish. Bake, uncovered, at 350° for 30 minutes.

Sauce:

  1   **cup chicken broth**
  ¾   **cup tangerine juice**
  ¼   **cup cider vinegar**
  ¼   **cup brown sugar, firmly packed**
  ⅛   **teaspoon dry mustard**
  ¼   **teaspoon ground ginger**
2½   **teaspoons cornstarch**
  3   **tangerines, peeled and broken into sections**

Combine the broth, tangerine juice, vinegar, and brown sugar, in a saucepan and cook over low heat. Mix the mustard, ginger, and cornstarch and combine with enough of the juice mixture to make a smooth paste. Slowly stir the mustard mixture into the juice mixture, then bring to a boil, stirring constantly. Boil for 1 minute. Remove from the heat and add the tangerine sections. Arrange the meat on the rice and pour the sauce over all.

Four servings

MEXICAN HOMINY CASSEROLE

  2   **cups cubed, cooked pork**
  2   **cans (16 ounces each) hominy, drained**
  1   **can (16 ounces) tomatoes, drained**
  2   **mild red chili peppers, chopped fine**
  1   **medium onion, chopped**

Combine all the ingredients and place in a buttered casserole. Bake, covered, at 325° long enough to heat through (about 30 minutes).

Six servings

SOUTH SEAS SUPPER

  2   **heaping cups cubed, cooked pork**
  1   **can (8¼ ounces) pineapple chunks, drained and juice reserved**

2   tomatoes, cut in thin wedges, or the equivalent in
        canned sliced tomatoes, juice included
2   tablespoons cornstarch
⅓   cup cider vinegar
½   cup dark brown sugar
2   tablespoons soy sauce
1   green pepper, cut in 1-inch squares
2   tablespoons finely cut preserved ginger
½   teaspoon salt

Measure the reserved pineapple juice and add water to make 1 cup; if using canned tomatoes, substitute tomato juice for the water. Mix the cornstarch and 2 tablespoons of the juice to a smooth paste. Add the remaining juice, vinegar, brown sugar, soy sauce, and salt and cook, stirring constantly, until smooth and thick.

Meanwhile, parboil the pepper pieces for 6 minutes. Drain and add, along with the meat, pineapple chunks, tomatoes, and ginger, to the cooked liquid. Cover and cook over low heat, watching carefully, for 10 minutes. Serve with hot rice.

Six servings

MALAY PORK AND SHRIMP WITH RICE

½   pound diced, cooked pork
¼   pound diced, cooked ham
2   cups raw rice
4   ounces sliced bacon, cut into quarters
3   tablespoons cooking oil
1   large onion, chopped
2   cloves garlic
1   teaspoon ground coriander
1   tablespoon chutney
1   tablespoon soy sauce
1   can (4½ ounces) shrimp
1   leek, sliced
¼   cup chopped celery
½   cucumber, peeled and diced
    Salt
    Pepper

Cook the rice in salted water until just tender. Drain well and dry over hot water. Fry the bacon in a heavy skillet. Remove and drain. Add the oil to the same skillet and cook the onion until golden. Add the garlic, coriander, chutney, soy sauce, salt, and pepper. Stir over low heat; gradually add the rice, turning gently to keep the grains separated and to coat them with the seasonings. Add the meat and two-thirds of the shrimp. Then add the vegetables and heat thoroughly. Salt and pepper to taste. To serve—pile on a hot serving platter, garnish with the remaining shrimp.

Four servings

Chopped, Cubed, and Ground Pork

Uncooked pork can be ground or cut into small pieces and easily lends itself to recipes calling for such treatment. Using pork this way permits extending its good flavor into the other ingredients in casserole, loaf pan, stewing kettle or frying pan. It may be cooked on skewers, rolled into balls, tossed into a stew, or baked in a loaf. It seems to us the cook is helped by our grouping together recipes calling for small pieces of pork since they do not require any particular retail cut. Calculating servings in these recipes is not an exact science, but we have evaluated them carefully, based on considerable testing. In general, servings have been calculated on the generous side.

PORK AND SHRIMP HAWAIIAN

1	pound lean pork, cubed
½	pound fresh shrimp, cleaned and cooked
2	tablespoons shortening
1	clove garlic, crushed
1	small onion, sliced
1	package (8 ounces) fine noodles
¼	cup finely chopped peanuts
¼	cup crisply cooked, crumbled bacon
1	teaspoon salt
⅛	teaspoon freshly ground pepper

Heat the shortening in a large, heavy skillet. Add the garlic and cook for a few minutes, then remove and discard. Add the onion and cook until tender. Add the pork, cover, and simmer very gently until the pork is cooked and tender. Add the shrimp, salt, and pepper.

Meanwhile, cook the noodles in boiling salted water until tender.

147

Drain thoroughly and add to the skillet. Mix gently, then reheat carefully. Serve accompanied by small dishes of the peanuts and bacon.

Four servings

WASHINGTON PORK

2 pounds lean pork, cut in 1-inch cubes
1 tablespoon shortening
½ cup water
2 tablespoons red wine vinegar
½ teaspoon dry mustard
¼ teaspoon ground cloves
1 can (16 ounces) tart, pitted red cherries, drained and liquid reserved
½ cup granulated sugar
2 tablespoons cornstarch
½ cup slivered almonds
1 teaspoon salt
   Hot, cooked rice

Heat the shortening and brown the pork evenly. Season with salt, then add the water, vinegar, mustard, and cloves. Cover and cook slowly until the meat is tender (30 to 45 minutes). Combine the cherry liquid, sugar, and cornstarch and add to the pork. Cook, stirring, until the sauce is clear and thick. Fold in the cherries. Heat through, sprinkle with the almonds, and serve on a platter, with a border of rice.

Six servings

GROUND PORK TROUANT

3   pounds ground lean pork
3   teaspoons sage
3   teaspoons salt
1½ teaspoons freshly ground pepper
    Butter or margarine, if necessary

Combine all the ingredients except the butter and cook, covered, in a heavy skillet for 30 minutes, stirring often. If the meat is very lean and there appears to be danger of its sticking, add a small quantity of butter or margarine. Uncover and cook for another 30 minutes.

Eight servings

CUBED PORK À LA DIXON

2   pounds lean pork, cubed
2   cups water
½   cup vinegar
1   clove garlic
1   tablespoon shortening
2   tablespoons soy sauce
4   teaspoons salt
1   teaspoon pepper
     Hot, cooked rice

Simmer the pork in the water and vinegar, along with the garlic, salt, and pepper, until the meat is tender and about ½ cup of liquid remains. Remove the pork and garlic and drain thoroughly. Reserve the liquid and discard the garlic. Fry the meat in the shortening until brown, then add the ½ cup of liquid and the soy sauce. Simmer for 5 minutes. Serve over the hot rice.

Six servings

GREEN PEPPERS AND PORK JULIENNE

1   pound lean pork, cut in ½-inch strips
¼   cup cooking oil
2   green peppers, cut in strips
2½   cups sliced tart apples
1   cup chicken bouillon
2   tablespoons cornstarch
3   tablespoons soy sauce
½   cup vinegar
½   cup granulated sugar
½   teaspoon salt
¼   teaspoon pepper

Brown the pork on all sides in the oil. Add the peppers, apple slices, and ⅓ cup of the bouillon and cook, covered, over low heat for 30 minutes. Combine the cornstarch with the remaining bouillon, then add the soy sauce, vinegar, sugar, salt, pepper. Stir into the meat mixture and cook, stirring constantly, until clear and thick. May be served over rice or Chinese noodles.

Four servings

SPANISH PORK AND RICE

1   pound pork, cubed
1   tablespoon shortening
1   medium onion, diced
1   clove garlic, minced
½   teaspoon marjoram
½   teaspoon basil
½   teaspoon savory
½   teaspoon thyme
½   teaspoon Worcestershire sauce
½   teaspoon soy sauce
¼   teaspoon chili powder
1   medium tomato, diced
1½ cups beef or chicken consommé, more if necessary
½   teaspoon pepper
¼   cup sherry
¾   cup raw rice

Brown the pork in the shortening. Add all the other ingredients except the sherry and rice and bring to a boil. Add the sherry, then stir in the rice. Cook without stirring until the rice is tender, checking occasionally and adding more liquid if necessary.

Four servings

CANADIAN PORK STEW

2   pounds lean pork, cubed
6   tablespoons all-purpose flour
2   tablespoons cooking oil
6   scallions, including tops, chopped
2   large stalks celery, chopped
3   sprigs parsley
1   small bay leaf
3   whole cloves
3   peppercorns
½   teaspoon thyme
1   garlic clove, minced
8   medium carrots, cut in large pieces
6   medium potatoes, cut in large pieces

Minced parsley
1   **teaspoon salt**
¼   **teaspoon pepper**

Combine 4 tablespoons of the flour with the salt and pepper in a shallow dish and roll the pork cubes in it. Heat the oil in a large, heavy saucepan or Dutch oven. Add the pork and brown well on all sides. Add scallions and celery and cook gently for 5 minutes. Sprinkle in the remaining 2 tablespoons of flour, stirring constantly. Remove from the heat and add enough water to cover the meat. Stir, return to the heat and bring to a boil.

Tie the parsley, bay leaf, cloves, peppercorns and thyme in a small cheesecloth bag and drop into the stew. Add the garlic, cover tightly, and turn the heat to low. Simmer about 30 minutes, or until the meat is just beginning to get tender, then add carrots and potatoes. Cover again and continue simmering until everything is tender, about 45 minutes. Lift out the bag of seasonings and discard. Sprinkle with minced parsley and serve.

Six servings

SCRAPPLE

1   **pound pork (neck bones or other inexpensive cut)**
2   **fresh pig's feet (or omit and use another pound of meat)**
1   **quart water**
1   **cup yellow cornmeal**
2   **tablespoons finely chopped onion**
½   **teaspoon sage**
2   **teaspoons salt**
⅛   **teaspoon pepper**

Place the meat in a large pan and pour in the water. Cover and simmer until the meat drops from the bones. Remove the meat and grind it fine, then strain the broth into the top of a large double boiler. Add water if necessary to make 4 cups. Stir in the cornmeal. Place over direct heat and cook, stirring constantly, for 5 minutes. Add the meat, onion, and seasonings. Cook over boiling water for 30 minutes. Pack into a small loaf pan that has been rinsed in cold water and chill until firm. Then slice ½ inch thick and pan fry until crisp and brown. Serve hot, with maple syrup.

SWEET-SOUR PORK BALLS

Meat balls:

1½   pounds ground lean pork
¼   cup minced scallions
½   teaspoon ground ginger
2   tablespoons soy sauce
1   slice white bread, broken into crumbs
3   tablespoons milk
1   egg, lightly beaten
¼   teaspoon garlic salt
3   tablespoons cooking oil
¼   teaspoon salt
⅛   teaspoon pepper

Sauce:

2   tablespoons cornstarch
½   cup cider vinegar
⅓   cup soy sauce
1   tablespoon Worcestershire sauce
1   can (1 pound 4 ounces) pineapple chunks, drained, but juice reserved
¼   cup brown sugar
1   green pepper, cut in strips
1   can (16 ounces) bean sprouts
1   can (8 ounces) water chestnuts, drained and sliced
1   teaspoon salt
⅛   teaspoon pepper

Combine all the meat-ball ingredients except the cooking oil and chill thoroughly in the refrigerator. Shape into balls and brown well, in the oil, on all sides, in a heavy skillet. Remove the balls as they brown.

Drain all but 2 tablespoons of drippings from the skillet. Stir the cornstarch into the drippings, then remove from the heat and add the vinegar, soy sauce, Worcestershire sauce, and reserved pineapple juice, stirring until well blended. Return to moderate heat and bring to a boil, stirring constantly. Add the sugar, salt, and pepper. Return the meat balls to the skillet. Add the pineapple and green pepper and cook for 5 minutes. Add the bean sprouts and water chestnuts and cook for 5 minutes longer. Serve with hot, cooked rice.

Six servings

PORK-VEAL-BEAN BAKE

1½   pounds lean pork, cubed
1   pound veal, cubed
¼   cup finely diced salt pork
1   package (16 ounces) navy beans
10   cups water
2   medium onions, chopped
1   clove garlic, minced
¼   cup chopped fresh parsley
¼   teaspoon thyme
1   small bay leaf, crumbled
¼   cup cooking oil
1   can (8 ounces) tomato sauce
1   teaspoon dry mustard
2   teaspoons salt

Wash the beans. Cover with 4 cups of the water and allow to stand overnight.

The next day, pour the beans and their soaking water into a large kettle. Add the salt pork, 1 teaspoon of the salt, half the chopped onion, the garlic, parsley, thyme, bay leaf, and 6 cups of water. Bring to a boil. Turn down the heat, cover, and cook gently until the beans are tender (1 to 2 hours). Drain, saving the liquid.

Heat the oil in a Dutch oven. Add the veal, pork, and remaining chopped onion. Cook, stirring constantly, until the meat is browned. Drain off any fat. Combine the tomato sauce, mustard, and remaining salt. Add the meat. Bake, covered, at 350° until the meat is tender.

In a 2½-quart casserole, put alternate layers of beans and meat, beginning with beans. Combine the bean and meat liquids and add enough to the casserole to nearly cover the meat and beans. Bake, uncovered, at 325° for 2 hours, or until the beans have browned and most of the liquid has been absorbed.

Eight to ten servings

ITALIAN STEW

3   pounds lean boneless pork, cut in 1-inch cubes
3   tablespoons olive oil
2   cloves garlic, crushed
2   medium carrots, cut fine
½   teaspoon rosemary
¼   teaspoon white pepper
1½ cups dry white wine
1   cup canned chicken broth
3   green peppers, cut in 1-inch squares
1   can (16 ounces) Italian tomatoes, drained and chopped, liquid
     reserved
     Finely chopped parsley
2   teaspoons salt

Heat 2 tablespoons of the oil in a heavy, flameproof casserole. Cook the garlic in the oil until golden but not brown, then discard it. Stir the pork into the olive oil in the casserole. Cook, stirring, for 5 minutes, not to brown, just to coat with oil. Stir in the carrots, and sprinkle the seasonings over all. Add the wine and chicken broth and bring to a simmer. Place in the oven and bake, covered, at 325° for 1½ to 2 hours, or until the pork is tender. Skim off the fat.

Lightly sauté the green peppers in the remaining tablespoon of olive oil. Add to the stew, stir in the tomatoes and cook 15 minutes longer, adding the tomato liquid if needed. Sprinkle with chopped parsley and serve.

Eight servings

PORK WITH SAUERKRAUT

1½ pounds lean pork, cut in finger slices
2   tablespoons cooking fat
3   cups sauerkraut
1   onion, grated
2   cups white wine
1   teaspoon salt
     Freshly ground pepper

Fry the pork slowly in the fat for 20 minutes, or until brown on all sides. Salt and pepper the meat, then remove and keep warm. Put the sauerkraut in the same pan, add the onion and stir until thoroughly mixed. Add the wine and place the pork on top. Cover closely and steam without boiling until the sauerkraut is thoroughly heated.

Four servings

KIDNEY BEAN CASSOULET

½   **pound pork shoulder, cut in cubes**
4   **slices bacon**
1   **pork sausage, fried and sliced**
½   **pound veal, cubed**
1   **package (16 ounces) dried kidney beans**
1   **small onion**
2   **tablespoons butter**
1   **cup dry white wine**
2   **tablespoons catsup**
2   **tablespoons bread crumbs**
   Salt
   Pepper

Soak the beans overnight. The next day, drain them and place in a kettle with water to cover. Add salt and the onion and simmer for 2 hours.

Meanwhile, heat 1 tablespoon of the butter in a frying pan and brown the pork and veal cubes. Season with salt and pepper, add the wine and catsup and simmer for 1 hour. Place the meat mixture in a baking dish, top with the drained beans, and arrange the bacon and sausage over the beans. Sprinkle with bread crumbs, dot with the remaining butter. Bake, uncovered, at 325° for 1½ hours.

Six servings

PORK AND VEAL CASSEROLE

1   pound pork, cut in cubes
1   pound veal, cut in cubes
    All-purpose flour
4   tablespoons shortening, more if necessary
1   medium onion, chopped
1   green pepper, chopped
1   cup sliced celery
1   cup sliced mushrooms
1   package (8 ounces) medium-width noodles
3   beef bouillon cubes
6   cups boiling water
½   cup buttered bread crumbs
    Salt
    Pepper

Flour the meat. Then brown in the shortening in a heavy skillet. Remove to a casserole and season with salt and pepper. In the same skillet, sauté the onion, green pepper, celery, and mushrooms, adding more shortening if necessary. Dissolve the bouillon cubes in the water and cook the noodles for 7 minutes, or as directed on the package. Combine all ingredients in the casserole and bake, covered, at 325° for 45 minutes, adding more stock if needed. Cover the top with buttered bread crumbs and bake for 15 minutes longer.

Six to eight servings

FRIED PORK BURGERS

1½   pounds ground pork
½   teaspoon thyme
½   teaspoon marjoram
4   dashes Worcestershire sauce
1   egg, lightly beaten
1   cup fine, dry bread crumbs
3 to 4 tablespoons butter or margarine
2   teaspoons salt
⅛   teaspoon pepper

Season the pork with the salt, pepper, thyme, marjoram, and Worcestershire sauce, blending thoroughly. Shape the pork into thick patties. Dip in the beaten egg, then roll in bread crumbs. Fry in the butter until brown on both sides and cooked through.

Three or four servings

GOULASH

1   **pound lean pork, cubed**
1   **tablespoon bacon drippings**
1   **large onion, chopped**
1   **clove garlic, minced**
1   **can (6 ounces) tomato paste**
1   **can (16 ounces) sauerkraut**
1   **cup sour cream or sour half-and-half**
1   **teaspoon paprika**
½   **cup water**
    Salt
    Pepper

Brown the pork in the drippings in a large skillet, then add the onion and garlic and let them brown. Pour off excess fat. Combine the tomato paste, paprika, and water and add to the meat mixture. Season with salt and pepper. Simmer, covered, for 15 minutes. Add the sauerkraut. Simmer for 45 minutes longer. Stir in the sour cream and heat through; do not allow the mixture to boil.

May be served over hot noodles.

Four servings

GINGER PORK

1½   pounds lean pork, cut in 1-inch cubes
2   tablespoons cooking oil
5   pieces preserved ginger, sliced
      or
¾   teaspoon ground ginger·
¾   can (10½ ounces) cream of mushroom soup
¼   cup water
½   cup dry white wine
1½   teaspoons salt
¼   teaspoon freshly ground pepper

Brown the pork cubes in the cooking oil, then remove to a casserole. Sprinkle with the preserved or ground ginger. Combine the soup and water, and add the wine, salt, and pepper. Pour the mixture over the meat. Bake, covered, at 350° for 1½ hours, or until the sauce is thick and the meat is well done.

Six servings

SUKIYAKI

1½   pounds pork, cut in 1½- x ½-inch strips
¼   cup vegetable oil
6   tablespoons soy sauce
¼   cup granulated sugar
1   can (8 ounces) bamboo shoots, cut in strips
1   cup sliced fresh mushrooms
1   cup sliced scallions
2   tablespoons sake or white wine
3   cups cooked rice

Brown the meat in the oil in a heavy skillet. Add the soy sauce and sugar and simmer for 10 minutes. Add the bamboo shoots, scallions, and mushrooms. Simmer for 5 minutes. Add the sake, mix thoroughly, and serve with rice.

Six servings

PORK BALLS WITH LIMA BEANS

1   **pound ground pork**
½   **cup coarse bread crumbs**
¼   **teaspoon thyme**
1   **egg, lightly beaten**
½   **cup milk**
½   **cup fine, dry bread crumbs**
2   **tablespoons butter or margarine**
1   **green pepper, cut in julienne strips**
1   **medium onion, sliced thin**
2   **cups canned green lima beans, drained, and liquid reserved**
1   **can (8 ounces) tomato sauce**
2   **tablespoons cornstarch**
¾   **cup water**
1   **teaspoon salt**
¼   **teaspoon pepper**

Combine the pork, coarse crumbs, thyme, egg, and milk. Season with salt and pepper, then shape into balls 1 inch in diameter. Coat with the fine crumbs. Brown on all sides, in the butter, in a heavy skillet. Remove and keep warm.

Sauté the green pepper and onion in the skillet. Add the liquid from the beans, the tomato sauce, and ½ cup of the water. Bring to a boil. Combine the cornstarch with the remaining ¼ cup water, mixing until smooth. Stir into the skillet mixture. Cook until thick and smooth. Season with salt and pepper, remove from the heat, and add the meat and lima beans. Return to the heat and simmer, covered, for 20 minutes.

Six servings

PORK WITH SQUASH

- 2 pounds pork, cut in 1-inch cubes
- 2 tablespoons butter
- 2 tablespoons all-purpose flour
- 1 can (16 ounces) peeled tomatoes, drained
- 1 teaspoon paprika
- ½ teaspoon thyme
- 1 bay leaf
- ½ teaspoon rosemary
- 1 teaspoon basil
- 1 teaspoon ground ginger
- 1½ cups beef bouillon
- 1 medium butternut squash, peeled and cut into ½-inch cubes
- 1 large zucchini, sliced ½ inch thick
- ⅓ pound fresh mushrooms, sliced, or 1 can (8 ounces)
- 1 cup dry white wine
  Freshly grated Romano cheese
- 1 teaspoon salt
- ½ teaspoon ground pepper

Lightly brown the pork cubes, in the butter, in a Dutch oven. Season with the salt and pepper, then sift the flour lightly over the meat. Stir until the flour browns. Add the tomatoes, all the herbs and spices, and the bouillon. Simmer for 1½ hours. Add the butternut squash and simmer 20 minutes longer, then add the zucchini, mushrooms, and the wine. Simmer for 10 minutes longer, or until both squashes are tender. Serve with cheese sprinkled on top.

Four or five servings

PORK PASTIES

- 1½ pounds ground pork
- 1 clove garlic, chopped
- 2 onions, chopped
- 2 tablespoons butter or margarine
- 2 large potatoes, peeled and cubed
- 2 tomatoes, peeled and chopped
- ⅛ cup vinegar

Beef stock
½   teaspoon ground ginger
½   teaspoon ground cloves
1   teaspoon ground coriander
    Whole cloves
1   package (10 ounces) pie-crust mix
2   teaspoons salt
¼   teaspoon freshly ground pepper

Sauté the onions and garlic, in the butter, in a heavy skillet. Add the meat and brown lightly. Add the potatoes, tomatoes, vinegar, salt and pepper, and sufficient stock to make a moist, juicy mixture. Add the ginger, cloves, and coriander and simmer, covered, until the meat and potatoes are done.

Meanwhile, prepare the pie-crust mix. Roll to thickness of ⅛ inch and cut in 3-inch squares. Distribute the meat mixture on each of the squares; fold the corners to the center, moisten, and crimp to seal. Fasten each with a whole clove, prick the tops, and bake at 450° until brown (about 15 minutes).

PORK HASH

2   pounds ground pork
½   pound chorizo or other spiced pork sausage
1   small onion, chopped fine
1   tablespoon butter or margarine
2   large tomatoes, peeled, seeded, and chopped
¼   cup lemon juice
¼   cup chopped parsley
2   hard-boiled eggs, chopped fine
    Salt
    Pepper

Sauté the onion in the butter in a large skillet for 2 minutes. Add the tomatoes and cook over high heat until most of the liquid has evaporated. Skin and chop the sausage, then add it and the pork to the skillet mixture. Cook for 20 minutes, mixing thoroughly. Add the lemon juice, salt, and pepper to taste and cook for 5 minutes longer. Transfer the hash to a hot serving dish, garnish with the parsley and egg.

Four to six servings

ECONOMY CASSEROLE

2   **pounds pork shoulder, cut in 1-inch cubes**
2   **tablespoons butter or margarine**
¾   **cup chopped onion**
¼   **cup chopped fresh parsley**
½   **teaspoon caraway seeds**
¼   **teaspoon ground allspice**
½   **cup beer or beef broth**
5   **cups shredded cabbage**
3   **red apples, unpeeled but cored**
1   **teaspoon salt**
¼   **teaspoon pepper**

In a large Dutch oven, brown the meat in the butter. Season with the salt and pepper, then add the onion and parsley and cook for 5 minutes. Add the caraway seeds and allspice and stir in the beer. Simmer, covered, for 15 minutes. Slice the apples in thin wedges. Add the apples and the cabbage and cook, covered, for 10 to 15 minutes more, or until the apples are tender.

Six servings

PORK WITH DRIED FRUIT

2   **pounds pork shoulder, cut in 1-inch cubes**
1   **onion, stuck with 2 cloves**
6   **cups water**
1   **pound mixed, dried fruit (cooked)**
3   **tablespoons butter or margarine**
¼   **cup all-purpose flour**
3   **teaspoons granulated sugar**
⅛   **teaspoon ground cloves**
1   **teaspoon salt**

Put the meat, onion, water, and salt in a large saucepan. Bring to a boil, then reduce the heat and simmer, covered, for 40 minutes. Remove the onion and cloves and discard. Add the fruit and simmer for 15 minutes longer. Drain off the liquid, reserving 4 cups. In another large saucepan, melt the butter, slowly stir in the flour and cook over low heat, stirring constantly, for about 3 minutes. Remove from the heat and slowly stir in the reserved liquid. Mix the sugar and ground cloves and add to the sauce. Simmer for about 5 minutes. Add the pork and fruit and cook over moderate heat until the sauce has thickened.

Four servings

JELLIED PORK À LA SARAH

1   **pound cubed pork**
1   **very small onion, stuck with 5 whole cloves**
2   **carrots, peeled and sliced**
2   **stalks celery, including leaves, cut in small pieces**
1   **teaspoon thyme**
3   **sprigs fresh parsley, chopped fine**
1   **tablespoon Worcestershire sauce**
1   **tablespoon (1 envelope) unflavored gelatin for every 2 cups water used**
1   **teaspoon salt**
⅛   **teaspoon pepper**

Place all the ingredients except the gelatin in a kettle. Add water, 1 cup at a time, until the contents are covered (remember the amount of water used) and bring to a boil. For each 2 cups of water used, dissolve 1 envelope of gelatin in ½ cup cold water. Add to the boiling kettle. Lower the heat and simmer, covered, for 1 hour, then remove the meat, carrots, and celery with a slotted spoon. Place them in a serving bowl. Strain the broth through a fine sieve and pour it over the meat and vegetables. Refrigerate for 12 hours.

Four servings

PORK AND VEAL POT-AU-FEU

1   pound pork, cut into 1-inch cubes
1   pound veal, cut into 1-inch cubes
8   slices bacon, cut in 1-inch pieces
1½   pounds cabbage, shredded
4   white turnips, peeled and sliced thin
4   potatoes, peeled and cut in 1-inch cubes
1   medium onion, chopped
4   cups chicken broth
3   teaspoons salt
½   teaspoon pepper

In a large Dutch oven, make layers using half each of the pork, veal, bacon, cabbage, turnips, potatoes, and onions. Sprinkle with half the salt and half the pepper. Repeat these layers once and sprinkle with the remaining salt and pepper. Pour the chicken broth over all. Bring to a boil over high heat. Then reduce the heat to low and simmer, covered, for 1½ hours. Cook, uncovered, for 30 minutes longer, or until the meats and vegetables are tender and the liquid is reduced.

Eight servings

EASY PORK LOAF

1   pound ground pork
1   pound ground ham
1   cup cracker crumbs
1   can (10½ ounces) tomato soup
1   egg
½   cup milk
½   teaspoon salt
¼   teaspoon pepper

Mix all the ingredients thoroughly, reserving ½ cup of the soup. Shape into a loaf, place in a baking pan, and pour the remaining soup over the top. Bake, uncovered, at 350° for 1½ hours.

Eight servings

HAITIAN MEAT AND RICE CASSEROLE

1   pound lean pork, chopped fine
¼   pound salt pork, chopped fine
1½ pounds mushrooms
5   cups water
3   tablespoons cooking oil
4   cups raw rice
2   tablespoons butter or margarine
¼   teaspoon thyme
    Pinch of ground cloves
2 or 3 drops Tabasco sauce
½   teaspoon salt

Wash the mushrooms and cook them in the water for 20 minutes. Strain the liquid through a fine cheesecloth into a large saucepan and squeeze the mushrooms to extract as much liquid as possible. Reserve the mushrooms for another purpose. Sauté the pork and salt pork in the oil until they are thoroughly cooked. Add to the mushroom broth the rice, butter, salt, thyme, cloves, and Tabasco. Cover the saucepan and cook over low heat until the rice is barely tender, then add the meat and cook until the mixture is hot and the flavors are blended.

Eight servings

PORTUGUESE PORK

1¾ pounds lean pork, cut in 1 inch cubes
1   tablespoon lard or shortening
1   cup dry white wine
1   garlic clove, minced
1¼ teaspoons ground coriander
1¼ teaspoons ground cumin
4   thin slices lemon, cut in quarters
1½ teaspoons cornstarch
1½ teaspoons water
    Salt
    Pepper

Sauté the pork in the shortening in a heavy skillet until brown. Pour in ¾ cup of the wine. Add the garlic, coriander, and cumin. Bring the liquid to a boil, reduce the heat and simmer for about 45 minutes or until the meat is tender. Transfer the pork to a serving dish and keep it warm. Add the other ¼ cup of wine and the lemon slices to the liquid in the pan. Reheat. Add the cornstarch, which has been mixed with the water, and cook gently until thickened. Add salt and pepper to taste. Pour over the meat. Serve with noodles or boiled rice.

Four servings

PORK STROGANOFF

1½ pounds pork shoulder, cut into 2-inch x ½-inch strips
1 tablespoon all-purpose flour
1 tablespoon cooking oil
½ cup chopped celery
½ cup chopped green pepper
1 clove garlic, minced
1 chicken bouillon cube, dissolved in 1 cup hot water
½ cup sour cream
1 package (8 ounces) narrow egg noodles, cooked and drained
3 tablespoons butter or margarine
Paprika
Chopped fresh parsley
Salt
Pepper

Coat the pork with flour by tossing in a paper bag. Heat the oil in a large skillet and brown the meat. Drain off the excess fat. Add the celery, green pepper, and garlic and cook for 5 minutes. Stir in salt, pepper, and the bouillon. Simmer, covered, for 45 minutes, or until the pork is tender. Stir in the sour cream and heat thoroughly, but without boiling. Toss the noodles with the butter. Put the meat on top, sprinkle with paprika and parsley.

Four servings

STUFFED CABBAGE LEAVES

1   pound ground pork
8   large cabbage leaves
     Chicken bouillon or stock
1   large onion, chopped fine
4   chicken livers, chopped fine
½   pound fresh mushrooms, chopped fine
½   cup chopped fresh parsley
½   teaspoon thyme
4   tablespoons butter or margarine
     Salt
     Pepper

Boil the cabbage leaves for 3 minutes in the chicken bouillon. Drain on a towel, reserving the liquid. Sauté the pork, onion, livers, mushrooms, parsley, and thyme in the butter for 15 minutes in a heavy skillet. Remove with a slotted spoon. Place a portion of the mixture on each of the drained cabbage leaves. Season with salt and pepper, then roll the leaves and fasten with wooden picks. Place the rolls side by side in a shallow pan, cover with the bouillon, and poach gently for 30 minutes.

Four servings

NEW ORLEANS JAMBALAYA

1   pound lean pork, cubed
1   pound ham, cubed
1   tablespoon butter
1   tablespoon olive oil
1   large onion, chopped
1   cup raw rice
3   cups water
½   cup sherry
1   teaspoon dry mustard
½   teaspoon celery salt
½   teaspoon summer savory
½   teaspoon thyme
¼   teaspoon freshly ground pepper

Heat the butter and olive oil in a skillet and brown the pork and onion. Add the ham and sauté for 4 minutes, then transfer the contents of the skillet to a casserole. Cover with the rice and set aside. Add the water, sherry, and seasonings to the skillet and bring to a boil. Pour into the casserole, stir gently, and bake, covered, at 325° for 35 to 40 minutes, or until the liquid is absorbed. Stir once with a fork during the cooking.

Four servings

STURTEVANT PORK PIE

1½   pounds ground lean pork
2   onions, chopped fine
1   cup water
2   soda crackers, crushed
½   teaspoon poultry seasoning
¼   teaspoon ground allspice
1½   teaspoons salt
⅛   teaspoon pepper
     Pastry for a 2-crust pie

Place the pork, onions, and water in a heavy saucepan. Cook over low heat for 2 hours, then remove from the heat and stir in the crackers and seasonings. Make two pie crusts, using your favorite recipe or mix. Fill with the pork mixture and bake at 450° for 20 minutes, or until browned.

Four servings

SWEET AND SOUR PORK SKILLET

1   pound lean pork, cut in ¾-inch cubes
2   tablespoons cooking oil
1   can (13¼ ounces) pineapple chunks, drained and juice reserved
2   tablespoons cider vinegar
½   teaspoon garlic salt
1   cup converted rice
1   green pepper, cut into small squares and parboiled
1   tomato, cut into thin wedges
¼   cup sliced water chestnuts
1½   teaspoons salt

Brown the pork, in the cooking oil, in a 10-inch skillet. Remove and drain. Add enough water to the reserved pineapple juice to make 2½ cups. Add this liquid, the vinegar, salt, and garlic salt to the pork. Stir and bring to a boil, then reduce the heat, cover, and cook over low heat for 20 minutes. Stir in the rice and continue to cook for about 25 minutes, until the liquid is absorbed and the pork is tender. Stir in the pineapple chunks, green pepper, tomato, and water chestnuts. Heat thoroughly.

Four servings

SALT PORK WITH RICE PILAU

¼ pound salt pork
¾ cup raw rice
2 medium onions, chopped fine
3 cups hot chicken broth or stock
¼ cup finely chopped fresh parsley
¼ cup chopped dry-roasted peanuts
¼ cup raisins, plumped in hot water and drained
   Pinch of ground allspice
½ teaspoon salt
   Pinch of freshly ground pepper

Cut the salt pork into small pieces and fry, over low heat, until crisp. Remove from the pan. Add the rice and onions and cook, stirring constantly, until the rice is golden brown. Add the hot broth gradually, then cover and cook over low heat until the rice is tender (about 15 minutes). Add the parsley, pork, and seasonings and cook a few minutes longer. Mix in the peanuts and raisins.

Four servings

QUICK AND GOOD BAKED BEANS

¼   pound salt pork, cut into 6 pieces
1   package (9 ounces) precooked navy beans
3½   cups boiling water
¼   cup catsup
3   tablespoons brown sugar
¼   cup dark molasses
2   tablespoons finely diced onion
½   teaspoon dry mustard
1   teaspoon salt

Place the beans (no soaking necessary) in a 2-quart bean pot or casserole. Mix all other ingredients together and pour into the bean pot. Stir well, then cover and bake at 450° for 30 minutes. Uncover, stir well, and bake 15 minutes longer.

Six servings

SALT PORK AND APPLE RINGS

12   slices salt pork
    Milk
    All-purpose flour
    Shortening
2   large, tart apples, cored and cut in ¼-inch rings
    Granulated sugar
3   tablespoons butter

Put the meat in a heavy skillet and fill with cold water. Boil for 5 minutes, then drain the slices and dip them first in milk and then in flour. Dry the skillet, grease with shortening, and fry the meat slices very slowly until crisp. Remove, drain on paper, and keep warm.

Dip the apple rings in sugar and fry them in the butter, turning frequently with a pancake turner until brown on both sides. When the apples are tender, place them on the meat and serve hot.

Four servings

Outdoor Cookery Dishes

Man's earliest cooking experience was with outdoor cookery. The art has come a long way from the smudge beside the cave entrance. Now it is done much more for pleasure than from necessity, and has acquired an almost ritualistic procedure.

Outdoor cookery requires its own skills. We consider these important enough to be treated separately (see page 281).

A basic rule in barbecuing ham slices, chops and steaks is to trim off the outer edge of the fat to reduce the possibility of excessive dripping and the resulting flare-ups. Have some baking soda to use in event of a flare-up. Score the edges to prevent cupping, or cook the meat in a wire holder to keep it flat.

Here we include representative samples of basic pork recipes that are relatively easy to carry out and sure to be appreciated. As the outdoor cookery devotees acquire skill and confidence, they can ring almost endless changes and variations on them.

BARBECUED LOIN

1	pork loin (4 to 6 pounds), boned and tied
⅓	cup finely chopped onion
1	clove garlic, minced
1	tablespoon shortening
1	can (6 ounces) tomato paste
⅔	cup honey
½	cup red wine vinegar
3	tablespoons soy sauce
1	teaspoon celery seed
1	teaspoon dry mustard
1	teaspoon salt

171

Balance the roast on the spit, tighten the prongs, and place in the rotisserie holder. Insert a meat thermometer and start the machinery. Cook, allowing about 25 minutes to the pound, until the thermometer registers 170°.

Sauté the onion and garlic in the shortening without browning. Add all the remaining ingredients, and mix well. Simmer, covered, for 15 to 20 minutes. Brush the roast with sauce several times during the last 30 minutes of cooking. Serve the remaining sauce with the meat.

Eight servings

ORANGE-GLAZED ROTISSERIE ROAST

   1   **center-cut pork loin (4 to 5 pounds), prepared for roasting**
   1   **can (6 ounces) frozen orange juice concentrate, defrosted**
  ⅓   **cup water**
  ½   **cup honey**
   1   **teaspoon prepared mustard**
   1   **teaspoon soy sauce**
5 or 6 **drops Tabasco sauce**
   4   **teaspoons cornstarch**
  ¼   **cup orange liqueur**
  ½   **cup sour cream**
  ¼   **teaspoon salt**

Combine all the ingredients except the meat, in a saucepan and bring to a boil. Set aside and allow to cool. Carefully slide the pork into a plastic bag. Pour the sauce into the bag, close the bag, and place in a shallow baking dish. Marinate in the refrigerator for 4 to 6 hours, or overnight, turning several times. Remove the pork from the marinade. Retain the marinade, reserving 1 cup for sauce.

Thread one prong into rotisserie spit, points away from handle. Thread spit through the roast, end to end, balancing meat on the rod perfectly. Put the second prong into the spit. Push the prongs firmly into the roast and tighten the screws. Attach the rod to the rotisserie motor and start the motor. Roast over low, glowing coals until the meat is tender (about 2¾ to 3 hours).

Meanwhile, combine 1 cup of the marinade with the cornstarch. Blend, then heat, stirring constantly, until thick and clear. Stir in the orange liqueur. Heat, without boiling, then blend the marinade mixture into the sour cream. Serve with the roast.

Four to five servings

ROTISSERIE PORK

1   pork loin (4 to 6 pounds), bones cracked, tied
⅓   cup finely chopped onion
1   clove garlic, minced
1   tablespoon shortening
1   can (6 ounces) tomato paste
¾   cup honey
½   cup red wine vinegar
3   tablespoons soy sauce
1   teaspoon celery seed
1   teaspoon dry mustard
1   teaspoon salt

Balance the roast on the spit, tighten the prongs, and place in rotisserie. Insert a meat thermometer. Cook, allowing about 25 minutes to the pound.

Sauté the onion and garlic in the shortening, without browning. Add the remaining ingredients and mix well. Simmer, covered, 15 to 20 minutes. Baste the roast with this sauce at least four times during cooking. Serve the remaining sauce with the meat.

Eight servings

ROAST STUFFED WITH PRUNES

1   pork loin (6½ to 7 pounds), with bones cracked and pockets cut every 1¼ inches on the meaty side
3   pitted, dried prunes for each pocket
2½   cups orange juice or sherry, or equal parts of each
1   jar (4¾ ounces) puréed prunes (baby food)

Soak the dried prunes in the baby food and orange juice for at least 2 hours. Stuff the prunes into the pockets in the meat, reserving the juice. Tie the whole roast lengthwise to keep the pockets closed and insert a thermometer in the meatiest part, away from bone and fat. Cook on a covered grill over a bed of coals for 2 hours, or until the thermometer reads 170°. Baste several times with the orange juice mixture while roasting.

Six servings

MANDARIN TENDERLOIN

2 **pork tenderloins (1 pound each)**
1 **cup soy sauce**
1 **garlic clove, minced**
3 **tablespoons honey**
1 **tablespoon ground ginger**
1 **tablespoon dry mustard**
½ **cup vegetable oil**
½ **cup orange marmalade**
2 **tablespoons vinegar**
1 **tablespoon chopped pimiento**
⅛ **teaspoon paprika**
⅛ **teaspoon salt**

Combine the soy sauce, garlic, honey, ginger, mustard, and vegetable oil. Pour over the meat and refrigerate for 24 hours, turning occasionally. Combine the marmalade, vinegar, pimiento, paprika, and salt in a saucepan and heat them.

Remove the tenderloins from the marinade and grill them over hot coals until well done, turning as the meat browns. Cut the meat into ½-inch slices and serve with the marmalade sauce.

Four servings

BARBECUED TENDERLOIN

2 **pork tenderloins (¾ to 1 pound each)**
½ **cup soy sauce**
¼ **cup sake or dry sherry**
¼ **cup salad oil**
2 **cloves garlic, crushed**
1 **teaspoon ground ginger**
1 **cup converted rice**
1 **tablespoon butter or margarine**
2¼ **cups water**
¼ **cup sliced scallions, tops included**
1 **can (8 ounces) water chestnuts, diced (optional)**
1 **teaspoon salt**

Prepare a marinade for the pork by combining the soy sauce, sake, oil, garlic and ginger. Mix well. Cut the tenderloins into ½-inch slices and place in a shallow glass or porcelain dish. Pour the marinade over the meat. Cover and refrigerate for 4 hours, turning the meat occasionally. Drain off and reserve the marinade.

Arrange the pork slices flat sides up and thread them horizontally, on skewers. Use 2 parallel skewers through the slices to make turning easy. Broil 5 inches above the coals for about 15 minutes, turning 3 times and brushing the slices lightly each time with the reserved marinade.

Before starting to cook the meat, place the rice, butter, salt, water and ¼ cup of the reserved marinade in a saucepan. Bring to a boil, cover, and cook over low heat until the rice is tender and all the liquid has been absorbed (about 20 minutes). Just before serving, add the scallions and water chestnuts. Toss gently to mix well.

Six servings

GRILLED MARINATED CHOPS

4   rib or loin pork chops, 1 inch thick
½   cup olive oil
½   cup white wine vinegar
1   clove garlic, minced
1   bay leaf, crushed
2   peppercorns
¼   teaspoon dry mustard
½   teaspoon salt
⅛   teaspoon pepper

Trim the fat from the chops and then place them in a shallow pan. Combine all the other ingredients and pour over the chops. Cover, and marinate in the refrigerator overnight or all day, turning occasionally. When ready to use, drain the chops. Grill them over charcoal, turning once, until tender. Serve immediately.

QUICK-SERVE SMOKED CHOPS

6   smoked pork chops
⅓   cup melted butter
    Juice of 1 lemon

Combine the melted butter and the lemon juice in a small pan. Place the chops; fat trimmed off, on a grill set about 4 inches above the coals. Brush the chops with the butter, then turn them over and brush the other side. Continue to brush and turn for 6 minutes, or until you are sure the chops are cooked through. Serve with warm, spiced applesauce or your favorite fruit sauce.

SPARERIBS BARBECUED WITH PLUM GLAZE

4   pounds spareribs
    Bottled browning sauce
½   teaspoon ground ginger
1   tablespoon vinegar
¼   cup plum jam
    Dash of garlic salt
    Salt

Cut the spareribs in 3- or 4-rib pieces. Put in a kettle and barely cover with water. Simmer for 30 minutes. Drain. Place on a grill over hot coals for 10 minutes. Then brush with browning sauce and turn them frequently for another 10 minutes.

Stir the ginger, vinegar, garlic, and salt into the plum jam, breaking up the plums with a fork. Cook the ribs 15 minutes longer, basting frequently with the sauce.

Four servings

RIBS WITH SUPER SAUERKRAUT

6   pounds spareribs or back ribs
1   pound sauerkraut
2   apples, peeled and diced
1   onion, sliced
1   carrot, coarsely chopped
½   bay leaf
10 peppercorns
    Chicken broth or bouillon
    Salt to taste

Before starting the spareribs, put the sauerkraut, apples, vegetables, and seasonings in a large saucepan. Cover with broth, or use half broth and half water. Cover and simmer for 2 to 3 hours. If possible, prepare the sauerkraut well ahead of time and reheat it when needed.

The ribs should be placed, bone side down, on a slow fire with the grill as high above it as possible. Turn the meat after 30 minutes. In another 30 minutes check for doneness (no pink showing when cut into). If the thinner end of the ribs gets done before the thicker end, slide a piece of foil under the thinner end. Serve the ribs with the warm sauerkraut, from which the peppercorns and bay leaf have been removed.

Six servings

WINE GLAZED HAM

1   center-cut ham slice, about 1 inch thick
½   cup sauterne or other white dinner wine
¼   cup orange juice
¼   cup maple syrup
½   teaspoon dry mustard
¼   teaspoon ground ginger
2   teaspoons wine vinegar
1   tablespoon cornstarch

In a saucepan, combine all the ingredients except the ham. Bring to a boil, then lower the heat and simmer a few minutes. Trim the fat from the edge of the ham and grill the meat over charcoal, brushing frequently with sauce, until tender, about 10 minutes on each side. Spoon the remaining hot sauce on the meat when it is served.

SPIT-ROASTED CANNED HAM

1   canned ham (5 pounds)
2   tablespoons butter
2   tablespoons honey
½   teaspoon ground cloves
½   teaspoon mustard
½   teaspoon ground cinnamon

Remove the ham from the can. Scrape off the gelatin and set it aside. Score the surface of the ham lightly, if desired. Balance the ham on the spit and tie securely with string. Attach the spit to the motor and start the rotisserie. Cook over low, glowing coals that give off an even heat.

Meanwhile, prepare the basting sauce. Melt the reserved gelatin and add enough water to make ¾ cup of liquid. Add the remaining ingredients and heat. Baste the ham frequently with the sauce during the last 30 minutes of roasting. Check the label on the can for length of cooking time.

Eight to ten servings

FRESH HAM MARINATED IN WINE

1   fresh ham, boned and rolled (about 5½ pounds)
¾   cup dry white wine
2   tablespoons soy sauce
2   tablespoons salad oil
2   tablespoons chopped onion
1   teaspoon ground ginger

Make a marinade of the wine, soy sauce, salad oil, onion, and ginger. Mix thoroughly. Marinate the ham for 1 hour. Remove the ham from the marinade and roast on a spit, over medium coals, for 6 hours, basting frequently with marinade.

Twelve servings

SKEWERED PORK, INDONESIAN STYLE

2   pounds lean pork, cut into 1-inch cubes
2   tablespoons ground coriander
2   cloves garlic
¼   teaspoon Tabasco sauce
1   cup sliced onion
¼   cup fresh lemon juice
2   tablespoons brown sugar
¼   cup soy sauce
8   tablespoons melted butter or margarine
½   cup beef bouillon

In an electric blender, combine all the ingredients except the meat, butter, and bouillon. Blend to a fine purée. Transfer the purée to a saucepan and bring to a boil. Add the butter and bouillon. Remove from the heat. Place the pork cubes in a nonmetallic container. Pour the purée over them and let stand at least 3 hours.

Remove the meat cubes from the purée and carefully thread them on skewers. Broil slowly over charcoal, turning frequently to make sure the meat browns on all sides. If any purée remains it may be heated and served over the meat.

Four to six servings

Roasts

Roasts are the pork fare par excellence. Nothing tastes better, looks more festive, gives the cook more satisfaction, or earns her more praise than a skillfully prepared crown roast. It is unsurpassed in appetizing quality and decorative value. The most uncertain carver can hardly make a mistake in cutting it into equal and attractive portions.

There are other pork roasts, for plain or fancy events, and the variety of recipes in this section shows that no one need fall back on the old, tired stand-bys. Despite an understandable hankering for any good old days there may have been with their homey, old-timey methods, we recommend modern, tested procedures for roasting.

Be sure to buy a roast large enough and thus avoid anxiety after the first two or three generous portions have been served. Any roast not used at the first serving will make excellent planned-overs.

The chart in chapter 1 is a *guide* to servings per pound. Many factors enter into estimates of numbers of servings. All roasts shrink during cooking; a cheap cut shrinks more. Some hosts are generous servers; some are not. When the servings are given with a recipe they have been carefully estimated to give you as much help as possible in buying. They are not given as absolute amounts.

The roasting time table given here is based on meat taken from the refrigerator immediately before roasting. Roasting time adjustments must be made if you prefer to allow the roast to come to room temperature before cooking.

Always roast on a rack, unless the bones themselves form a rack. Roast fat side up and, unless a heat change is specified in the recipe, don't make it. Cook throughout at an even temperature.

Roasting temperatures have been worked out fairly accurately. Several factors influence time, but the thermometer takes most of the uncertainties out of timing and ensures doneness throughout the roast. We

180

encourage all cooks, no matter how experienced, to use it and to follow the individual recipe instructions. A meat thermometer should be inserted in the thickest part of the roast; it must not touch the bone, nor rest in the fat. The thermometer dial should be as far from the source of heat as possible. If you can't resist pricking for doneness, remember red juice means insufficiently cooked pork and light yellowish means well done. Shades in between indicate degrees of doneness. All pork must be thoroughly cooked.

In general, roasts are cooked uncovered and no water is added. Our recipes specify if and when to cover. Do not stuff a roast until you are ready to cook it.

After the roast is cooked allow it to "set" before carving. This is especially important for a rib roast. Unless it sets it will give the carver endless trouble, because it is not firm enough to cut well. Pork roasts need 15 to 30 minutes to set. Before serving, rolled roasts should have all strings removed, except for a few to keep it in shape.

ROASTING TIME TABLE

Fresh　　　　　Roast in a slow oven, 325°-350°

CUT	Weight in Pounds	Meat Thermometer Temperature	Minutes Per Pound *
Loin			
Center	3 to 5	170°	30 to 35
Half	5 to 7	170°	35 to 40
Blade loin or sirloin	3 to 4	170°	40 to 45
Crown	4 to 6	170°	35 to 40
Picnic shoulder			
Bone-in	5 to 8	170°	30 to 35
Boneless	3 to 5	170°	35 to 40
Blade Boston shoulder	4 to 6	170°	40 to 45
Leg (fresh ham)			
Whole (bone-in)	12 to 16	170°	22 to 26
Whole (boneless)	10 to 14	170°	24 to 28
Half (bone-in)	5 to 8	170°	35 to 40

Smoked   Roast at Oven Temperature 300° to 325°

CUT	Weight in Pounds	Meat Thermometer Temperature	Minutes Per Pound *
Ham (cook-before-eating)			
Whole	10 to 14	160°	18 to 20
Half	5 to 7	160°	22 to 25
Shank or butt portion	3 to 4	160°	35 to 40
Ham (fully cooked)			
Whole	10 to 14	140°	15 to 18
Half	5 to 7	140°	18 to 24
Loin	3 to 5	160°	25 to 30
Picnic shoulder			
Cook-before-eating	5 to 8	170°	30 to 35
Fully cooked	5 to 8	140°	25 to 30
Shoulder roll (butt)	2 to 4	170°	35 to 40

* Based on meat taken directly from the refrigerator

(Adapted from *National Live Stock and Meat Board*)

CROWN ROAST WITH HERB RICE

1   crown roast of pork (7 to 8 pounds), prepared for roasting
1½ cups raw, long-grain rice
3   tablespoons butter
3   cups chicken broth
1   lemon wedge
3   tablespoons chopped fresh parsley
3   tablespoons chopped scallion
    Salt
    Freshly ground pepper

Season the meat with salt and pepper. Place in a shallow roasting pan, without a rack, and insert a thermometer away from bone and fat. Roast at 325° for 2½ to 3 hours, or until the thermometer reads 170°.

Combine the rice, butter, broth, salt, and lemon in a large saucepan. Heat to boiling, stirring thoroughly, then simmer, covered, at reduced heat until the liquid is absorbed. Remove from the heat and stir in the parsley and scallion, tossing lightly. Spoon into the center of the roast about 10 minutes before the roast is done.

Eight to ten servings

SHERRY ROAST

1   pork loin (4 pounds), bone cut for easy carving
½   cup sherry
½   cup brown sugar, firmly packed
1   tablespoon grated orange rind
⅓   cup orange juice
1   teaspoon horseradish
1   teaspoon prepared mustard

Place the roast, ribs down, on a rack in a roasting pan. Insert a meat thermometer. Combine all the other ingredients in a saucepan and bring to a boil over medium heat, then pour over the meat. Roast, uncovered, at 325° for about 3 hours, or until the meat thermometer registers 170°. Baste the meat frequently during the first 2 hours.

Six to eight servings

ROAST WITH MUSTARD AND CLOVES

1 pork loin (4 to 5 pounds), prepared for roasting
2 tablespoons shortening
2 tablespoons prepared mustard
18 whole cloves
¼ cup fine, dry bread crumbs
1½ teaspoons salt

Sprinkle the meat with the salt, spread with the shortening, coat with the mustard, and stud with the cloves. Sprinkle on the bread crumbs, making an even coating. Insert a meat thermometer in the meatiest part of the roast, away from bone and fat. Roast, in a shallow pan, at 350° for 2 to 2½ hours, or until the thermometer reads 170°.

Eight to ten servings

ROAST LOIN À L'ORANGE

1 pork loin roast (4 to 5 pounds)
½ teaspoon ground ginger
1½ teaspoons salt

Orange Sauce:

1 cup orange marmalade
1 cup orange juice
2 tablespoons grated orange rind
2 tablespoons cornstarch
½ teaspoon salt
½ teaspoon ginger
1 cup seedless or seeded grapes, halved
⅓ cup orange-flavored liqueur

Rub the meat with a mixture of the salt and ginger. Insert a meat thermometer in it, then place the roast, ribs down, on a rack in a shallow baking pan. Bake, uncovered, at 325° for 2¾ to 3 hours, or until the meat thermometer registers 170°. Brush ⅓ cup of orange sauce, made as described below, over the roast 30 minutes before the end of the roasting time.

To make the sauce, combine the marmalade, orange juice and rind, cornstarch, salt, and ginger in a saucepan. Heat, stirring constantly, until thick and clear. Reserve ⅓ cup of this sauce for glazing. Just before serving, fold in the grapes and heat but do not boil. Stir in the liqueur and serve with the meat.

Eight to ten servings

SWEET-SOUR ROAST

1   **pork loin or shoulder (4 to 5 pounds)**
¼   **cup pickle relish**
¼   **cup chopped onion**
1   **tablespoon brown sugar**
1   **tablespoon vinegar**
1   **tablespoon Worcestershire sauce**
1   **can (10½ ounces) tomato soup**

Place the roast on a rack in a shallow pan. Insert a meat thermometer in the thickest part of the meat and roast at 325° until the thermometer reads 170° (about 35 minutes per pound). Thirty minutes before the roast is done, drain off the drippings. Add the relish, onion, sugar, vinegar, and Worcestershire sauce to the soup. Mix thoroughly, then spread over the roast. Continue roasting until done.

Eight to ten servings

LOIN WITH APRICOTS

1   **pork loin roast (3 to 4 pounds)**
¼   **teaspoon thyme**
¼   **teaspoon basil**
½   **teaspoon paprika**
1   **clove garlic, minced**
8   **canned apricot halves, including juice**
2   **teaspoons salt**
¼   **teaspoon pepper**

Combine the salt, thyme, basil, pepper, paprika, and garlic; rub into the roast. Place in a roasting pan and insert a meat thermometer. Roast at 375° for 30 minutes, then pour off the fat. Add the apricots and juice, reduce the heat to 350°, and roast for 1½ to 2 hours, or until the meat thermometer registers 170°. Baste frequently.

Six to eight servings

ROAST BOULANGÈRE

1   **pork loin roast (3½ pounds)**
½   **cup chopped onion**
½   **cup coarsely chopped fresh parsley**
2   **pounds potatoes, peeled and sliced very thin**
3 to 4 **cups beef bouillon**
1   **tablespoon all-purpose flour**
1   **teaspoon sage**
1   **teaspoon paprika**
½   **teaspoon garlic salt**
1   **teaspoon salt**
¼   **teaspoon pepper**

In a bowl, combine the onion, parsley, salt, and pepper. Toss with a fork to mix well. Place the potatoes in layers in a 13½ x 8½-inch casserole, sprinkling each layer with some of the onion-parsley mixture. Arrange the top layer of potatoes in an attractive pattern and press down well. Pour on enough beef bouillon to be just level with the top layer of potatoes.

Trim the fat from the loin, leaving a layer ¼ inch thick. With a knife, score the fat in a diamond pattern. Combine the flour, sage, paprika, and garlic salt, and rub into the meat. Place it on top of potatoes in the casserole and roast, uncovered, at 350° for 1½ to 2 hours (about 30 minutes per pound of meat).

Five or six servings

LOIN ROAST WITH HERBS

1   pork loin (4 to 5 pounds)
    Olive oil
    All-purpose flour
¼   teaspoon thyme
¼   teaspoon oregano
¼   teaspoon ground fennel seed or aniseed
1   large onion, sliced thin
1   teaspoon salt
¼   teaspoon freshly ground pepper

Rub the roast with olive oil, then sprinkle with the flour. Mix the herbs, salt and pepper and sprinkle them on the roast. Fasten the slices of onion all over the roast, using wooden picks. Wrap the roast in waxed paper or aluminum foil and let stand in the refrigerator for about 12 hours. Remove and insert a meat thermometer. The meat may then be cooked on a rotisserie or baked, uncovered, in the oven at 350° for 2½ hours, or until the thermometer registers 170°.

Eight to ten servings

ROAST WITH MINCEMEAT AND APPLES

1   pork loin (3 pounds), prepared by the butcher for roasting
6   baking apples, cored but unpeeled
6   tablespoons mincemeat
¼   cup chopped onion
⅛   teaspoon dried dill weed, crushed
2   tablespoons butter or margarine
1   can (10 ounces) chicken giblet gravy
¼   cup sour cream

Insert a meat thermometer and roast the loin on a rack at 350° for 1 hour. Stuff the apples with the mincemeat and put them around the roast. Bake for 45 minutes longer, or until the thermometer reads 170° and the apples are tender. Meanwhile cook the onion and dill in butter until the onion is tender. Stir in the gravy, then lower the heat and stir in the cream. Heat through, but do not allow to boil. Serve with the meat and apples.

Six servings

ROAST WITH SAUERKRAUT

1 pork loin (5 pounds), prepared for roasting
2 cans (1 pound 11 ounces each) sauerkraut, rinsed
1 pint sour cream
2 tablespoons caraway seeds   Salt
   Hot mustard   Pepper

Mix the sauerkraut, caraway seeds and sour cream in a heavy baking pan. Spread the mustard over the meat, sprinkle with salt and pepper, and place on the sauerkraut. Bake, covered, at 375°for 3 hours (or at 325° for 4 to 5 hours).

Eight to ten servings

ROAST WITH BANANAS AND ORANGES

1 pork loin roast (3½ pounds)
2 tablespoons finely chopped crystallized ginger
¼ cup soy sauce
8 slightly under-ripe medium bananas, peeled
1 medium orange, cut in small chunks
2 tablespoons orange juice
2 tablespoons lemon juice
⅓ cup granulated sugar
¼ teaspoon ground cinnamon
·¼ teaspoon nutmeg
   Watercress

Make several small slits in the meat. Insert 1 tablespoon of the ginger in the slits. Combine the remaining ginger and the soy sauce.

Place the meat, fat side up, in a shallow roasting pan without a rack. Brush the pork with part of the soy sauce mixture. Insert a meat thermometer in the meatiest part of the roast, away from bone or fat. Roast, uncovered, at 350° for 1 hour 45 minutes, or until the thermometer reads 170°. Brush with the soy sauce mixture several times during roasting.

Meanwhile, place the bananas in a shallow baking dish. Add the remaining ingredients except the watercress and bake, uncovered, at 325° for 20 to 30 minutes, until the bananas are golden and tender. Serve with the roast, garnished with watercress.

Six servings

BONED LOIN WITH MUSTARD SAUCE AND ORANGE SECTIONS

1   boneless pork loin roast (3 to 4 pounds)
1⅛   teaspoons dry mustard
1⅛   teaspoons marjoram, crushed
2   teaspoons grated orange peel
½   cup orange juice
1   tablespoon brown sugar
3   tablespoons all-purpose flour
1½   cups water
2   oranges, peeled and sectioned
1   teaspoon salt
    Freshly ground pepper

Place the roast on a rack in a shallow baking pan. Combine 1 teaspoon each mustard, marjoram, and salt. Rub this on the surface of the roast. Insert a meat thermometer and roast at 350° for 2 hours. Skim the fat from the roasting pan and discard. Combine the orange peel and juice and brown sugar, and spread the mixture over the roast. Return to the oven and cook 30 minutes longer, basting frequently, until the thermometer reads 170°. Remove the meat to a serving platter.

    Drain off 3 tablespoons of clear fat from the pan juices. In a saucepan combine it with the flour, ⅛ teaspoon mustard, and ⅛ teaspoon marjoram. Blend over moderate heat, then stir in the water. Cook until thick and bubbly; season with salt and pepper as desired. Add the orange sections. Serve this sauce with the roast.

Six to eight servings

BONED LOIN ROAST, GLAZED AND GARNISHED

1   pork loin (5 pounds), boned and rolled
1   clove garlic, cut in half
    All-purpose flour
1   tablespoon chopped onion
1   tablespoon chopped apple
2   tablespoons melted butter
1   tablespoon tomato purée

1   **tablespoon prepared mustard**
    Prunes
    Spiced vinegar
    Salt
    Freshly ground pepper

Rub the roast with salt, pepper, and garlic, then with the flour. Place it, fat side up, in a roasting pan. Insert a meat thermometer and bake, uncovered, at 350° for 2½ hours, or until the thermometer registers 170°.

Fry the onion and apple in the melted butter until soft. Add the tomato purée and mustard, stirring until well blended. Spoon this sauce over the roast about 10 minutes before it is done. Simmer the prunes in vinegar until they are plump, then drain and use them to garnish the roast.

Eight to ten servings

SHOULDER ROAST IN A BAG

1   **fresh pork shoulder (4 to 5 pounds), boned and rolled**
1   **teaspoon rosemary**
2   **medium onions, peeled**
1   **small carrot, sliced**
1   **sprig parsley**
½   **cup dry white wine or vermouth**
    All-purpose flour or cornstarch
½   **teaspoon salt**
⅛   **teaspoon pepper**

Mix together the rosemary, salt, and pepper. Rub into the outside of the roast. Place it in an oven bag, put the bag in a roasting pan, and add the onions, carrot, and parsley. Pour in the liquid and close the bag with a twist tie. Puncture 5 holes in the top of the bag with a knife and insert a meat thermometer through one of them. Roast at 325° for 2 to 2½ hours, or until the thermometer registers 170°.

To make a sauce or gravy, snip a corner of the bag and drain off the juice, leaving the meat in the bag until ready to serve. Mix the juice with water and 1 tablespoon of flour or ½ tablespoon cornstarch for each cup of liquid (water or wine may be added to the juice to increase the quantity). Bring the juice to a boil, add the thickening mixture and stir until smooth and thick. To serve the roast, slit the bag with scissors and transfer to a warm serving platter.

Four to six servings

GLAZED ROAST WITH PEARS

1   **pork shoulder (4 to 4½ pounds)**
½   **cup catsup**
1   **tablespoon brown sugar**
1   **teaspoon dry mustard**
1   **can (16 ounces) pear halves, drained**
1½ **teaspoons salt**
⅛   **teaspoon freshly ground pepper**

Place the roast on a rack in a shallow roasting pan. Season with salt and pepper and insert a meat thermometer. Roast at 350° for 2 to 2½ hours, or until the thermometer reads 170°. Mix the catsup, brown sugar, and mustard, and half an hour before the roast is done spread this mixture on it. Fifteen minutes before the roast is done put the pear halves around the meat.

Four servings

PENNSYLVANIA DUTCH STUFFED SHOULDER

1   **pork shoulder (5 to 6 pounds), boned**
4   **cups sauerkraut, drained**
    All-purpose flour
1   **tablespoon brown sugar**
    Salt
    Freshly ground pepper

Sprinkle the meat inside and out with salt and pepper. Fill the shoulder with the sauerkraut and skewer or sew the opening together. Score the top in a diamond pattern, as for baked ham. Dredge with a mixture of flour and brown sugar, then insert a meat thermometer and roast at 350°

for 30 to 35 minutes per pound or until the thermometer registers 170°. Baste occasionally. Thirty minutes before the roast is done, pour off most of the drippings. Complete the roasting.

Four to six servings

POT-ROASTED BUTT

1   **fresh Boston (shoulder) butt (4 to 5 pounds), with blade bone removed**
¼   **cup lemon juice**
½   **cup water, more if necessary**
2   **tablespoons cornstarch**
1   **teaspoon caraway seeds**
2   **teaspoons salt**
¼   **teaspoon freshly ground pepper**

Brown the butt on all sides in a Dutch oven. Add the salt, pepper, lemon juice, and ¼ cup of water. (More water may be added later if necessary.) Cover the pot and simmer over low heat until the meat is tender (about 2 hours). Remove the meat to a hot platter.

Measure the pan juice and add water to make 2 cups. Return the juice to the pan and stir in any bits adhering to the pan. Mix the cornstarch with ¼ cup of water until smooth, then add to the pan juice and cook, stirring constantly, until thick and clear. Add the caraway seeds and serve the sauce with the meat.

Four servings

SHOULDER WITH RED WINE

1   **pork shoulder (2 pounds), boned and rolled**
2   **cups red wine**
5   **juniper berries**
2   **bay leaves**
2   **tablespoons butter**
    Salt
    Freshly ground pepper

Cover the meat with the red wine, then add the seasonings. Allow to stand 8 to 10 hours in the refrigerator. Drain well and wipe, then brown in the butter in a skillet. Add the marinade, cover, and simmer 1½ hours, or until tender. Serve sliced thin.

Four servings

STUFFED SHOULDER

1   pork shoulder (3 pounds), boned
2   cups packaged herb-seasoned stuffing
1   cup diced pitted prunes
½   cup chopped onion
½   teaspoon rosemary
½   teaspoon sage
¾   cup dry white wine
¾   cup water
¼   cup all-purpose flour
1   teaspoon salt
¼   teaspoon pepper

Trim all the fat from the pork. Dice enough of the fat to make ¼ cup. Place in a heavy Dutch oven over low heat to render the fat (about 15 minutes); do not remove the crisp bits from the hot fat.

Prepare the stuffing according to the package directions, then add the prunes and onion. Spoon the stuffing into the cavity of the pork and close the opening with skewers. Mix the rosemary, sage, salt, and pepper. Rub the mixture into the pork. Brown the meat on both sides in the fat, then pour in the wine and ½ cup of the water. Cover, reduce the heat, and cook slowly for about 1½ hours, or until the meat is tender. Remove the meat and keep warm.

Skim off as much fat as possible from the pan juices. Make a smooth paste of the flour and remaining ¼ cup of water, and add to the pan juices. Cook, stirring constantly, until thickened. Serve with the meat.

Six servings

STUFFED FRESH HAM

1   **fresh ham (8 pounds), boned**
⅓   **cup chopped mushrooms**
2   **tablespoons butter**
½   **cup fine, dry bread crumbs**
2   **tablespoons chopped parsley**
½   **teaspoon grated onion**
¼   **teaspoon poultry seasoning**
¼   **teaspoon rosemary**
2   **cups apple cider**
    Paprika
1   **tablespoon salt**
1   **teaspoon pepper**

Wipe the ham with a damp cloth and rub ½ tablespoon of the salt into it. Sprinkle with pepper. Sauté the mushrooms, in the butter, in a skillet. Add all the remaining ingredients except the cider and mix well. Stuff the meat with the mixture and tie securely. Place, fat side up, in a roasting pan that has been lined with foil. Insert a meat thermometer, then roast, uncovered, at 350° for 4 hours, or until the thermometer registers 170°. Baste occasionally with drippings to which a little of the cider has been added. About 45 minutes before the ham is finished, pour on the remaining cider.

Twelve to fourteen servings

FRESH HAM WITH CIDER

½   **fresh ham (about 4 pounds)**
1   **teaspoon dry mustard**
2   **teaspoons paprika**
½   **cup cider**
½   **cup water**
2   **teaspoons salt**
¼   **teaspoon pepper**

Mix together the mustard, salt, pepper, and paprika. Rub into the ham, then place the ham in a roasting pan and roast at 350° for 1½ hours. Pour off the fat. Add the cider and water and roast about 1 hour 15 minutes longer, or until tender, basting frequently.

Ten to twelve servings

BAKED FRESH HAM

½   fresh ham (6 to 8 pounds)

Ask the butcher to score the ham rind in a diamond pattern. Place the ham on a rack in a roasting pan, with the scored side up. Insert a meat thermometer, then roast, uncovered, at 325° until the thermometer registers 170°, allowing 35 to 40 minutes to the pound. When serving, cut slices to include a portion of the crisp rind.

Ten to twelve servings

MARINATED FRESH HAM

1   butt half fresh ham (5 to 6 pounds)
1   small piece ginger root
2   pints beer
2   whole cloves
½   teaspoon sage
4 or 5 peppercorns
1½ cups cold water
1   cup light brown sugar
1   teaspoon cornstarch
1   teaspoon salt
¼   teaspoon white pepper

Place the meat in a large, deep crock. Crush the ginger root, add the beer, cloves, sage, salt, white pepper, and peppercorns. Warm this mixture and pour over the pork. Marinate, covered, for 24 hours in a cool place, turning once.

Remove the pork from the crock and place on a rack in a deep roasting pan. Strain the marinade and pour over the meat. Insert a meat thermometer, then roast, at 350°, for 3 to 3½ hours, or until the thermometer registers 170°, basting every 20 minutes. Each time the roast is basted add ¼ cup of the cold water.

After roasting 2 hours, pour off 1 cup of pan juices. Mix the brown sugar into the juices and carefully cover the top of the roast with this to produce a glaze.

When the pork is done, place on a hot platter. Mix the cornstarch with a little cold water and add to the pan juices, stirring well. Reheat and strain a little of this gravy over the meat. Serve the remaining gravy in a sauceboat.

Twelve to fourteen servings

FOIL-WRAPPED FRESH HAM

1   **butt or shank half fresh ham (6 pounds)**
6   **teaspoons red or white rock salt**
6   **teaspoons liquid smoke flavoring**
6   **teaspoons soy sauce**
4   **unpeeled bananas**
6   **medium sweet potatoes, scrubbed but not peeled**
6   **lettuce leaves**
¾   **cup water**

Place the meat on a large sheet of heavy foil. Sprinkle it with the rock salt, smoke flavoring, and soy sauce. Arrange the bananas and potatoes around the roast (the bananas are for flavor only and should be discarded when the roast is cooked), then pull the foil up around the meat, bananas, and potatoes. Cover the roast with the lettuce leaves and add the water. Finish wrapping the meat in foil, using several sheets if necessary to seal it tightly. Put the package in a shallow pan and allow it to stand for several hours in a cool place or overnight in the refrigerator, turning it several times to distribute the juices and to allow the flavor to penetrate the meat on all sides. Place the meat and pan in a 500° oven for 1 hour, then lower the temperature to 400° and roast 4 hours longer.

Twelve to fourteen servings

Sausage

It is said there are two hundred kinds of sausage. We have not counted them, but considering the ancient use and geographic distribution of this good product, the number seems likely. The Romans ate sausage two thousand years ago and they were late-comers in appreciating it. It was known in other Mediterranean areas a thousand years before that. Now there are said to be some four thousand sausage processors in the United States grinding out five billion pounds a year!

The best sausage, according to some authorities, is made from ham, shoulder, picnic ham, and loin (only occasionally). It includes three parts lean to one part fat.

Sausage is available in a variety of forms. It may be fresh, smoked, cooked, dry, or semi-dry. These distinctions and the ingredients are usually listed on the label. The ingredients under "spices" are not always specified, as they provide the special brand flavor and are the trade secret of the producer.

Cooking time adequate to guard against trichinae is generally indicated on the label, which should be read carefully. All sausage should be refrigerated until cooked. It should never be tasted for flavor before it is thoroughly cooked.

SAUSAGE CASSEROLE

1   **pound bulk sausage**
2   **medium onions, chopped**
1   **cup raw rice**
4   **medium carrots, cut in ½-inch pieces**
¼   **teaspoon thyme**
2½   **cups canned tomatoes**
½   **cup fine, dry bread crumbs**
¼   **cup melted butter**
1½   **teaspoons salt**
¼   **teaspoon pepper**

Put the sausage in a cold, heavy skillet and heat gently until the pan is well greased. Add the onion. Cook and stir until the sausage meat is browned. Arrange the meat-onion mixture, the rice, and the carrots in layers in a 2-quart casserole. Add the salt, pepper, and thyme to the tomatoes. Blend and add to the casserole. Combine the crumbs and butter and sprinkle over the top. Bake, covered, at 350° for 30 minutes. Then uncover and bake until browned and the rice has absorbed most of the liquid, about 30 minutes.

Four servings

SAUSAGES IN WHITE WINE

6   **country sausages**
1   **tablespoon butter**
1   **onion, chopped fine**
½   **cup dry white wine**
1   **cup Sauce Espagnole**
6   **pieces toasted bread, slightly larger than a sausage**
1   **teaspoon chopped fresh parsley**

Brown the onion in the butter and add the wine. Prick the sausage skins, add them to the onion-wine mixture. Simmer for 5 minutes. Heat the Sauce Espagnole and add to the sausage mixture. Simmer for 20 minutes, skimming off any fat that rises. Place one sausage and some of the sauce on each piece of toast, sprinkle with parsley, and serve.

Six servings

SAUSAGES IN ALE

1¼   pounds pork sausage links
2   tablespoons butter
1   cup ale
4   servings hot mashed potatoes

Prick the sausages. Melt the butter in a frying pan and, when hot, put in the sausages and brown rapidly on all sides. Pour off the fat and allow the sausages to cool slightly. Add the ale and bring to a boil. Cover tightly and simmer for 30 minutes. Put the sausages in a ring of mashed potatoes and pour some of the liquid over them.

Four servings

SAUSAGE LINKS WITH SWEET POTATOES AND APPLES

8   sausage links
4   sweet potatoes or yams
4   apples
2   tablespoons butter or margarine

Cook the sausage links until the fat has cooked out and they are browned on all sides. Drain. Boil the sweet potatoes until tender, then peel and slice them. Peel, core, and slice the apples into rounds. Put the slices of sweet potatoes in the bottom of a buttered casserole. Dot with more butter. Place the apples on the potatoes. Top with the sausage links. Bake, covered, at 325° for 30 minutes.

Four servings

SPANISH RICE WITH SAUSAGES

16   small sausage links, lightly cooked and drained
6   strips bacon, cut in small squares
2   cups raw rice
1   large onion, chopped
1   green pepper, diced

1   can (16 ounces) tomatoes
2   tablespoons all-purpose flour
¼   teaspoon chili powder (optional)
1   teaspoon salt
¼   teaspoon pepper

Cook the rice and drain thoroughly. Fry the bacon until brown, then remove from the fat and add to the rice. Add the onion and green pepper to the hot bacon fat and cook until the onion is yellow or wilted. Sprinkle in the flour. Add the tomatoes and cook until hot and well blended. Season with the salt, pepper, and the chili powder. Add to the cooked rice. Place in a baking dish. Put the sausage links on top. Bake, uncovered, at 350° until the sausage is browned.

Eight servings

SAUSAGE AND BEAN CASSEROLE

1   pound bulk sausage
1   can (16 ounces) cut green beans, drained
1   can (16 ounces) creamed corn
½   cup light cream
    Salt
    Pepper

Place the sausage in a shallow baking dish, spreading it about ½ inch thick. Bake, uncovered, at 400° for 25 minutes, then remove from the oven and drain off the excess fat. Mix the beans with the corn, add the cream, add salt and pepper, and stir gently. Spread evenly on top of the sausage. Return to the oven and bake for 20 minutes at 425°.

Four servings

FRIED APPLES AND SAUSAGES

8   large sausage links
3   tablespoons brown sugar
3   apples, cored and cut in thick rings

Fry the sausages until well done, then drain and keep warm. Combine the sugar with the drippings in the skillet. Place the apple rings in the pan. Cook, covered, over low heat, until tender, basting occasionally. Serve the sausages on top of the apple rings.

Four servings

SAUSAGES AND RICE IN A SKILLET

12   sausage links
 2   medium onions, sliced thin
½   cup chopped green pepper
 2   cups cooked rice
 1   can (10½ ounces) tomato soup
½   cup beef broth or bouillon
 1   teaspoon salt

Brown the sausages in a heavy iron skillet or an electric skillet. Remove and drain. In the same skillet, sauté the onions and green pepper until tender. Remove from the skillet, then pour out the drippings. Cover the bottom with the rice, sprinkle with salt. Top evenly with onion and green pepper. Arrange the sausages on top.

Gradually stir the broth into the tomato soup. When smooth, pour it over the mixture in the skillet. Do not stir. Cook, covered, over low heat for 15 to 20 minutes.

Six servings

SAUSAGE MIXED GRILL

4   large pork sausages, partially cooked
4   lamb chops, 1 inch thick
4   lamb kidneys, split in halves
4   thick slices tomato
4   large mushroom caps
2   tablespoons melted butter
    Salt
    Pepper

Heat the broiler. Rub the rack with fat. Place the lamb chops, kidneys, and sausages on the rack. Broil for 7 minutes. Then turn the meats and add to the broiler the tomato slices and mushroom caps. Brush the vegetables liberally with melted butter and sprinkle with salt and pepper. Broil until the chops and sausages are done (about 6 minutes).

Four servings

HOMINY CREOLE

1½   **cups sausage meat**
3   **cups canned hominy, drained**
3   **tablespoons chopped onion**
½   **teaspoon savory**
1   **can (10½ ounces) tomato soup**
½   **cup buttered bread crumbs**
¾   **teaspoon salt**

Combine the sausage, hominy, onion, and savory and sauté in a skillet until brown. Put the mixture in a buttered casserole. Dilute the soup with one half can of water and pour into the casserole. Stir gently. Top with the buttered crumbs. Heat thoroughly in a 325° oven, but do not allow to dry out.

Four servings

SAUSAGE AND CORNBREAD CASSEROLE

8   **pork sausages, partially cooked**
4   **servings of creamed chicken (frozen or freshly made)**
1   **package (12 ounces) corn muffin mix**

Put the creamed chicken in a rather shallow casserole or baking dish. (If using frozen chicken it must be thawed and heated first.) Prepare the muffin mix according to the package directions. Spread it in a thin layer over the chicken. Arrange the sausages on top of the mix. Bake at 400° for 15 to 20 minutes, or until the muffin mix is brown and cooked through.

Four servings

SAUSAGE AND NOODLE CASSEROLE

1   pound bulk sausage
1   medium onion, chopped
1   green pepper, chopped fine
2   cans (16 ounces each) tomatoes
3   quarts boiling water
1   package (8 ounces) medium noodles
¼   cup buttered bread crumbs
1½   teaspoons granulated sugar
1   tablespoon plus 1 teaspoon salt
⅛   teaspoon pepper

Fry the sausage in a heavy skillet, breaking it up into small pieces. Remove when brown and add the onion and green pepper to the skillet. Cook until soft. Break up the tomatoes and add them, along with the sausage, sugar, the 1 teaspoon salt, and the pepper. Simmer gently for about 15 minutes, stirring occasionally.

Meanwhile, cook the noodles in the boiling water with the 1 tablespoon salt. Drain. In a greased 2-quart casserole alternate layers of noodles and the sausage mixture. Top with the buttered crumbs. Bake, uncovered, at 350° for 25 to 30 minutes.

Four to five servings

SAUSAGE IN ACORN SQUASH

2   pounds bulk sausage
4   medium acorn squash, cut in half lengthwise
½   cup brown sugar
    Salt
    Pepper

Remove the seeds and pulp from the cut squash. Sprinkle each half with salt and pepper and 1 tablespoon of the brown sugar. Put in a large, shallow baking dish, pour in enough water to cover the bottom, and cover with foil. Bake at 350° until almost tender.

Meanwhile, form the sausage into eight equal patties the size of the squash cavities. Brown them in a heavy skillet, pouring off the excess fat. When the squash is ready, place the sausage patties in the cavities. Return to the oven for at least 20 minutes.

Eight servings

SAUSAGE AU GRATIN

1   pound bulk sausage
2   tablespoons water
2   tablespoons butter or margarine
2   tablespoons all-purpose flour
1   cup milk
½   cup grated Cheddar cheese
1   teaspoon prepared mustard
2   cups sliced, boiled potatoes
1   package (10 ounces) frozen peas, cooked
¾   teaspoon salt
⅛   teaspoon pepper

Form the sausage into eight patties. Put them and the water in a cold frying pan. Simmer, covered, over low heat for 5 minutes, then remove the cover, pour off the drippings, and brown the patties.

In another pan melt the butter. Stir in the flour, salt, and pepper. Add the milk, stirring constantly, until the mixture has thickened. Add the cheese and mustard. Stir until the cheese melts, then gently mix in the potatoes and peas. Transfer to a casserole. Place the patties on top. Bake, uncovered, at 350° for 30 minutes.

Four servings

SAUSAGES WITH APPLES

1   pound link sausages
4   tart cooking apples
¼   cup brown sugar
¼   teaspoon ground cinnamon
½   cup dried currants
2   tablespoons butter or margarine
¼   cup red wine

Peel and core the apples and cut them into quarters. Put them in a bowl, sprinkle with the sugar and cinnamon. Cover tightly. Allow them to stand for 2 to 3 hours. Wash the currants and plump them in hot water. Drain. Prick the sausages. Heat the butter in a skillet and lightly brown the sausages. Put in the skillet as many of the apple slices as can be fitted in beside the sausages. Scatter in the currants. Cover, and cook over low heat, turning the apples over once or twice.

When they are done, remove, keep hot, and replace with more of the apple quarters. When all have been cooked, arrange the sausages and apples on a hot platter. Pour the wine into the pan, heat it, and then pour it over the apples and sausages.

Four servings

SAUSAGE BALLS IN PINEAPPLE SAUCE

2   pounds bulk sausage
2   tablespoons water
1   can (8¼ ounces) pineapple chunks, drained and juice reserved
2   tablespoons butter or margarine
¼   cup granulated sugar
2   tablespoons cornstarch
½   cup apple juice
2   tablespoons red cinnamon candies
8   maraschino cherries

Form the sausage into small balls. Place them in a cold skillet. Add the water, and cover tightly. Cook slowly for 5 minutes. Remove the cover, pour off the drippings, and brown the balls.

Add enough water to the reserved pineapple juice to make 1 cup. Melt the butter in a heavy saucepan. Combine the sugar and cornstarch and stir it into the melted butter. Add the pineapple juice, apple juice, and candies. Cook over medium heat, stirring constantly, until thick and clear. Add the meat balls, pineapple chunks, and cherries. Cook for 5 minutes over very low heat. Serve hot over waffles or pancakes.

Eight to ten servings

SAUSAGE AND PANCAKES WITH CHERRY SAUCE

1½ pounds bulk sausage
 2 cups pancake mix
 1 egg
 2 tablespoons melted shortening
 2 cups milk
 1 can (16 ounces) cherry pie filling
 ½ cup ginger ale

Shape the sausage into sixteen thin patties about 3 inches in diameter. Brown them on both sides. Combine the pancake mix, egg, shortening, and milk and stir until the mix is thoroughly moistened. Use to make twenty-four 3-inch pancakes on a moderate griddle. Place eight of the pancakes in an 8 x 12-inch baking dish. Put a sausage on top of each one, add another pancake, another patty and top with a pancake. Combine the cherry filling and ginger ale. Pour over the pancake stacks and bake, uncovered, at 375° for 15 minutes.

Eight servings

SAUSAGE SAVORY

 1 pound sausage links
 ½ cup sliced onion
2½ cups canned tomatoes
 1 cup chopped celery
 ½ cup chopped green pepper
 1 teaspoon granulated sugar
12 ounces wide egg noodles, cooked
 1 pound American cheese, grated
 ¼ teaspoon salt
 ⅛ teaspoon pepper

Fry the sausages until nicely browned and cooked through. Drain them, reserving 1 tablespoon of the drippings. Cut the sausages into 1-inch pieces and set aside. Combine the onion, tomatoes, celery, and green pepper in a casserole. Stir in the sugar, salt, pepper, and sausage drippings. Bake, covered, at 300° for 1½ hours. Add the sausages, noodles, and cheese, and heat thoroughly.

Four servings

SAUSAGE AND EGG CASSEROLE

6   **sausage links**
2   **tablespoons butter or margarine**
1   **can (16 ounces) tomatoes**
1   **tablespoon all-purpose flour**
½   **teaspoon sugar**
½   **teaspoon dried basil**
½   **teaspoon oregano**
6   **eggs**
1½   **teaspoons salt**
¼   **teaspoon pepper**

Sauté the sausages in 1 tablespoon of the butter until brown and cooked through. Combine the tomatoes, flour, sugar, herbs and ½ teaspoon of the salt in a saucepan. Cook slowly until thick. Pour into a shallow baking dish. Arrange the sausages on top, as spokes in a wheel. Break the eggs and drop them carefully between the spokes. Sprinkle with the remaining salt and pepper, dot with the remaining tablespoon of butter. Bake, uncovered, at 400° for 6 to 8 minutes, until the eggs are set but not hard.

Six servings

SAUSAGES WITH SWEET POTATOES

1   **pound sausage links**
2   **cans (16 ounces each) sweet potatoes, drained**
¼   **cup raisins, plumped in hot water and drained**
1   **can (8 ounces) pineapple chunks, drained**
½   **teaspoon salt**

Brown the sausage links. Mash the sweet potatoes. Add to them the raisins, pineapple, and salt. Place in a 1½-quart casserole. Arrange the links on top. Bake, uncovered, at 350° for 20 minutes, or until heated through.

Four servings

ALMOND-TOPPED SAUSAGE CASSEROLE

2   pounds bulk sausage
2½ cups chopped celery
¾   cup chopped onion
1   cup chopped green pepper
1   can (10½ ounces) chicken noodle soup
1¼ cups boiling water
1   cup raw rice
1   cup slivered almonds
1   tablespoon butter
½   teaspoon salt

Brown the sausage in a large skillet. Add the celery, onion, and green pepper and sauté until the vegetables are tender. In a saucepan combine the soup, boiling water, rice and salt. Simmer for 20 minutes. Combine the rice and sausage mixture and put in a greased casserole. Sauté the almonds in the butters, sprinkle on top. Bake, uncovered, at 375° for about 20 minutes.

Eight servings

SAUSAGES WITH ZUCCHINI AND TOMATOES

1   pound sausage links, browned and drained
2   medium zucchini, sliced ¼ inch thick
¼   teaspoon oregano
1   teaspoon paprika
½   cup fresh bread crumbs
2   large tomatoes, peeled and coarsely chopped
½   cup fine, toasted bread crumbs
½   teaspoon salt
⅛   teaspoon freshly ground pepper

Place the sausages in an ovenproof casserole. Add a layer of zucchini. Mix the seasonings and sprinkle half of the mixture over the zucchini. Add a layer of fresh bread crumbs and a layer of tomatoes. Sprinkle with the remaining spice mixture, top with the toasted crumbs. Bake, covered, at 350° for 1 hour.

Four servings

SAUSAGE AND APPLE STUFFING

1   pound bulk sausage
1   cup chopped celery
1   can (10 ounces) chicken giblet gravy
1   cup water
4   cups dry rye bread crumbs
4   cups dry white bread crumbs
1   cup chopped apple
½   cup raisins
1   tablespoon poultry seasoning
1   teaspoon salt

Brown the sausages in a skillet, stirring to separate. Add the celery and cook until tender, then add half of the gravy. Stir until well blended. Add the water and stir again.

Put the crumbs, apples and raisins in a large bowl. Sprinkle on the seasoning. Add the sausage mixture, and toss until the crumbs are evenly moistened, adding the remaining gravy, if necessary.

Enough to stuff a 12-pound bird

SAUSAGE-SAUCED SPAGHETTI

1   pound sausage links, sliced diagonally
1   green pepper, cut in strips
½   cup finely chopped onion
½   pound fresh mushrooms, sliced, or 1 can (2 ounces)
3   tablespoons olive oil
¼   teaspoon garlic salt
12   large, stuffed green olives, sliced
1   can (1 pound 12 ounces) tomatoes
1   can (8 ounces) tomato sauce
1   package (8 ounces) spaghetti, cooked
½   cup grated Parmesan cheese

Cook the sausage, green pepper, onion, and mushrooms in the olive oil until browned. Add the garlic salt, olives, tomatoes, and tomato sauce. Simmer for 2 hours, until thoroughly blended and thick. Serve over the hot spaghetti and sprinkle with the cheese.

Four servings

SAUSAGE SAUCE FOR PASTA

2   pounds sweet Italian-style sausage
2   tablespoons olive oil
1½ cups chopped onion
2   teaspoons minced garlic
12 cups (about 6 pounds) diced ripe tomatoes
½   cup chopped parsley
1½ teaspoons salt
¼   teaspoon pepper

Place the sausage, casing removed in a large, cold skillet. Cook over moderate heat until browned (about 20 minutes), stirring with a spoon to break it up. Remove to a plate and keep warm.

Discard the drippings and clean the skillet with a paper towel. Slowly heat the oil in the skillet, then add the onion and garlic. Cook until soft, stirring often. Mix in the sausage, tomatoes, salt, and pepper. Cover and simmer for 15 minutes, stirring two or three times to prevent sticking. Uncover and increase the heat to moderately high and cook for 5 minutes longer, stirring frequently, until the mixture is slightly thickened. Add the parsley just before serving.

Makes seven cups

SAUSAGE AND VEGETABLE CASSEROLE

1 pound pork sausage, bulk or links
1 large onion, sliced
3 large white potatoes, peeled and sliced thin
1 can (8 ounces) whole kernel corn, well drained
1 can (8 ounces) tomatoes
   Salt
   Freshly ground pepper

Put the onion slices in the bottom of a greased casserole. Add the potatoes. Salt and pepper lightly. Then make a layer of the corn. Drain the tomatoes. Add the tomatoes and about one half of their juice. Place the links, or thin patties made of the sausage, on top. Bake, uncovered, at 350° for 1 hour or until the potatoes are tender.

Six servings

Soups, Salads, and Sandwiches

MORE THAN A SNACK AND LESS THAN A MEAL

These recipes are the answer to the short-order cook's prayer. Most of them provide variety and plenty of nourishment in a hurry. Some can be prepared ahead of time and refrigerated or frozen. Some are simple enough to be prepared by children. Some are good enough for luncheon party fare.

DEMBERG PORK AND SAUERKRAUT SOUP

1 **pork shoulder (5 to 6 pounds)**
8 **peppercorns**
2 **bay leaves**
  Barley
1 **large can (27 ounces) sauerkraut**
  Sour cream
2 **teaspoons salt**

Place the meat in a large kettle with water to cover. Add the salt, peppercorns, and bay leaves. Simmer gently for 2 hours, or until the meat is tender. Remove the pork from the liquid and refrigerate both overnight.

Next day, skim all the fat off the liquid. Measure it as you return it to the large kettle. For each quart of broth add ¼ cup of barley. Then put in the sauerkraut and simmer over very low heat for 40 minutes. Put the meat in the soup and heat for 20 minutes or until hot. Remove the meat and cut into thick slices. Put these in large soup bowls. Fill the bowls with the soup. Put a generous tablespoonful of sour cream in each, and serve with slices of pumpernickel.

Six to eight servings

212

LENTIL SOUP WITH SOUR CREAM

1   smoked ham hock or meaty ham bone
1   package (16 ounces) lentils, washed
6½ cups water, more if necessary
1   carrot, sliced
1   medium onion, chopped
1   stalk celery, sliced
1   tablespoon chopped fresh parsley
2   tablespoons all-purpose flour
2   tablespoons bacon drippings
4   tablespoons sour cream
1   teaspoon salt

Soak the lentils overnight in 6 cups of the water in a large kettle. The next day add the meat, vegetables, parsley, and salt. Cook slowly, covered, until the lentils are soft, then remove from the heat and allow to cool slightly. Take out the bone and cut up the meat. Return it to the liquid.

Mash the meat and vegetables with a potato masher or put through a food mill. Brown the flour in the bacon drippings. Add ½ cup of water and stir until thick and smooth. Pour this into the soup (more water may be added if the soup seems too thick), and heat thoroughly. Just before serving, stir in the sour cream. This soup keeps well in the refrigerator or it may be frozen.

Six servings

SPLIT PEA SOUP WITH HAM

1   meaty ham bone
1   package (16 ounces) green split peas
2½ quarts water
1   cup sliced onion
1   cup diced celery
1   cup sliced carrots
1   teaspoon parsley flakes
¼   teaspoon marjoram
    Salt

Cover the peas with water and soak overnight. The next day, drain and put them in a large kettle with the water, ham bone and onion. Bring to a boil, reduce the heat, cover, and simmer for 2 hours, stirring occasionally. Remove the bone and cut off the bits of meat. Add the meat to the soup, along with the celery, carrots, parsley, marjoram, and salt to taste. Cook slowly for an additional 45 minutes.

Eight servings

HAM BALLS AND PEA SOUP DE LUXE

1	ham bone
1	package (16 ounces) split peas
8	cups water
1	large onion, cut up fine
1	bay leaf
1	can (1 pound 12 ounces) tomatoes
1½	cups diced potatoes
1½	cups chopped celery
1½	cups sliced carrots
2	teaspoons salt
½	teaspoon pepper

Ham balls:

1½	cups ground, cooked ham
2	tablespoons all-purpose flour
1	egg, lightly beaten
2	tablespoons minced parsley

Soak the peas overnight in water to cover. The next day, drain. Put the peas, water, ham bone, onion, bay leaf and seasonings in a large kettle. Cover and simmer for 1½ hours. Remove the bone and the bay leaf. Add the vegetables, cover, and continue cooking for 30 minutes. Meanwhile, mix the ground ham, flour, egg, and parsley. Drop from a teaspoon into the soup. Simmer very gently for 12 minutes longer. Serve immediately.

Twelve servings

LENTIL SOUP

1   **leftover ham bone**
2   **cups lentils**
2   **quarts cold water**
1   **cup chopped celery, including leaves**
½   **cup chopped carrots**
½   **teaspoon crushed bay leaf**
4   **sprigs fresh parsley**
2   **tablespoons all-purpose flour**
1   **tablespoon lemon juice**
1½ **teaspoons salt**
⅛   **teaspoon pepper**

Wash the lentils, and soak overnight. The next day, drain and put them with the water and ham bone, in a large kettle. Bring to a slow boil, uncovered, skimming when necessary. Simmer for 1½ to 2 hours, then add the celery, carrots, bay leaf, and parsley. Cover and simmer for 30 minutes longer. Put the soup through a food mill or fine strainer and chill.

Remove the grease from the chilled soup, reserving 2 tablespoons. Melt the reserved grease in a small skillet. Add the flour and blend. Add 1 cup of the soup and cook until thick. Stir this into the rest of the soup. Season the soup with salt and pepper. Add the lemon juice just before serving.

Eight servings

BLENDER KIDNEY BEAN SOUP

4   **slices bacon, cooked crisp and crumbled**
1   **tablespoon bacon drippings**
1   **small onion, sliced**
1   **stalk celery, sliced**
1   **can (15 ounces) red kidney beans**
1   **can (8 ounces) tomato sauce**

Place the bacon drippings in a large skillet. Add the onion and celery and cook until tender. Add the beans and tomato sauce and cook, covered, for about 10 minutes. Purée the soup in a blender at low speed for a very short time. The texture should be rather coarse. Add enough hot water to make 48 ounces. Return the soup to the skillet and reheat. Just before serving, stir in the bacon.

Six servings

BACON AND BEAN SOUP LUNCH

2   slices bacon, cut in small pieces
3   cups water
1   envelope (from a 3½-ounce package) vegetable beef soup mix
1   can (16 ounces) baked beans in tomato sauce

Cook the bacon until crisp. Drain. Put the water and soup mix in a saucepan and bring to a boil. Lower the heat and simmer for 5 minutes, stirring occasionally. Stir in the beans, and add the bacon. Cook for 5 minutes longer.

Four servings

CORN CHOWDER

6   slices bacon
¼   medium green pepper
4   pieces pimiento
¼   teaspoon thyme
    Dash of Tabasco sauce
2   tablespoons all-purpose flour
2   cups milk
2   cans (16 ounces each) cream-style corn
    Chopped fresh parsley
¼   teaspoon salt
⅛   teaspoon pepper

Fry the bacon until crisp. Remove from the skillet and drain. Add the green pepper to the skillet and fry in the bacon drippings until tender. Put the bacon, green pepper, pimiento, thyme, Tabasco, flour, 1 cup of the milk, 1 can of corn, and the seasonings in a blender. Blend until the corn is well chopped up. Pour into a saucepan. Blend the rest of the corn and milk. Pour into the saucepan. Heat but do not boil the soup. (If you cannot keep your eye on it, use a double boiler.) Serve the soup sprinkled with the parsley.

Four servings

CARROT CHOWDER

4   slices bacon, cooked and crumbled
1   can (16 ounces) sliced carrots
1   tablespoon grated onion
¼   cup finely diced celery
2½ cups chicken broth

Put the can of carrots, including the liquid, into the blender. Turn on at low speed for a few seconds. The carrots should be very coarsely chopped. To make the broth use 3 packets of instant broth dissolved in 2½ cups of boiling water. Place all of the ingredients except the bacon in a saucepan and cook over very low heat until the celery is barely tender. Just before serving, stir in the bacon.

Four servings

BACON AND BAKED BEAN CHOWDER

6   slices bacon, cut up
½   cup chopped onion
2   tablespoons all-purpose flour
3   cups milk
2   medium potatoes, peeled and diced
1   can (21 ounces) baked beans in brown sugar sauce
¼   teaspoon thyme
4   tablespoons chopped fresh parsley
1   teaspoon salt
⅛   teaspoon pepper

Cook the bacon lightly in a large skillet. Add the onion and cook until it is tender, then blend in the flour. Pour in the milk, stirring constantly, and cook until the mixture thickens. Add the potatoes, salt, pepper and thyme. Cover and simmer until the potatoes are tender, then stir in the beans and heat thoroughly. Serve topped with the parsley.

Four servings

SUCCOTASH SOUP WITH BACON

6   slices bacon, cooked, drained, and crumbled
4   cups beef broth or bouillon
⅛   teaspoon savory
1   package (10 ounces) frozen baby lima beans
2   cups cream-style corn
1   cup evaporated milk, undiluted
3   tablespoons all-purpose flour
4   tablespoons water
1   teaspoon salt

Heat the broth to boiling in a large saucepan. Add the savory, salt and lima beans and cook as indicated on the package. Put the corn and milk in a blender. Blend until corn is well broken up, then add to the soup mixture. Mix the flour and water to a smooth paste. When the soup is hot, add the paste and stir thoroughly. Cover and simmer for 10 minutes. Serve in warm soup bowls and garnish with the bacon.

Four or five servings

SPLIT PEA SOUP

1   2-inch cube salt pork
1   package (16 ounces) dried split peas
2   quarts cold water
2   medium white onions, chopped fine
½   cup chopped celery, including leaves
½   teaspoon crushed bay leaf
1   medium potato, peeled but left whole
2   tablespoons barley
2   tablespoons chopped fresh parsley
2   teaspoons salt
⅛   teaspoon pepper

Soak the peas overnight. The next day, drain, and put in a large saucepan. Add the cold water and bring to a boil. Skim and lower the heat. Add all the remaining ingredients except the salt and pepper. Cover, and boil slowly for 1½ to 2 hours. Remove the pork and discard. Lift out the potato, put it through a fine strainer, and stir into the soup. Add the salt and pepper. Bring to a boil before serving.

Eight servings

TOMATO CHOWDER

¼   pound salt pork, cut in thin strips
2   small white onions, sliced thin
1   teaspoon all-purpose flour
1   can (8 ounces) tomatoes
3   cups water
¼   cup raw rice
2   tablespoons granulated sugar
    Grated Parmesan cheese
2   teaspoons salt
¼   teaspoon pepper

Put the pork in a fairly hot frying pan. When it begins to melt, add the onions and fry until both pork and onions are lightly browned. Sprinkle in the flour and stir to blend. Turn into a large, heavy saucepan. Add all the other ingredients except the cheese. Simmer, covered, for 1 hour, stirring occasionally. Serve in warm bowls, with the grated Parmesan cheese sprinkled over the top.

Six servings

FISH CHOWDER

¼   cup diced salt pork   Salt
1   pound haddock fillets   Pepper
1   cup water
2   cups cubed potatoes
1   small onion, chopped
3   cups milk
1   tablespoon butter or margarine
¼   teaspoon paprika

Put the fish and water in a saucepan. Cook slowly (about 10 minutes) until the fish flakes easily when tested with a fork. Remove and separate it into flakes. Add the potatoes to the cooking water. Cook them until tender but still firm.

Meanwhile, put the salt pork in a skillet and fry it over low heat until the fat melts. Add the onion and cook until golden. Add to the potatoes. Pour 1 cup of the milk into the onion pan and stir, then pour it and the remaining milk into the saucepan. Heat thoroughly but do not boil. Just before serving, add the butter, paprika, and salt and pepper to taste. This chowder is even better if made one day and served the next. But it must be reheated over hot water and, again, not allowed to boil.

Four servings

SAUSAGE AND VEGETABLE SOUP

¾　pound kielbasa (Polish sausage)
1　pound salt pork
½　cup Great Northern dried beans
1　large carrot, diced
1　turnip, diced
1　leek, cut in ¼-inch slices
1　celery stalk
1　onion, sliced
6　sprigs fresh parsley
¼　teaspoon thyme
1　bay leaf
3　cups shredded cabbage
2　potatoes, peeled and cut into ½-inch cubes
¼　pound green beans, cut into 1-inch lengths
2　teaspoons salt
　White pepper

Toast:

1　egg yolk
½　cup Parmesan cheese, freshly grated
　Dash of cayenne
6　slices French bread, 1 inch thick, toasted and buttered

Place the salt pork in a saucepan and add water to cover. Bring to a boil. Reduce the heat and simmer for 1 hour. With a slotted spoon remove to a warm dish and set aside.

Boil the dried beans in 2 cups of water for 2 minutes. Remove from the heat and allow to soak for 1 hour, then drain the beans and transfer to a large kettle. Add 9 cups of hot water. Cook over low heat for 45 minutes, then add the carrot, turnip, leek, celery, and onion. Put the parsley, thyme, and bay leaf in a cheesecloth bag. Add to the vegetable kettle. Add the pork and season with salt. Bring to a boil, then reduce the heat and simmer for 45 minutes. Add the sausage, cabbage, potatoes, and green beans and simmer for 30 minutes, or until the vegetables are tender. Remove and discard the celery and the cheesecloth bag. Lift out the pork and sausage and cut into ½-inch slices. Return to the kettle and season with salt and pepper to taste. Garnish with the toast, made as follows:

Combine the egg yolk, cheese, and cayenne. Spread on the toast. Place on a baking sheet and broil for 3 minutes, or until the cheese has melted. Serve 1 slice on top of each bowl of soup.

Six servings

SLICED PORK IN MINT ASPIC

8 slices cold roast pork
1 envelope (1 tablespoon) unflavored gelatin
1 cup beef bouillon
1 cup mint sauce, bottled or homemade
1 package (10 ounces) frozen green peas, cooked according to
     package directions
⅓ cup mayonnaise
2 tablespoons cream
   Mint sprigs or watercress
   Salt

Soften the gelatin in ¼ cup of the bouillon. Heat the mint sauce, and add the gelatin, stirring until it dissolves. Then add the remaining bouillon. Allow the sauce to cool.

Arrange the pork slices around the edge of a shallow platter. Salt very lightly. When the sauce starts to set, pour it over the meat and refrigerate until firm.

Meanwhile, mix the peas with mayonnaise which has been thinned with cream. When ready to serve mound the peas in the center of the platter. Garnish with mint or watercress.

Four servings

PORK AND MACARONI SALAD

3   cups cooked, slivered pork
¼   cup olive oil
2   tablespoons white wine vinegar
2   tablespoons minced chives
¾   teaspoon dry mustard
3   cups seeded, diced cucumbers
¾   cup mayonnaise
1   teaspoon curry powder
4   cups cooked elbow macaroni
    Shredded chicory
    Sliced radishes
    Salt
    Pepper

Combine the olive oil, vinegar, chives, mustard, salt, and pepper. Add the pork to the mixture and marinate at room temperature for 1 hour, tossing several times. Place the cucumbers in a colander, sprinkle with ½ teaspoon salt, and drain for 30 minutes. Meanwhile, combine the mayonnaise and curry powder.

Combine the pork mixture, mayonnaise, and macaroni. Line a platter with chicory and place the salad mixture on this. Garnish with radishes.

Six to eight servings

COLD PORK AND CELERY SALAD

1½   cups julienne-cut, cooked lean pork
1½   cups julienne-cut celery
4   hard-boiled egg yolks
2   teaspoons Dijon mustard

¼ **cup olive oil**
¼ **cup salad oil**
1 **tablespoon wine vinegar**
¼ **teaspoon lemon juice**
2 **cups shredded iceberg lettuce**
2 **tablespoons heavy cream or undiluted evaporated milk, more if necessary**
¾ **teaspoon salt**
¼ **teaspoon cayenne pepper**

The ideal size for the strips of pork is 1½ inches x ½ inch. In cutting up the celery, make the strips as nearly as possible the same size as the strips of pork. Soak the celery strips in ice water for 1½ hours. Allow the meat to stay at room temperature.

Make a dressing by mashing together the egg yolks and the mustard to a smooth paste. Beat in the combined oils, about ½ teaspoon at a time. This mixture will be thick. Thin it by blending in the vinegar and lemon juice. Sprinkle in the salt and cayenne and beat in the cream. If the dressing still seems too thick, add more cream, a little at a time.

Put the lettuce, which has been washed and dried and chilled in the refrigerator, in the bottom of a cold glass or china salad bowl. Put the pork over it. Dry the celery carefully and spread the strips over the top. Pour on the dressing. Carry to the table, toss, and serve on cold salad plates.

Four servings

ELEGANT HAM MOUSSE

2 **cups cooked ham, finely ground**
4 **tablespoons butter**
¼ **cup all-purpose flour**
1 **cup hot milk**
½ **teaspoon nutmeg**
¼ **cup brandy**
2 **egg yolks**
½ **cup heavy cream**
2 **envelopes (2 tablespoons) unflavored gelatin**
½ **cup cold water**

½   **cup hot chicken broth**
¼   **teaspoon salt**
⅛   **teaspoon pepper**
        Stuffed olives (optional)
        Hard-boiled eggs (optional)
        Thin-sliced cucumber (optional)

Melt the butter in a heavy saucepan and stir in the flour. Cook over low heat for 2 minutes. Gradually pour in the hot milk, stirring constantly until the mixture has thickened. Season with nutmeg, salt, and pepper. Stir in the brandy.

In a small bowl mix the egg yolks with the cream. Stir in a little of the hot sauce, then pour into the sauce in the pan. Cook over low heat, stirring, until blended and thickened. Do not allow it to boil. Soften the gelatin in the cold water, then dissolve in the hot broth. Blend into the sauce. Stir in the ham. Pour the mixture into a 4- or 5-cup mold. Chill until the mousse is firm and thoroughly set.

When ready to serve, unmold on a platter. May be garnished with stuffed olives, hard-boiled eggs or thin-sliced cucumber.

Six to eight servings

SIMPLE HAM MOUSSE

2   **cups chopped, cooked ham**
1   **envelope (1 tablespoon) unflavored gelatin**
¼   **cup cold water**
1   **cup mayonnaise or salad dressing**
½   **cup chopped celery**
½   **cup chopped green pepper**
1   **teaspoon grated onion (optional)**
½   **cup heavy cream, whipped**
        Watercress

Sprinkle the gelatin over the water in a saucepan. Warm slowly, over low heat, stirring constantly until the gelatin has dissolved. Add this to the mayonnaise, stirring constantly until smooth. Chill until the mixture just begins to thicken. Stir in the ham, celery, green pepper, and onion. Fold in the whipped cream and chill until firm. Unmold to serve and garnish with watercress.

Four servings

HAM SALAD WITH SOUR CREAM DRESSING

2 cups (1 pound) diced, cooked ham
1 can (16 ounces) sliced potatoes
1 cup sour cream
¼ cup chili sauce
¼ cup chopped sweet pickles
1 tablespoon lemon juice
¼ teaspoon dill weed
1 package (9 ounces) frozen artichoke hearts, cooked and drained
Salad greens

Drain the potatoes well. Add ⅓ cup of dressing made by combining the sour cream, chili sauce, pickles, lemon juice, and dill. Chill the potatoes, artichoke hearts, and the remaining dressing for at least 1 hour. Line a salad bowl with greens and place the potatoes in center. Surround with artichoke hearts and ham and pour the remaining dressing over.

Six to eight servings

CAESAR HAM SALAD

⅓ pound cooked ham, cut in ½-inch strips
1 garlic clove, crushed
1 large head romaine
3 tablespoons olive oil
1 egg, simmered for 1 minute
1½ tablespoons lemon juice
4 anchovy fillets, chopped
⅓ cup grated Parmesan cheese
1 cup toasted croutons
Salt
Pepper

Rub a salad bowl with the crushed garlic clove. Break the romaine into bite-sized pieces and put in the bowl. Pour on the oil, and mix until well coated, then break the egg into the salad and toss. Sprinkle with lemon juice. Add the anchovies and cheese and mix thoroughly. Add the croutons and ham strips and mix well. Season with salt and pepper to taste and serve at once.

Two or three servings

HAM AND TURKEY SALAD WITH TOKAY GRAPES

1   cup julienne-cut, cooked ham
2   cups Tokay grapes
1   cup diced, cooked turkey or chicken
½   cup mayonnaise
1   cup sliced celery, including a few minced leaves
¼   cup pickle relish
¼   teaspoon tarragon
¼   cup chopped green pepper
    Lettuce
½   teaspoon salt

Halve and seed the grapes and combine in a bowl with the turkey and
ham. Mix well the remaining ingredients, except the lettuce. Add to the
Tokay mixture, and toss lightly. Chill and serve on lettuce.

Five or six servings

HAM AND RICE SALAD

1½   cups julienne-cut, cooked ham
1½   cups cooked rice
 ½   cup diced green pepper
 2   tablespoons granulated sugar
 2   teaspoons soy sauce
 1   tablespoon finely chopped onion
 1   can (11 ounces) mandarin oranges, drained
 ½   cup French dressing
     Salad greens

Toss all the ingredients together lightly except the greens. Chill
thoroughly. Serve on crisp salad greens.

Four servings

HOT BACON AND GREEN BEAN SALAD

½   pound bacon
2   eggs
⅓   cup vinegar
½   cup water
3   tablespoons granulated sugar

1½ **pounds fresh beans, cooked,**
                    or
2   **cans whole green beans**
2   **tablespoons diced pimiento**
¼   **teaspoon salt**

Cook the bacon until crisp. Drain, reserving ¼ cup of the drippings, and crumble. Beat the eggs and blend in the vinegar, water, sugar, and salt. Add the egg mixture to the drippings and cook over low heat until thickened. Meanwhile, cook the beans, drain, and put them in a serving dish. Pour the hot dressing over them and sprinkle with crumbled bacon and pimiento.

Six servings

ONWENTSIA A B C SALAD

Bacon, cooked crisp, crumbled
Lettuce
Small curd cottage cheese
Ripe avocado
French dressing

For each serving, make a bed of crisp lettuce. In the center put a generous scoop of small curd cottage cheese. Surround this with slices of ripe avocado. Pour French dressing (or your favorite salad dressing of the oil and vinegar type) over this. Top with a very generous quantity of crisp, crumbled bacon.

WILTED SPINACH SALAD

5   **slices of bacon, diced, cooked crisp, and drained**
1   **pound fresh spinach**
2   **tablespoons wine vinegar**
1   **tablespoon lemon juice**
1   **teaspoon granulated sugar**
4   **scallions, sliced**
2   **hard-boiled eggs, sliced**
½   **teaspoon salt**
¼   **teaspoon coarsely ground black pepper**

Wash the spinach thoroughly and discard the stems. Dry and tear into bite-sized pieces in a large bowl. Add the scallions and pepper.

Add the vinegar, lemon juice, sugar, and salt to the bacon drippings. Heat to boiling, then pour over the contents of the bowl, tossing gently until all the leaves are coated and slightly wilted. Add the bacon and serve at once, garnished with the egg slices.

Four servings

GERMAN POTATO SALAD

6   slices bacon
2   small onions, diced
2   tablespoons flour
1   cup vinegar
1   cup sugar
6   medium white potatoes, boiled, peeled, and sliced
2   teaspoons salt
¼   teaspoon pepper

Cut up the bacon and cook until crisp. Drain and crumble. Cook the onions in the bacon fat until they are light brown.

Combine the flour, salt, vinegar, sugar, and pepper in a saucepan and cook, stirring constantly, until clear. In the top of a double boiler combine the potatoes, bacon, onions, bacon drippings, and the dressing. Stir gently and allow to stand for 2 to 3 hours. To serve, reheat over boiling water.

Six servings

DEVILED HAMWICHES

1   can (2¼ ounces) deviled ham
1   tablespoon finely chopped celery
1   hard-boiled egg, chopped fine
¼   teaspoon curry powder
½   teaspoon salad oil
1   tablespoon mayonnaise
6   slices whole-wheat bread
    Butter or margarine, softened
    Lettuce

Combine the ham, celery, and egg. Moisten the curry powder with salad oil and stir it into the mayonnaise. Add to the ham mixture. Spread 3 slices of bread with softened butter and the remaining 3 slices of bread with the ham mixture. Top with lettuce. Then put on the buttered bread. To serve, cut the sandwiches in half.

Makes six small sandwiches

BROILED HAM AND CHEESE SANDWICHES

6   slices cooked ham
2   tablespoons softened butter
1   teaspoon chopped fresh parsley
1   teaspoon thyme
6   slices bread
6   slices Fontina cheese
    Salt
    Pepper

Combine the butter with the parsley and thyme. Add salt and pepper to taste. Toast the bread on one side. Spread the other side with the butter mixture. Put on the ham and top with the cheese. Arrange the sandwiches (open face) on a cookie sheet. Put under a preheated broiler for 3 minutes, or until the cheese is melted and slightly browned.

Six servings

TRIPLE TREAT SANDWICH

1   cup diced, boiled ham
½   cup chopped celery
½   cup chopped apple
½   cup mayonnaise
1   teaspoon Beau Monde seasoning
6   slices Swiss cheese
12   slices rye bread, buttered
12   crisp lettuce leaves

Combine the ham, celery, apple, mayonnaise, and seasoning in a bowl. Place 1 slice of cheese on each of 6 slices of bread. Spread the ham mixture on top of the cheese, then put on the lettuce leaves. Top with remaining slices of bread.

Six servings

CROQUE-MONSIEUR
(French style ham and Swiss cheese sandwich)

For each sandwich use:

1   slice cold cooked ham
1   slice Swiss cheese
2   slices sandwich bread, crusts trimmed off
3   tablespoons butter or margarine

Put the ham and cheese between the slices of bread. Press together firmly. Sauté the sandwich in the butter in a heavy skillet until it is brown and crisp on both sides.

HAM SALAD SANDWICH FILLING

2   cups ground, cooked ham
½   cup pickle relish
½   cup mayonnaise or salad dressing

Mix all the ingredients. Refrigerate until ready to use, but do not freeze.

Makes about two cups

HAM ON WAFFLES

1¼   cups ground, cooked ham
2   teaspoons prepared mustard
   Milk
1   package (6) frozen waffles
1   egg
1½   tablespoons butter or margarine

Mix the ham with the mustard. If it is too crumbly to hold together, add a few drops of milk. Spread the mixture on 3 unthawed waffles. Top with 3 more waffles and press them together to make sandwiches. Beat the egg lightly and stir in ⅓ cup milk. Place the waffle sandwiches in the egg-milk mixture. Allow to stand for a minute or two, and then turn. Melt the butter in the skillet, and when it is hot sauté the sandwiches on both sides until golden brown.

Three servings

HAM–ASPARAGUS SOUP SANDWICH

4 slices baked or boiled ham
4 slices buttered toast
1 can asparagus tips
⅓ cup milk
¼ cup mayonnaise
1 can (10 ounces) cream of chicken soup
1 tablespoon chopped pimiento

Put the slices of toast on a cookie sheet. Top each with a slice of ham and some of the asparagus tips. Blend the milk and mayonnaise into the soup, then add the pimiento. Pour this over the sandwiches and broil until hot.

Four servings

HEARTY BACON ROLLS

8 bacon slices
4 hard rolls (bakery or brown-and-serve)
     Prepared Polynesian-style mustard
1 package (8 ounces) sliced sharp Cheddar cheese
4 frankfurters

Split the rolls. If necessary, cut off a small amount of the tops in order to make a flat surface. Spread the inside of each half with mustard. Cover the bottom halves with cheese slices cut to fit the rolls, then put 1 frankfurter on each. Top with another slice of cheese. Replace the top halves and wrap each roll with 2 slices of bacon, securing with wooden picks. Place top down on a rack and bake at 400° for 5 minutes. Turn and bake for 5 to 10 minutes longer, or until the bacon is cooked. Remove the picks and serve hot.

Four servings

TOMATO AND BACON WITH CHEESE SAUCE

12　slices bacon
 6　thick slices tomato
 ½　soup can milk
 1　can (10½ ounces) Cheddar cheese soup
 3　English muffins, sliced in half
　　Butter or margarine

Cook the bacon in a heavy skillet. Drain and set aside to keep warm. Pour all but a small amount of bacon fat from the skillet and fry the tomato slices, turning once, until thoroughly hot. Meanwhile, add the milk to the soup and heat. Toast and butter the muffin halves.

To assemble, put a muffin half on a plate, top each with a hot tomato slice, and pour some of the cheese sauce over each. Lay two bacon strips in a cross on each sandwich.

Six servings

BACON-CHEESE SANDWICH

 ¼　cup cooked crumbled bacon
 1　cup shredded Cheddar cheese, firmly packed
 2　tablespoons mayonnaise or salad dressing
 1　tablespoon heavy or sour cream

Combine all the ingredients and mix until well blended. Spread on rye or cracked wheat bread.

Makes about 1¼ cups

BACON–TOMATO SOUP SANDWICH

8   slices bacon, cooked
4   slices buttered toast
8   thin slices tomato
⅓   cup milk
1   teaspoon minced dried onion
½   teaspoon Worcestershire sauce
1   can (10½ ounces) cream of mushroom soup

Put the slices of buttered toast on a cookie sheet. Top each with 2 slices of tomato and 2 slices of bacon. Stir the milk, onion, and Worcestershire into the soup. Pour over the sandwiches. Broil until hot and bubbly.

Four servings

EASY PIZZAS

12 sausage links
4   slices Mozzarella cheese
4   slices bread, toasted
½   teaspoon oregano
1   can (8 ounces) tomato sauce

Place a slice of cheese on each slice of toast. Brown the sausage and arrange 3 links on top of the cheese. Combine the oregano and tomato sauce. Put some on each sandwich. Place on a cookie sheet. Bake at 450° for 6 to 8 minutes.

Four servings

SIMPLE SANDWICH

Slices, left-over shoulder roast
Cracked wheat bread

Cut medium-thick slices from a left-over shoulder roast (see page 191). Butter the desired number of slices of cracked wheat bread. Place a meat slice on each. Salt generously and sprinkle with freshly ground pepper.

This is not only quick and easy, but delicious without any additions.

Spareribs

Spareribs come several ways, but they come superbly into their own for outdoor barbecuing. No cut of meat better serves the outdoor cook. Spareribs may also be baked or simmered. They are just what their name says, ribs sparely covered with meat. "Country-style" spareribs are cut from the shoulder end of the loin. They are a little meatier. All spareribs have a very special flavor that has won them many devoted admirers. These recipes are among the best to show off their flavor and to delight their admirers.

BAKED SPARERIBS AND SAUERKRAUT

4	pounds spareribs, cut in 2- or 3-rib pieces
2	cans (1 pound 11 ounces each) sauerkraut, undrained
2	cups diced green apples
1½	teaspoons caraway seed
¾	cup diced onion
1½	teaspoons salt
½	teaspoon pepper

Place the spareribs in a large roasting pan. Sprinkle with the salt and pepper and roast at 450° for about 30 minutes, turning the ribs occasionally until well browned. Reduce the heat to 350° and cook, uncovered, for 30 minutes longer.

Remove the ribs from the oven and drain off the fat. Add the undrained sauerkraut, apples, caraway seed, and onions to the pan, then cover and return to the oven. Continue baking at 350° until the ribs are tender (about 1 hour), turning occasionally. Add water, if necessary during this time, to keep the sauerkraut from drying out.

Four servings

RED-GLAZED SPARERIBS

4 to 5 pounds spareribs, cut in 3-rib sections
½ teaspoon garlic salt
½ cup currant jelly
⅓ cup port
⅓ cup honey
1 tablespoon soy sauce
½ teaspoon ground ginger
¼ teaspoon red food coloring
1½ teaspoons salt
Melon or pineapple slices or fresh mint (optional)

Place the spareribs in a shallow pan. Combine the garlic salt and regular salt and sprinkle over the ribs. Cover tightly with foil and bake at 350° for 1½ hours.

Meanwhile, combine the jelly, port, honey, soy sauce, ginger, and food coloring in a saucepan. Bring slowly to a boil, stirring gently, to melt the jelly.

Thirty minutes before the ribs have finished cooking, take them from the oven. Remove the foil and drain off the drippings, then return the ribs to the oven and baste thoroughly several times with the jelly mixture until the ribs are cooked. The ribs may be garnished with melon or pineapple slices or fresh mint.

Four servings

SPARERIBS BAKED WITH BARBECUE SAUCE

6 pounds spareribs, cut in 2-rib pieces
2 cloves garlic, minced
2 tablespoons butter or margarine
2 tablespoons prepared mustard
2 tablespoons Worcestershire sauce
1 tablespoon celery seed
¼ cup brown sugar
1½ cups water
1 cup catsup
¾ cup chili sauce
2 dashes Tabasco sauce
½ teaspoon salt

Place the spareribs on a rack in a shallow baking pan and bake, covered, at 450° for 45 minutes.

Meanwhile, in a saucepan, cook the garlic in the butter, over low heat for 4 to 5 minutes. Blend in all the other ingredients and bring to a boil. Remove the meat and rack from the pan and drain off the fat. Replace the ribs in the pan and pour on the sauce. Bake, uncovered, at 350° for 1½ hours, occasionally brushing the meat with the sauce.

Six servings

SPARERIBS POLYNESIAN STYLE

4 pounds spareribs, cut in serving-size pieces
1 cup brown sugar, firmly packed
1 teaspoon celery salt
1 teaspoon ground ginger
3 tablespoons cornstarch
1 can (8 ounces) crushed pineapple, undrained
1 tablespoon shredded orange rind
¼ cup soy sauce
½ cup water
¼ cup minced onion
⅓ cup cider vinegar
2 tablespoons Worcestershire sauce
4 dashes Tabasco sauce

Place the spareribs in a shallow roasting pan, meat side up. Bake, covered with foil, at 375° for 1 hour. Drain off the fat.

Combine the sugar, celery salt, ginger, and cornstarch in a saucepan. Stir in the remaining ingredients and cook over low heat, stirring constantly until thick. Brush the meat generously with this sauce, then turn the meat and pour the remaining sauce over it. Bake, covered with foil, at 325° for 30 minutes. Uncover and bake until brown and tender.

Four servings

SPARERIBS WITH GINGERSNAP CRUMBS

4 pounds spareribs, cut in serving-size pieces
½ cup sliced scallions, including tops
½ cup diced celery

2   **tablespoons butter or margarine**
3   **cups cooked rice**
⅔   **cup diced dried apricots**
½   **cup gingersnap crumbs**
¼   **cup lemon juice**
½   **cup honey**
½   **teaspoon ground allspice**
½   **teaspoon salt**
⅛   **teaspoon pepper**

Parboil the spareribs for 1 hour, or until tender. Drain, reserving ½ cup of the broth. Cook the scallions and celery in butter until soft but not brown. Add the rice, apricots, pepper, and reserved broth. Turn into a baking pan. Place the ribs, meat side up, on the rice mixture. Mix the gingersnap crumbs, lemon juice, honey, allspice, and salt in a saucepan. Boil until thick, then brush on the meat. Bake, uncovered, at 350° for 30 minutes, brushing with the honey mixture every 10 minutes. Serve with the remaining sauce.

Four servings

SPARERIBS WITH ALMOND STUFFING

4   **pounds spareribs, cut in 3-rib pieces**
¼   **cup chopped onion**
1   **tablespoon shortening**
¼   **cup slivered almonds, toasted**
1   **can (8 ounces) crushed pineapple**
2   **cups soft bread crumbs**
½   **cup seedless raisins**
¼   **teaspoon ground ginger**
½   **teaspoon ground cinnamon**
¼   **teaspoon grated nutmeg**
2½ **teaspoons salt**
⅛   **teaspoon pepper**

Season the ribs with the pepper and 2 teaspoons of the salt. Place half the pieces, rib ends up, on a rack in a roasting pan. Brown the onion lightly in the shortening. Add all the other ingredients, mixing lightly. Place 2 tablespoons of this stuffing on each piece of meat in the roasting pan. Cover with the remaining sections, rib ends down, and bake, covered, at 350° for 1 hour. Uncover and bake for 45 minutes longer.

Four servings

OVEN-BARBECUED SPARERIBS

6   pounds spareribs, cut in 3-rib pieces
½   cup chopped onion
1   clove garlic, crushed
¼   cup cooking oil
2   cups tomato purée
8   tablespoons light brown sugar
¼   cup lemon juice
¼   cup vinegar
4   teaspoons Tabasco sauce
1½ teaspoons dry mustard
6   bay leaves
⅓   cup all-purpose flour
1½ teaspoons salt

Arrange the spareribs in one layer in a roasting pan and bake at 325° for 1 hour, turning occasionally, until they are lightly browned. Drain most of the fat from the ribs.

In a skillet, sauté the onion and garlic in oil until the onion is soft. Stir in the tomato purée, 5 tablespoons of the sugar, the lemon juice, vinegar, Tabasco, mustard, salt, and bay leaves. Bring this mixture to a boil and baste the spareribs with half of it. Bake the ribs for 1 hour longer, basting with the remaining sauce and turning the ribs occasionally.

In a bowl, blend the flour and remaining 3 tablespoons brown sugar. Sprinkle the spareribs with the mixture and bake them until they are browned.

Six servings

SWEET-SOUR SPARERIBS

2   pounds spareribs, cut in 2-rib pieces
2   slices bacon
1   large onion, sliced

1 can (8 ounces) pineapple chunks, drained, juice reserved
2 medium green peppers, chopped
½ cup brown sugar
¼ cup vinegar
2 tablespoons soy sauce
2 tablespoons cornstarch
2 tablespoons water

Fry the bacon, then remove from the pan and chop into small pieces. Brown the spareribs and onion in the bacon drippings. Pour off the fat, add the reserved pineapple juice, and simmer for 1 hour 40 minutes. Add the green pepper, pineapple, brown sugar, vinegar, bacon, and soy sauce. Blend the cornstarch and water and stir into the meat mixture, then simmer, covered, until the sauce is thick, about 20 minutes.

Four servings

TEXAS SPARERIBS

5 pounds country-style spareribs
½ cup lemon juice
1 small onion, grated
1 cup chili sauce
1 cup chopped celery
1 cup water
½ clove garlic, minced
⅓ cup granulated sugar
1 tablespoon Worcestershire sauce
1 tablespoon chili powder
1 dash Tabasco sauce
2 teaspoons salt

Place the ribs, meat side up, on a rack in a shallow baking pan. Mix 2 tablespoons of the lemon juice, the grated onion, and 1 teaspoon of the salt. Spread this evenly over the meat and bake, covered with foil, at 350° for 1 hour.

Meanwhile, combine the remaining ingredients and simmer, covered, for about 15 minutes. Remove the baking pan from the oven and drain off the drippings. Brush the ribs with the sauce and return to the oven. Bake, uncovered, at 350°, for 1 hour longer, or until tender. During the last 20 minutes baste frequently with the sauce.

Five servings

SPARERIBS FOR A PICNIC

4 or 5 pounds spareribs, cut into 1-rib pieces
- **1 cup soy sauce**
- **2 tablespoons honey**
- **½ cup sherry**
- **1 clove garlic, chopped**

The night before the picnic, put all the ingredients except the meat in a shallow, nonmetallic pan. Mix thoroughly. Marinate the ribs in this for at least 2 hours, turning once. Drain the ribs and reserve the marinade.

In the morning, bake the spareribs at 350° for 50 minutes, basting frequently with the marinade and turning them once. At the end of 50 minutes brush the ribs with a little honey and glaze them under the broiler for 10 minutes, being careful not to let them burn. Immediately wrap them in foil and put into a thermal container. Take along some hot mustard to serve with them. If the ribs are used as an appetizer, this quantity will serve six.

Six servings

Steaks

Steaks are one of the most advantageous pork cuts. There are blade steaks from the Boston shoulder, arm steaks from the picnic shoulder. Slices cut from the center of the whole leg, fresh or smoked, are also often called steaks. All of these cuts provide a convenient piece of tender meat. Their thickness may be adjusted to the buyer's need. They are an economical cut, usually having only one small bone, and they do not present a carving problem. In many recipes steaks are interchangeable with chops. It is easy to calculate, by looking at a steak, the number of servings it will provide.

STEAKS NIÇOISE

4   pork shoulder steaks
½   teaspoon garlic powder
1   tablespoon vegetable oil
½   cup canned tomato sauce
¼   cup dry sherry or dry white wine
¼   teaspoon dried basil or oregano
1   green pepper, cut in lengthwise strips
½   cup pitted ripe olives, cut in halves
1   teaspoon salt

Trim the steaks and rub with the salt and garlic powder. Heat the oil in a heavy skillet and brown the meat. Drain off the excess fat, then add the tomato sauce, sherry, and basil to the skillet. Place the pepper strips on the meat and simmer, covered, over low heat for 25 minutes. Add the olives and simmer 35 minutes longer, or until meat is tender. This dish is usually served with rice or macaroni shells.

Four servings

STEAKS WITH APRICOT AND SHERRY SAUCE

4   medium pork steaks
3   tablespoons sherry or port
6   tablespoons granulated sugar
1   tablespoon ground cinnamon
6   tablespoons soy sauce
1½   cups mashed fresh or canned apricots
2   tablespoons lime juice
½   teaspoon dry mustard

Place the meat in a baking dish. Combine the sherry, sugar, cinnamon, and soy sauce and pour over the meat. Bake, covered, at 325° for 30 minutes, then turn the steaks and bake for 30 minutes longer.

Meanwhile, blend the apricots, lime juice, and mustard. When ready to serve, place this mixture in the bottom of a serving dish and place the steaks on top.

Four servings

STEAKS WITH CAPERS

4   pork shoulder steaks
¼   cup all-purpose flour
2   tablespoons butter or margarine
¼   cup water
2   teaspoons cornstarch
2   tablespoons capers, drained
1   teaspoon salt
¼   teaspoon pepper

Trim any fat off the steaks. Dredge with the flour and brown in the butter over medium heat. Sprinkle with salt and pepper. Add the water and simmer, covered, over low heat for 40 minutes or until the meat is tender. Blend the cornstarch and water and add to the pan juice, stirring until thick and smooth. Add the capers and cook, for 5 minutes longer.

Four servings

STEAKS NEW BRUNSWICK

6 pork steaks, ½ inch thick
6 slices bacon
¼ cup finely chopped green pepper
½ cup finely chopped onion
1 can (16 ounces) stewed tomatoes
1 can (16 ounces) cream-style corn
1 cup water
½ package (4 ounces) fine noodles
½ teaspoon salt
⅛ teaspoon pepper

Dice the bacon and fry it until crisp, then remove from the pan. Brown the steaks in the bacon fat. Remove. Cook the green pepper and onion in the fat, over low heat, for 3 to 4 minutes. Add all the other ingredients, including the noodles and the bacon. Place the steaks on top, and simmer, covered, over low heat for 45 minutes, or until the steaks are tender.

Six servings

STEAKS BASQUE

4 pork steaks, 1 inch thick
1 tablespoon olive oil
1 clove garlic, minced
1 red onion, sliced
1 green pepper, sliced in rings
1 teaspoon basil
½ cup tomato juice
1 teaspoon salt

Heat the olive oil and garlic in a heavy skillet. Add the steaks and brown over high heat. Line a shallow baking pan with heavy foil, allowing enough extra to cover the steaks completely. Scatter half the onion slices, half the pepper rings, and half the basil in the pan. Place the steaks on top, sprinkle with salt, and cover with the remaining onions, green pepper, and basil. Add the tomato juice, fold the foil over the steaks, and seal tightly. Bake at 350° for 1½ hours.

Four servings

STEAKS MEXICAN STYLE

4   pork steaks, ¾ inch thick
½   cup chopped onion
¼   cup chopped green pepper
3   tablespoons vegetable oil
    All-purpose flour
1   can (8 ounces) tomato sauce
½   cup beef bouillon or chicken stock
½   cup chopped ripe olives
¼   cup seedless raisins
1   clove garlic, minced
1½   teaspoons chili powder
    Salt
    Freshly ground pepper

Sauté the onion and green pepper in the vegetable oil until the onion is golden brown. Remove from the skillet. Trim the steaks, sprinkle with salt and pepper, and dredge with flour. Brown lightly on both sides in the oil remaining in the skillet, then return the vegetables to the skillet. Mix the remaining ingredients and add them to the skillet. Simmer, covered, for 45 minutes or until the meat is tender. Serve with hot rice.

Four servings

STEAKS WITH FIGS

6   pork steaks
1   tart apple, cored and sliced
6   dried figs, sliced
2   tablespoons brown sugar
½   teaspoon ground cinnamon
1   tablespoon apple-mint jelly
    Salt
    Freshly ground pepper

Place the steaks in a large, shallow baking dish, and season with salt and pepper. Top with a layer each of apple slices and figs, sprinkle with sugar and cinnamon, and dot each steak with jelly. Bake, covered, at 350° for 40 minutes. Uncover and bake for 20 minutes longer.

Six servings

Tenderloin

Tenderloin, whole or in patties, ranks high among the elegant pork cuts. It will grace any dinner party. This cut is a long, tapering, boneless piece of meat from the underside of the loin. It is about 12 inches long and weighs from ¾ pound to 1 pound. Usually it is sold with the loin roast or with loin chops and for this reason is not readily available in the markets. In flavor and texture it is equal to a crown roast. It amply rewards the cook who treats it with due consideration and it lends itself to special garnishing. Serving it is easy, a delight to the host, who is spared any carving problems.

TENDERLOIN PATTIES WITH VERMOUTH

10   pork tenderloin patties
 3   tablespoons butter or margarine
 ½   cup sweet vermouth
1½   cans (10½ ounce size) cream of chicken soup
     Salt
     Freshly ground pepper

Brown the patties in the butter, then season with salt and pepper and place in a casserole. Add the vermouth to the chicken soup, stirring until smooth. Pour over the patties and bake, covered, at 350° for 30 to 45 minutes.

BAKED TENDERLOIN PATTIES

4   pork tenderloin patties
2   tablespoons bacon fat
1   cup fresh bread crumbs

245

1   tablespoon water
2   tablespoons melted butter or margarine
2   tablespoons all-purpose flour
1   cup milk
1   teaspoon minced dried onion
2   teaspoons salt
¼   teaspoon pepper

Brown the patties in the bacon fat in a skillet, then remove to a baking dish. Set the skillet aside, reserving the fat for the gravy. Bake the patties, covered, at 325° for 30 minutes. Season the bread crumbs with salt and pepper and moisten with the water and melted butter. Cover the meat with this bread mixture and bake, uncovered, for another 30 minutes.

Mix the flour with the bacon fat in the skillet. Cook for 2 minutes, blend in the milk and onion. Cook, stirring, until the gravy is thick and smooth. Spoon it over the patties before serving.

TENDERLOIN PATTIES WITH MUSHROOMS AND CIDER

4   thick pork tenderloin patties
2   tablespoons shortening
1   medium onion, chopped
½   cup chopped fresh mushrooms
2   tablespoons all-purpose flour
2   tablespoons water
4   tablespoons cider
    Salt
    Freshly ground pepper

Brown the patties, in the shortening, in a heavy skillet, then remove to a baking dish. Sauté the onion and mushrooms in the skillet. Remove to the baking dish. Sprinkle with salt and pepper. In a saucepan, combine the flour and water and mix until smooth. Add the cider and heat. Pour this over the patties and bake, covered, at 350° for 45 minutes, or until the patties are tender.

ENGLISH TENDERLOIN PATTIES

4   **thick pork tenderloin patties**
1   **cup pitted prunes**
1   **cup, plus 2 tablespoons, dry white wine**
⅓   **cup red currant jelly, melted**
3   **tablespoons butter or margarine**
3   **tablespoons heavy cream**
  Salt
  Freshly ground pepper

In a saucepan, soak the prunes in the 1 cup of wine for 15 minutes. Bring to a boil, add the currant jelly and simmer for 3 to 5 minutes, or until the prunes are tender. Set aside.

Sprinkle the meat with salt and pepper. Brown on all sides, in the butter, in a skillet just large enough to hold them. Place in a shallow heat-resistant dish and keep warm. Stir the 2 tablespoons wine into the skillet juices and bring to a boil, stirring constantly. Pour it over the meat. Cover with foil and bake at 350° for 45 minutes, or until tender. Place in a serving dish and keep hot.

Add the prune and wine mixture to the skillet and bring to a boil. Stir in the cream, and when thoroughly heated, pour this sauce over the meat and serve.

TENDERLOIN BAKED WITH STUFFING

2   **pork tenderloins, ¾ to 1 pound each**
4   **cups packaged bread stuffing**
½   **cup melted butter**
1   **cup water**
1   **small onion, grated**
½   **teaspoon basil**
½   **teaspoon savory**
½   **package (3 ounces) pine nuts (pignolias)**
4   **slices bacon**
1   **teaspoon salt**

Cut each tenderloin in half lengthwise. Slightly flatten the pieces with a wooden mallet. Combine all other ingredients except the bacon. Place 2 tenderloin halves in a baking pan. Cover them with the stuffing mix, then place the remaining tenderloin halves on top and tie them together with string. Top with bacon strips and bake, covered, at 325° for 30 minutes. Uncover, baste with drippings, and bake another 30 minutes, or until tender.

Six to eight servings

TENDERLOIN PATTIES WITH CRANBERRIES AND PINEAPPLE

6	pork tenderloin patties
¼	cup all-purpose flour
2	tablespoons shortening
¼	cup brown sugar
1½	teaspoons cornstarch
½	teaspoon ground ginger
¼	teaspoon ground cinnamon
1	can (8 ounces) crushed pineapple
1	can (8 ounces) cranberry sauce
1	teaspoon salt
⅛	teaspoon pepper

Dredge the patties with the flour, salt and pepper. Brown in the shortening, then remove to a baking dish. Combine the brown sugar and cornstarch in a saucepan. Add the ginger, cinnamon, and pineapple, and combine with the cranberries. Bring to a boil, stirring constantly until the mixture thickens. Pour the sauce over the patties, and bake, tightly covered, at 350° for 45 minutes, or until the meat is tender.

TENDERLOIN EN BROCHETTE

1½	pounds pork tenderloin, cut in 1-inch cubes
8	mushroom caps
4	slices bacon, each cut into 4 pieces
4	tablespoons butter
6	tablespoons fine, dry bread crumbs

Raisin Rice:

1   tablespoon butter or margarine
1   cup raw long-grain rice
2½ cups chicken stock or broth
½   cup seedless raisins

Sour Cream Sauce:

2   shallots, chopped
4   tablespoons butter or margarine
2   tablespoons all-purpose flour
½   cup white wine
2   cups chicken stock or bouillon
2   tablespoons sour cream
1   teaspoon lemon juice

Arrange all the ingredients on four skewers. Start each one with a mushroom cap, then alternate bacon and tenderloin, using four of each on each skewer. End with a mushroom cap.

Melt the butter. Sprinkle over the filled skewers, and roll each one in bread crumbs. Place on a broiler pan, and cook and turn under moderate heat until browned on all sides (15 to 20 minutes). Serve with raisin rice and sour cream sauce, made as described below.

For the rice, melt the butter in a saucepan. Add the rice and cook 3 to 4 minutes, stirring constantly. Bring the stock to a boil and add to the rice. Cook, covered, without stirring, until the rice is tender and the liquid is absorbed (about 20 minutes). Remove from the heat, and allow to stand for 5 minutes. Meanwhile cover the raisins with boiling water and let stand until plump. Drain and stir into the rice.

To make the sour cream sauce, sauté the shallots in butter for about 5 minutes. Blend in the flour, then add the wine and stock, stirring constantly. Cook over low heat until thick and smooth. Add the sour cream and lemon juice, and blend thoroughly, but do not allow the sauce to boil. Serve the sauce separately.

Four to six servings

GARNISHED TENDERLOIN

```
 3   pork tenderloins, cut into serving pieces
 ¼   cup plus 2 tablespoons all-purpose flour
 ½   teaspoon paprika
 4   tablespoons butter or margarine
 ½   pound sliced, lean bacon, cut in 1-inch pieces
 4   medium onions, sliced
1½   pounds fresh mushrooms, sliced
 1   can (16 ounces) peas
 ¼   cup cream
 ¾   cup milk
 2   tablespoons water
 1   teaspoon salt
 ¼   teaspoon pepper
```

Combine the ¼ cup flour, salt, pepper, and paprika, and dredge the meat with this mixture. Melt 2 tablespoons of the butter in a skillet and brown the tenderloins on all sides. Place them in the bottom of a large casserole and set aside.

Fry the bacon until crisp. Drain and set aside. In the bacon fat, sauté the onions until transparent. Place the onions on top of the tenderloins and top them with the bacon. Sauté the mushrooms in the remaining butter. Lift them out with a slotted spoon and add them to the casserole. Drain the peas, reserving the liquid, and add them to the casserole.

Add the cream to the butter remaining in the skillet. Stir in the liquid from the peas, then add the milk and heat. Make a thin paste of the 2 tablespoons flour and the water. Add to the sauce, continuing to cook and stir until thick and smooth. Add salt and pepper to taste and pour over the ingredients in the casserole. Bake, covered, at 350° for 30 to 40 minutes.

TENDERLOIN PATTIES IN CREAMY SAUCE

6   pork tenderloin patties
1   egg, lightly beaten
1   tablespoon cold water
    Salted crackers to yield ¾ cup fine crumbs
5   tablespoons butter or margarine
½   pound fresh mushrooms, sliced
1   can (10½ ounces) cream of chicken soup
1   cup sour cream
¼   cup dry sherry
1   teaspoon salt
¼   teaspoon pepper

Mix the egg and water. Then mix the cracker crumbs with the salt and
pepper. Dip the patties in the egg mixture, then dip them in the cracker
crumbs. Melt 3 tablespoons of the butter in a heavy skillet and brown the
patties on both sides. Place them in a casserole. Sauté the mushrooms in
the remaining butter, add the soup, sour cream, and sherry and blend
thoroughly. Pour over the meat and bake, covered, at 350° for 45
minutes.

TENDERLOIN PATTIES WITH SOUR CREAM AND HORSERADISH

8   pork tenderloin patties
2   tablespoons all-purpose flour
½   teaspoon chili powder
2   tablespoons shortening or drippings
½   cup water
2   teaspoons prepared horseradish
¼   cup chopped onion
½   cup sour cream
1½   teaspoons salt
⅛   teaspoon pepper

Combine the flour and seasonings. Dredge the patties in this mixture and
brown them in the shortening. Pour off the drippings and add the water,

horseradish, and onion. Simmer, covered, for 45 minutes, then remove to a hot platter. Stir the sour cream into the pan. Heat through and pour over the patties.

TENDERLOIN WITH POTATOES

1	pound pork tenderloin, sliced ½ inch thick
3	medium potatoes, peeled and sliced thin
1¼	cups milk
1½	cups bread crumbs
¼	teaspoon sage
2	teaspoons melted butter
2	tablespoons minced onion
2	tablespoons butter
½	teaspoon salt
⅛	teaspoon pepper

Place the potatoes in a well-greased 2-quart casserole. Add 1 cup of the milk and sprinkle with salt and pepper. Combine the remaining milk, the bread crumbs, sage, melted butter, and onion. Spread this mixture over the potatoes.

Pound the tenderloin slices flat. Put on top of the dressing mixture, dot with the 2 tablespoons butter, and bake, covered, at 350° for 1 hour, or until both meat and potatoes are tender.

Four servings

TENDERLOIN PATTIES IN WINE SAUCE

8	large tenderloin patties
4	tablespoons butter or margarine, more if necessary
1	can (10½ ounces) cream of chicken soup
¾	cup white wine
1	teaspoon rosemary, crushed
1	heaping tablespoon dried powdered mushrooms
½	pound fresh mushrooms, sliced
1	cup sour cream
1	teaspoon coarse black pepper
1	teaspoon onion salt

Brown the patties in the butter. Place in a buttered casserole and season with the onion salt and pepper. Blend the chicken soup with the wine until smooth. Add the rosemary and powdered mushrooms, then pour over the patties and bake, covered, at 325° for 1 hour.

Sauté the sliced fresh mushrooms in the meat pan, adding more butter if necessary. Add the sour cream to the mushrooms and blend into the casserole mixture. Bake, uncovered, for 15 minutes longer.

Eight servings

SLICED TENDERLOIN WITH WINE AND MUSHROOMS

1½ pounds pork tenderloin, sliced ½ inch thick
4   tablespoons butter
1   medium onion, chopped fine
½   cup dry white wine or dry vermouth
    Juice of ½ lemon
½   pound fresh mushrooms, sliced
3   tablespoons all-purpose flour
1   can (10½ ounces) beef consommé
½   teaspoon garlic salt
¼   teaspoon thyme
¾   cup water
1   teaspoon salt
¼   teaspoon pepper

Brown the meat, in 2 tablespoons of the butter, in a heavy skillet. Add the onion, salt, and pepper, and cook for 5 minutes over low heat. Add the wine and lemon juice and simmer, covered, for 30 minutes.

Sauté the mushrooms in the remaining butter and set aside. Add the flour to the skillet, and stir to blend. Add enough consommé to make a smooth paste, then add the garlic salt and thyme. Pour in the remaining consommé and the water. Simmer until thick and smooth. Pour over the meat. Place in a serving dish and top with the mushrooms.

Six servings

TENDERLOIN CASSEROLE

12 slices pork tenderloin
 4 tablespoons butter
 1 mild onion, finely chopped
 1 cup sour cream
 ½ cup white wine
    Salt
    Freshly ground pepper

Brown the meat, in the butter, in a heavy skillet. Season with salt and pepper, then place in a casserole. Sauté the onion in the same skillet. Add the sour cream and blend in the wine. Pour over the meat. Sprinkle generously with paprika. Bake, uncovered, at 350° for approximately 50 minutes.

TENDERLOIN IN PASTRY

 2 whole pork tenderloins, ¾ to 1 pound each
 ½ teaspoon dry mustard
 ½ teaspoon thyme
 2 tablespoons butter or margarine
 1 teaspoon salt
 ¼ teaspoon pepper

The pastry:

 2 cups sifted all-purpose flour
 ⅔ cup butter or margarine
 1 egg, beaten
7 to 9 tablespoons cold water
 ¼ teaspoon salt

Combine the mustard, thyme, salt, and pepper on waxed paper. Roll the tenderloins in this seasoning, then brown them in the butter, turning frequently, for about 20 minutes. Add more butter if needed. Drain on absorbent paper.

To make the pastry, sift the flour and salt into a mixing bowl. Cut in the butter until the pieces are the size of small peas. Sprinkle with the cold water, a little at a time, mixing lightly until the dough begins to stick together. Turn out and press together on a lightly floured board or pastry cloth, then roll out into a 14 × 9-inch rectangle. Blend the egg with 1 tablespoon water and brush it on the pastry.

Cut the pastry in half crosswise and roll a tenderloin in each half. Seal the edges and ends, then place, seam side down, in a greased 13 × 9-inch baking dish. Brush with the remaining egg mixture, and bake, uncovered, at 425° for 20 to 25 minutes, or until golden brown.

Six to eight servings

TENDERLOIN WITH SOUR CREAM AND APPLES

4 pork tenderloin patties
1 tablespoon butter or margarine
2 cooking apples
4 tablespoons brown sugar
1 cup sour cream
½ teaspoon salt

Brown the patties in the butter. Salt them and place in a baking dish. Peel and core the apples, then cut them into 1-inch-thick rings. Place a ring on each patty. Fill the center of the apple slice with 1 tablespoon of the brown sugar. Heat the sour cream, and pour it over the patties, and bake, covered, at 350° for 45 minutes.

TENDERLOIN MARINATED IN SPICED SHERRY

1¾ pounds pork tenderloin
⅓ cup sherry
⅓ cup soy sauce
⅓ cup anisette
⅛ teaspoon ground cinnamon
⅛ teaspoon ground cloves
1 teaspoon cornstarch
2 teaspoons water

Mix the sherry, soy sauce, anisette, cinnamon, and cloves. Pour over the tenderloin and marinate for at least 2 hours. Drain, reserving the marinade, and remove to a baking pan. Bake, uncovered, at 325° for 1 hour, or until tender, basting frequently with the marinade. Remove the meat to a warm serving dish.

Moisten the cornstarch with the water, add to the pan juices, and simmer until thick, stirring constantly. Serve with the meat.

Six or seven servings

TENDERLOIN IN ORANGE SAUCE

2   whole tenderloins
2   tablespoons butter or margarine
¾   cup finely chopped onion
½   cup white wine
2   oranges
3   tablespoons granulated sugar
1   bay leaf
1   tablespoon chopped fresh parsley
1½   teaspoons arrowroot
1   tablespoon water
2   cups hot, cooked rice
2   teaspoons salt
¼   teaspoon freshly ground pepper

Sauté the tenderloins in the butter until golden brown, then remove from the skillet. Add the onion, salt, and pepper to the skillet, and cook until the onion is tender. Return the meat to the skillet. Add the wine, juice of 1 orange, sugar, bay leaf, and parsley. Simmer, covered, until the meat is tender, about 45 minutes. Remove the meat from the pan and keep warm.

Peel and section the remaining orange. Cut the orange peel in thin strips and boil in a little water until tender, then drain and set aside. Mix the arrowroot with the water and add to the wine and orange broth in the skillet. Stir until thickened.

Cut the tenderloin in thick slices. Place on top of the rice, pour the sauce over, and garnish with the orange sections and cooked peel.

TENDERLOIN PATTIES WITH APPLE BUTTER

 6 **pork tenderloin patties**
12 **slices bacon**
    Apple butter
 6 **thick cored, unpeeled apple rings**
    Salt

Cross 2 slices of bacon to make an X. Place a patty in the middle, season with salt, and spread with 2 teaspoons of apple butter. Place an apple ring on top. Bring the ends of the bacon slices together over the top of the apple and fasten with a wooden pick. Repeat for each patty, then place them in a shallow baking dish. Bake, uncovered, at 325° for 1 hour. During the last 5 minutes of baking, spoon more apple butter over each patty.

MARINATED TENDERLOIN SLICES

 2 **pounds pork tenderloin, cut in ½-inch slices**
⅔ **cup orange marmalade**
½ **cup soy sauce**
 1 **clove garlic, minced**
½ **teaspoon ground ginger**

Combine the marmalade, soy sauce, garlic, and ginger. Pour over the meat and marinate, covered, in the refrigerator overnight.

The next day, drain the meat and reserve ½ cup of marinade. Place the meat slices in a single layer in a baking dish. Pour the reserved marinade over the meat, and bake, uncovered, at 350° for 15 minutes. Turn the meat and bake 30 minutes longer.

Eight servings

Variety Meats

ALL THE PIG BUT THE SQUEAL

"Variety meats" is a term used in many areas of the United States to include the liver, heart, feet, hocks, brains, tongue, and chitterlings, and even the ears and tails of pigs. These parts of the hog, when referred to collectively, were once given more specific but less appetizing designations. However, even unappetizing names have never distracted a bargain-conscious shopper from appreciation of their nutritive value per dollar of price. Nearly all of them are boneless, fat free, and harbor no waste. They are all perishable and should be used soon after purchase.

They form the basis of most "soul food" recipes, having been less expensive and long associated with simple, although soul-satisfying southern cooking. A few may be available only in some parts of the country, but the appreciation of this style of cookery is now widespread.

HOCKS IN MUSTARD SAUCE

4   pork hocks
2   bay leaves
6   peppercorns
4   medium new potatoes, peeled
4   small onions
¾   cup sour cream
1   tablespoon Dijon mustard
½   tablespoon paprika
2   teaspoons all-purpose flour
½   teaspoon thyme
1   teaspoon salt

Place the hocks in a kettle with the salt and enough water to cover. Add the bay leaves and peppercorns, which have been tied together in a small piece of cheesecloth, and bring to a boil, skimming off any froth that forms. Reduce the heat and simmer for 1½ to 2 hours, or until the hocks are barely tender. Add the potatoes and onions, and cook until these are tender.

Remove the cheesecloth bag and open it. Discard the bay leaves. Crush the peppercorns and put them in a saucepan with the sour cream, ⅓ cup of the cooking liquid, the mustard, paprika, flour, and thyme. Simmer the mixture until it is thick and smooth. Place the hocks and vegetables in a warm serving dish and pour the sauce over them.

Four servings

HOCKS AND SAUERKRAUT

4   **pork hocks**
1   **quart sauerkraut**
1   **onion, sliced thin**
3   **cloves**
4   **peppercorns**
1   **teaspoon salt**
1   **pint beer (optional)**

Place the hocks in a large kettle, cover with cold water, and bring to a boil, then turn down the heat and simmer for 1½ hours. While the meat simmers, skim as needed, and replace water that has boiled off with additional hot water, cup by cup. Add the sauerkraut, onion, and seasonings, and continue to simmer for another hour, or until the hocks are fork-tender.

If you wish, you can cook the sauerkraut, onion, and seasonings separately in a pint of beer. They should cook about as long as the hocks.

Four servings

SMOKED HOCKS AND SUPER SAUERKRAUT

4   **smoked pork hocks**
    Super Sauerkraut (see page 177)

Simmer the hocks in water to cover for 1 hour. Pour off the water and cover again with fresh water, then simmer for 1 hour longer, or until tender. Remove the skin, bones, and fat. Place the lean meat on top of the Super Sauerkraut. Reheat and serve.

Four or five servings

PIG'S KNUCKLES AND CABBAGE

8   pig's knuckles, well scrubbed
4   peppercorns
4   medium potatoes, peeled
4   small carrots
1   onion, sliced thin
1   small head cabbage, quartered and core removed
1   teaspoon salt

Simmer the knuckles and seasonings in a large kettle of water for 2½ hours, skimming as necessary and replacing water that boils off. Add the potatoes, carrots, and onion, and simmer for 30 minutes. Add the cabbage and simmer for about 30 minutes longer, or until all the vegetables are tender.

Four servings

CHITTERLINGS

5 to 10 pounds chitterlings
1   large onion
1   stalk celery
1   teaspoon marjoram
1   tablespoon salt

If the chitterlings have been very thoroughly washed they need not be soaked. If there is any doubt, soak them overnight in salted water, then rinse.

Place the onion, peeled, in the bottom of a large kettle. Add the chitterlings, celery, salt, marjoram, and water to cover. Bring to a boil, then reduce the heat and simmer for 2 to 4 hours, or until the chitterlings can easily be cut with a fork. Drain. Season to taste and serve.

The traditional accompaniments are mustard or collard greens. Nowadays potato salad is frequently used. Some cooks put the drained chitterlings in a lightly greased frying pan for a few minutes to dry them. If left more than a very short time, however, they will become tough.

Two to six servings

PRESSURE-COOKED CHITTERLINGS

5 pounds chitterlings
2 tablespoons vinegar
2 cups water
1 tablespoon salt

Put the chitterlings, salt, vinegar, and water in the cooker. Cook at 15 pounds pressure for 25 minutes, then remove from the heat. When the pressure has gone down to zero, remove the chitterlings and drain them. Serve at once.

Two or three servings

CRACKLIN' BREAD

1 cup pork cracklings, cut into small dice
¾ cup corn meal
1 cup all-purpose flour
1 tablespoon baking powder
¼ cup granulated sugar
1 cup milk
1 egg, well beaten
2 tablespoons melted bacon drippings

Sift the dry ingredients together into a mixing bowl. Add the milk, egg, and drippings, and stir until well mixed and smooth. Fold in the cracklings. Bake in a shallow pan, 8 × 8 inches, at 425° for 20 minutes.

Six servings

PORK CHEESE

1   **pound lean pork**
1   **pound fat pork**
1½ **cups chopped scallions**
1   **tablespoon minced fresh parsley**
1   **cup aspic**
2   **teaspoons salt**
½   **teaspoon white pepper**

Chop the meat coarsely. Add the salt, pepper, scallions, and parsley, and mix well. Press into a loaf pan. Bake it in a moderate (350°) oven for 1 hour, then cool. Remove the loaf from the pan, and chill. Coat with the aspic, and slice to serve.

BRAWN

½   **pig's head**
     Few peppercorns
1   **stewing chicken**
1   **large onion**
1   **sprig fresh parsley**
     Salt
     Pepper

Cover the pig's head with salt. Leave it for 3 days in a cool place, then scrub off the salt and soak the head in fresh water for 2 hours. Put it in a large pan with peppercorns and simmer until tender. Cool. Discard the bones and pieces of skin, then skin the tongue, and coarsely chop the meat.

Cut up the chicken. Put in a large saucepan and add the giblets and just enough water to cover. Add the onion, salt to taste, pepper, and parsley and simmer, covered, until tender. Cool. Remove bones and skin and slice the chicken. Reserve the white meat for the bottom and sides of the mold.

Pack two or three large molds with meat, using alternate layers of pork and chicken. Combine the juice from the pig's head and the chicken and

boil rapidly to reduce the liquid. Season the liquid to taste. Pour the
liquid into the molds and refrigerate until firm. If correctly arranged, the
outer surface of the molds will show alternate layers of pink and white
meat when unmolded.

HEAD CHEESE

1 **pig's head**
2 **pig's feet**
   Coarse salt
2 **pounds onions, peeled**
2 **tablespoons sage**
   Salt
   Freshly ground pepper to taste

You will need a large kettle for this head cheese. Have the pig's head
split into halves and cleaned. Rub the pieces of the head and feet with
coarse salt, then pack closely in a large pan, and sprinkle with more salt.
Leave for 2 days in a cool place.

Wash the head and feet pieces with cold water and place in a kettle.
Cover with water, then bring to a boil. Skim well, and simmer gently for
about 3 hours, or until the meat is tender. Remove the pork, cool slightly
until it can be handled, and remove all the meat from the bones. Chop
the meat and the onions, season with the sage, and add salt and pepper
to taste.

Remove as much fat as possible from the liquid; add the chopped
meat and onions. Simmer for 20 minutes, stirring occasionally, then pour
into molds and chill. Head cheese is usually eaten cold as a sandwich
meat or with a "cold plate."

SOUSE

2 **pig's feet**
1 **pig's tongue**
   Vinegar (optional)
   Salt
   Pepper

Thoroughly scrub and rinse the feet and tongue. Put them in a kettle with water to cover and boil until the meat falls off the bones. Discard the bones, gristle, and skin. Cut the meat very fine and divide into custard cups or put in a small loaf pan.

Bring the broth to a boil. Season to taste with salt and pepper. (A very small amount of vinegar may be added if a sour souse is desired.) Strain the broth and pour it over the meat and stir. Cool until well set. To serve, unmold and slice.

STUFFED PIG'S STOMACH

1   pound fresh sausage
1   pig's stomach
8   large potatoes, peeled and cut into ½-inch cubes
¼   cup water
1   tablespoon salt

Combine the potatoes with the sausage and salt. Stuff into the pig's stomach and sew up the opening. Place in a roasting pan with the water, cover, and bake at 300° for 3 hours. Uncover for the last 30 minutes.

Eight to ten servings

PIG'S FEET WITH CABBAGE

4   pig's feet
1   medium onion, sliced
1   garlic clove, minced
½   lemon, sliced
1   bay leaf
1   small cabbage, coarsely shredded
1   teaspoon salt

Cover the pig's feet with water and add the salt. Bring to a boil over high heat, then reduce the heat and simmer, covered, for 3 hours, adding more boiling water if needed to keep the feet covered. Add all the remaining ingredients except the cabbage and simmer for 45 minutes longer. Add the cabbage and continue to simmer until the cabbage is tender.

Four servings

SPICY TROTTERS

3   pig's trotters
1   cup cooked prunes
1   cup cooked dried apricots
1   small onion, chopped
1   cup meat stock or broth
1   teaspoon brown sugar
3   tablespoons vinegar
¼   teaspoon ground cinnamon
¼   teaspoon ground cloves
½   teaspoon ground allspice
1   teaspoon salt

Remove the pits from the prunes. Cut the prunes and apricots into small pieces. Put the trotters, fruit, and onion in a kettle, add the stock, and simmer, covered, until the meat is tender. Remove the trotters, and allow to cool slightly, then separate the meat from the bone.

Mix the sugar, vinegar, cinnamon, cloves, allspice, and salt. Combine this mixture with the meat, drained fruit, and onion and place in a casserole. Bake, covered, at 350° for 30 minutes.

Two servings

COOKED AND PICKLED PIG'S FEET

6   pig's feet, split
3   cups distilled vinegar
1   large onion, sliced
1   bay leaf
5   whole cloves
10 peppercorns
1   tablespoon salt

Scrub the feet thoroughly and put them in a kettle. Cover them with water, add the vinegar, and heat to the boiling point. Skim, then add the remaining ingredients and simmer for 2 hours, or until fork-tender. Remove from the water, chill, and serve cold.

Six servings

DANISH LIVER PÂTÉ

1   **pound pork liver**
½   **pound bacon**
1   **small onion**
2   **eggs, lightly beaten**
2   **tablespoons all-purpose flour**
1   **teaspoon anchovy paste**
⅛   **teaspoon nutmeg**
     Pinch of ground cloves
1   **cup heavy cream**
1   **teaspoon salt**
½   **teaspoon crushed peppercorns**

Grind the liver, bacon, and onion separately twice, then combine them and put them through a food mill. In a large bowl mix them with the eggs, flour, anchovy paste, nutmeg, cloves, salt, and peppercorns. Stir in the cream, ¼ cup at a time.

Butter five 1-cup molds and fill them with the pâté. Cover the pâtés with foil and put on the lids of the molds. (If they do not have lids, cover with three more layers of foil.) Place them in a baking dish and pour in enough hot water to reach two-thirds of the way up the sides of the molds. Bake at 350° until they test done by inserting a skewer. When nothing is exuded from the pâté and the skewer comes out clean, they are done. If the skewer sticks at all, or any blood comes out, longer cooking is needed.

When the pâté is done, remove the molds from the pan, pour out the water, and return the molds to the pan. Remove the lids or the triple layers of foil, leaving intact the first (single) foil covering. Let the pâtés stand for 15 minutes and then put 1½- to 3-pound weights on each one. When they are cool, chill them thoroughly in the refrigerator. Remove the weights.

MARINATED LIVER, PORTUGUESE STYLE

1   pound pork liver, cut up
3   pounds fresh pork, cut in 2-inch cubes
1   cup white wine
½   cup water
2   cloves garlic, minced
1   teaspoon rosemary
1   teaspoon marjoram
1   teaspoon thyme
2   tablespoons paprika
    All-purpose flour
1   tablespoon salt
1   teaspoon pepper

Place the meat in a shallow glass or enameled dish. Combine all the other ingredients except the flour and pour over the meat. Marinate in the refrigerator for 24 hours. Transfer the marinade and meat to a saucepan and simmer for 1 to 2 hours, or until the meat is tender. Thicken the marinade with flour and serve as a stew.

Eight servings

Whole Hog: Suckling Pig

Now that you have seen the many ways of cooking the various cuts of pork, here is a way to go whole hog—with a suckling pig, the smallest pig that ever goes to market.

Charles Lamb maintained that man discovered the pleasure of eating cooked meat when a pig fell into the fire—undoubtedly the first roasted suckling pig. Whole roast pig is indeed an ancient dish. The Romans roasted a whole hog, stuffing it with thrushes, beccaficos, and other song birds, moistened with wine. The Irish cooked their pig in a caldron and were calculating in their servings to guests: the king was served a whole thigh or shoulder, a lord got a leg, while a philosopher came off with a backbone.

To serve this delicacy now is neither easy nor common. The first direction is the hardest: Get your pig! Suckling pigs are rarely available in the retail market. Sometimes a butcher will be able to order one. A farmer who raises hogs might be persuaded to produce one for a suitable price.

When a suckling pig is procured and served, it rewards the cook with a triumph of flavor and tenderness and enchants the guests with its contribution to a feeling of festivity and celebration. Cooked properly, the piglet's ears and tail retain their jauntiness; its jaws hold the bright red apple.

The instructions here are standard. A suitable-size piglet weighs about 12 pounds and requires about 2½ quarts of stuffing.

If you are among those who feel maybe you haven't lived unless you have experienced the roasting or barbecuing of a whole, full-grown hog, there are only two suggestions we can make for satisfying this urge. One is to join an organization that carries out this ritual feast. The other is to put it on the list of things to do when you visit Hawaii, where a luau is managed with style and verve and a prodigious amount of hard work by dozens of willing hands.

268

SUCKLING PIG

1 **10 to 12 pound suckling pig, cleaned and prepared by the butcher, heart and liver reserved**
2 **medium onions, chopped fine**
½ **cup butter**
8 **cups bread crumbs**
1 **egg, lightly beaten**
1 **tablespoon sage**
1 **tart apple, peeled and grated**
 Stock or beef bouillon
 All-purpose flour
 Small block of wood
1 **bright red apple, unpeeled**
 Salt
 Pepper

Simmer the heart and liver in salted water until tender. Drain and chop fine. Sauté the onion in some of the butter. Add to the heart and liver mixture. Add the bread crumbs, egg, sage, and grated apple, mixing well. Moisten with the stock and salt to taste. Stuff the pig with this mixture; don't overstuff. Sew up the opening. Insert the wood block between the pig's jaws; lower the eyelids and fasten shut. Skewer the legs, forelegs forward, hind legs in crouching position.

Melt the remaining butter and rub the whole pig thoroughly with it. Dredge with flour, salt, and pepper. To prevent burning, cover the ears and tail with paper towels soaked in fat and wrap with heavy foil. Place the pig on a rack in a heavy roasting pan. Bake, uncovered, at 450° for 15 minutes. Reduce the heat to 325° and roast until tender, allowing 35 minutes to the pound. Baste every 15 minutes with drippings; do not add water.

Remove the foil and paper towels 15 minutes before the roast is done. When completely cooked, remove the block and insert the apple in the pig's mouth.

Twelve servings

Pork Dessert

A pork dessert is no common thing, after a pork dinner or any other kind of dinner. This may well be the only one. We were not sure that one existed or could be created. That was a challenge. But research, imagination, and testing yielded their reward.

Novelty is not the only virtue of this dessert. It is relatively easy to make; ingredients are readily available. It keeps well. It goes with either luncheon or dinner menus. Above all, it tastes good.

Surprise Cake, made by the following recipe, will finish a meal not only with a happy surprise, but also with a flourish, and maybe with a guessing game!

We know it makes a fine end to a meal, and we consider it a fitting end to our recipes.

SURPRISE CAKE

½   **pound ground pork**
1   **cup boiling water**
½   **cup molasses**
1   **cup granulated sugar**
2¾   **cups all-purpose flour**
½   **plus ⅛ teaspoon baking soda**
1   **tablespoon ground cinnamon**
1½   **teaspoons ground cloves**
1½   **teaspoons grated nutmeg**
1⅓   **cups raisins**
2   **ounces citron**
⅓   **cup diced dates**
½   **cup chopped walnuts or pecans**
½   **cup gumdrops, cut up fine**
2   **tablespoons brandy**
¼   **teaspoon salt**

Pour the boiling water over the pork and allow it to stand until it is almost cool. Mix the molasses and sugar, add to the pork, and blend. Sift the flour. Add the soda, cinnamon, cloves, nutmeg, and salt and sift again. Add to the pork mixture and blend thoroughly. Fold in the raisins, citron, dates, nuts, and candy and pour the batter into a well-greased loaf pan, 5 × 9 × 4 inches. Bake at 275° for 2 hours, or until a cake tester comes out clean.

When the cake is cool, pour the brandy evenly over the top. Wrap in foil and allow to stand for a day or two before serving. This cake will keep for weeks in the refrigerator. It also freezes very satisfactorily.

OUTDOOR COOKERY

Cooking out-of-doors is one of the pleasantest of American enthusiasms. It gets everyone out of the kitchen at mealtime and allows the man of the house to demonstrate his prowess with the grill and rotisserie. Outdoor meals can be enjoyed on a rooftop in the city, in a postage-stamp-sized backyard, or on an elegant terrace in suburbia. There is something about the sizzle of the meat cooking, the glow of the embers, the aroma of the smoke, and the fresh air that appeals to young and old alike.

There are so many kinds of barbecue equipment that it will be best here if we just stick to the general rules for success. The first thing to do is to build your fire early enough so that it will have burned down to coals by the time you are ready to cook. A shallow bed of coals will do for chops or kebabs. A deeper fire is required for roasts and other thick cuts. It is important to be able to adjust the distance between the meat and the fire. This helps to hasten or to slow down the cooking process and gives much greater flexibility. Incidentally, in our lexicon, "to barbecue" means to cook over an open fire of glowing coals, whether wood or charcoal.

A very good way to shorten the time required for barbecuing certain cuts of pork is to precook them in the oven. You may wish to do this either for your own convenience or because this method is a good way to prevent the larger cuts from drying out. Spareribs and roasts are two good examples. If the ribs are cooked entirely over charcoal, the fat dripping into the fire causes flare-ups and the ribs may end up charred. You may precook the ribs by putting them in boiling water for 15 minutes. Then drain and grill them. If the ribs are given long, slow cooking in the oven, most of the fat is cooked out. During a short period over the coals, the ribs will absorb enough charcoal flavor and will be sufficiently cooked to be crisp and delicious. While over the charcoal, the ribs may be basted with a favorite barbecue sauce.

One very good way to precook a roast is to rub the outside with oil (do not season it) and bake it at 325° until it is three-quarters done. You can depend on minutes per pound (see chart) or use a meat thermometer. The roast can then be left at room temperature until you are ready to continue, or it can be taken to the outside fire at once. Before putting the roast over the charcoal, season it with salt and pepper or, if the meat or bones appear to be dry, add the seasonings to more oil and rub it over the roast.

Marinades play a very useful role in preparing pork for charcoal cooking. Depending upon their composition, they add subtle variations to the flavor of the meat. Primarily their purpose is tenderizing. When oil is one of the ingredients, it helps to keep the meat moist and juicy while it cooks. Many marinades should mellow for 12 to 24 hours before using. Many of them can also be used as a sauce, sometimes with a few additions, sometimes just as they are. When ready for use, the meat may be immersed in the marinade for as little as 2 hours or as much as 24. For short periods of time, marination is best accomplished at room temperature. For longer periods, it should be under refrigeration.

There are many recipes for marinades and except for the basic ingredients they can be varied as the cook sees fit. Some that are especially suited to pork are included in this book. In general it is best to use the homemade variety rather than a commercially prepared product. The latter tends to make the texture of the meat soft and pulpy rather than genuinely tender. If you do not marinate the meat you are charcoaling, it is advisable to rub the surface with olive or cooking oil or to use butter as described in the recipe for Quick Serve Smoked Chops.

The delicate, mild flavor of pork is especially suitable for barbecue sauces. A number of different types have been included in the glazes and sauces section. They lend variety, and the changes that may be made in ingredients are almost endless—another opportunity for the creative cook.

There are always unpredictables, besides the weather. The coals may be hotter than you thought, among the guests you may have late arrivals or slow drinkers. But no matter what the difficulties, guests and food must be ready at the same time. So choose your pork cut carefully, with all hazards taken into account. If you want a cut that will cook in minimum time, smoked chops are ideal. If you want something that does not require split-second timing but that is long and slow, a rolled roast is a good choice. In between, and in addition to these, there is a varied selection of pork for the barbecue. The recipes here go from the simple to the elaborate but all of them are delicious. They should give you pleasure and earn you compliments. So roll out the barbecue equipment and light the fire!

SOME HOW-TO HINTS FOR ROTISSERIE ROASTS

The rod must be inserted lengthwise through the center of the roast. A good way to test this is by supporting the two ends in the palms of your hands and rotating them gently to make sure that the meat does not slip. Fasten the meat securely. Insert a meat thermometer at a slight angle, making sure the tip is in the center of the roast and not touching the rotisserie rod or bone or resting in fat. The dial of the thermometer must clear the cooking unit and the drip pan while the meat is revolving. The meat should be removed from the heat and the rod removed when the thermometer registers 5° below the desired temperature because the meat will continue to cook even after being taken from the heat.

Some suggested cuts:

6- to 8-pound pork loin roll: allow 2½ to 3½ hours.

9- to 11-pound boneless leg of pork (also called fresh ham): allow 3½ to 4½ hours.

STORAGE ADVICE

If pork is to arrive at the table with its natural flavor unimpaired, this must be preserved at every step from producer to serving platter. An important part of this protective procedure includes proper preservation of the meat between purchase and cooking. This is usually the cook's responsibility.

Home storage is necessary; it requires both knowledge and skill. An adequately stocked refrigerator and freezer are reassuring, convenient, and economical. They allow for the unexpected guest and for sudden changes in family plans. They permit buying when quality is highest and cost is lowest.

Pork is tender and its flavor is delicate. It must be stored with care to protect both. The same storage periods do not apply to all meats; the timetable here applies only to pork. The following is a summary of the most important points to remember in refrigerating or freezing it.

A. *REFRIGERATION*

Fresh Pork

1. Do not wash.
2. Store in the coldest part of the refrigerator. Safest temperature is just above freezing.
3. Wrapping (other than self-service wrap) should be removed and the meat rewrapped loosely in waxed paper or aluminum foil. Store no longer than two days.
4. Self-service wrapped cuts should be refrigerated in the unopened original wrapper. Store no longer than two days.
5. Refrigerate variety meats and ground and cubed meats as above. Store for one to three days. For longer periods, freeze.
6. Do not try to freeze meats in the ice cube compartment. That is not its purpose.

Cured, Smoked Pork

1. Refrigerate all cured, smoked, cured and smoked pork, sausages, and ready-to-serve pork products in their original wrappings.

Canned

1. Do not freeze.
2. Refrigerate, unless directions on the container say otherwise.

Frozen

1. Put in the freezer or refrigerator immediately after purchase.

Home-Cooked

1. Cool quickly (within two hours), uncovered. Refrigerate tightly covered.

B. *FREEZING*

1. Keep the freezer at 0° or below at all times.
2. Wrap the meat properly (see below).
3. Freeze quickly.
4. Freeze meat while in top condition; freezing will not improve quality.
5. Do not refreeze defrosted meat. It should only be refrozen if it is still very cold. There will be some sacrifice of juiciness.
6. Keep all meat, wrappers, hands, and work surfaces clean; freezing does not sterilize.
7. Follow the freezer storage chart for correct lengths of safe, satisfactory freezer storage.
8. Thaw frozen meat in the refrigerator (in its wrapping) or during cooking.
9. Cook thawed meat promptly.

To Wrap

1. Use a moistureproof and vaporproof wrapping material.
2. Do not salt the meat.
3. Wrap in family-sized packages; place a double thickness of moistureproof paper or freezer wrap between each chop or steak or pattie before wrapping in a package.
4. Fold the wrapper tightly around the meat; make the package smooth; expel as much air as possible, otherwise you risk freezer burn.
5. Label with name, date, amount in weight or servings.

To Store

1. Allow space for air among packages during initial freezing time.
2. Arrange unfrozen packages against a refrigerated surface, not touching packages already frozen.

MAXIMUM PORK STORAGE TIME-TABLE

CUT	Refrigerator *36°–40° **	Freezer *0° or lower*
Pork (fresh)	2–4 days	3–6 months
Pork (ground)	1–2 days	1–3 months
Variety meats	1–2 days	3–4 months
Sausage (fresh)	1 week	2 months
Sausage (smoked)	3–7 days	
Sausage (dry and semidry, unsliced)	2–3 weeks	
Bacon	5–7 days	1 month
Smoked ham (whole)	1 week	2 months
Ham slices	3–4 days	2 months
Leftover cooked meat	4–5 days	2 to 3 months

* The range in time reflects recommendations for maximum storage time from several authorities.

PORK
FOR HEALTH
AND PLEASURE

For ages man has been concerned about what he eats and its relationship to his health and well-being. Egyptian documents as far back as 3000 B.C. attest to this. Scientific knowledge about food values, however, has only recently been acquired, coming into its own in the nineteenth and twentieth centuries.

Even a brief consideration of nutrition (all that is necessary here) begins with information about proteins and includes vitamins and minerals. Caloric values determine the energy-producing power of what we eat.

Meat makes one of the largest contributions of all foods to the requirements for proteins, which are essential to life and growth. They are the fundamental structural element of every cell in the body. They are well named; the word is of Greek derivation and means "of first importance."

Pork eaters are sure of getting their nutritional quota. The high-quality protein content of pork from all cuts easily supplies the recommended daily dietary need. For pleasure and health, a serving of pork one or more times a day would not be out of order. The many cuts and the great variety of ways to cook pork make this easy and pleasant.

Vitamins, although unnamed and unidentified, were known to exist in ancient times, by the effect of their absence rather than by knowledge of their essential nutritional elements. They were referred to as "necessary food factors" long before anyone knew what they were or how they worked.

Pork is an ideal source of thiamin, niacin and riboflavin, included in the vitamin B complex. Dietary needs are now well established, and modest pork servings can supply most of them.

Minerals, like some other body constituents, are small in amount but large in importance. Among the ten or more minerals most useful to the

278

body, iron, calcium, and phosphorus are of concern to dietitians. Pork can be depended on to supply a high percentage of the body's need for iron, a necessary constituent of red blood cells. Pork's yield of this mineral is among the highest of all meats.

In their cold calculation of calories and their hot pursuit of diet fads, weight watchers risk losing sight of the value of a balanced diet and thereby defeat their purpose. It is important for the overweight, the underweight, and those in between to remember that a healthful diet includes proteins, carbohydrates, and fats in accurate proportions. A 3½-ounce serving of lean, cooked pork provides approximately 28.5 grams of protein and 13 grams of fat, making a modest total of 240 calories. No matter what their source in the diet, all calories consumed in excess of those utilized for growth or maintenance or expended as energy are eventually stored in adipose tissue.

The healthy feeling of having enjoyed a meal, of having had plenty even with modest servings, depends largely on how slowly a meal is digested. The fat in marbleized pork slightly slows digestion and thus contributes to this pleasant, satisfied feeling. Several old notions about pork have been pushed aside by scientific information. One of these is that pork is hard to digest. This has been dispelled by a better understanding of fat in the digestive process. It is also true that hogs now go to market with a much lower fat content than their forebears. Another notion is that pork is not a summer food. This has also shared the fate of being outmoded by better knowledge. Pork, hot or cold, is a pleasant and healthful dish for all seasons.

All animal meats, including fats, contain some cholesterol. The controversy over this complex chemical, essential to life, is for the scientists. The cook may be aided by a few facts. Cholesterol is synthesized in the body as well as ingested. The amount of cholesterol in pork (exclusive of variety meats) is very low, being only 70 milligrams in 100 grams of an edible portion. Only a few foods rank lower than this. The polyunsaturated fats are of vegetable origin and the ones most often used in cookery are the oils from corn, soybeans, safflower, and sesame. These fats and the food products made from them are generally recommended by dietitians for those whose physiological chemistry is known to produce above-average cholesterol levels in the blood serum. Extensive studies of the relationship of the serum cholesterol level to coronary heart disease and circulatory conditions have been made.

Anyone with symptoms of heart or circulatory disease or anyone anxious about serum cholesterol levels should be under the care of a physician.

Although the number of hogs in the United States infected by trichinae (tiny worms that live in the hog's muscle) is low, the disease trichinosis may be contracted by eating insufficiently cooked pork. The basic health and cookery rule is cook pork thoroughly. This kills any parasites that might be present. It is impossible to identify an infected animal or the meat that comes from it by its appearance. Looking at the hog or the meat on the meat counter does not indicate presence or absence of the infecting parasite. The United States Department of Agriculture stresses thorough cooking for fresh, cured, and smoked pork and pork products—sausage, frankfurters, and so forth. Neither heat used in smoking nor temperatures and procedures used in home freezing destroy the parasite. The meat thermometer is a safe temperature guide for cooking all large cuts. It must register 170°. If pricking or making a small cut into chops or other pieces yields the least sign of pink juice, they must be cooked longer. Only tenderized hams stamped *Federally Inspected and Passed* have been processed to kill trichinae. The Department of Agriculture warns against even tasting any uncooked pork, such as sampling raw sausage for flavor, a taste test hard to resist.

After this brief survey of the natural content of pork and the health and pleasure it provides, we come to what growers, processors, cooks, and eaters add to it. Cooks since the beginning of cookery have enhanced the appearance of their culinary efforts with coloring and contributed to taste and preservation with spices and herbs. These early cooks would be bewildered by the thousands of "additives"—estimated at an individual annual consumption of five pounds for Americans—that producers and eaters now put into food. The cost of these is said to run into millions of dollars. Nearly a thousand have been determined safe under conditions of use. The record of some others is not so reassuring. They make the buyer's choice difficult, although they add to the attractiveness or to the preservation of many meats. The wary buyer can read the list of contents on the package and with diligent study become familiar with their significance.

METRIC MEASURE

The metric system of measures, based on decimals, was developed in France in the 1700's. Although the United States has been slow in adopting it for domestic and international trade, our country was the first large nation to use a decimal monetary system. Metric measurements were made legal, but not mandatory, in the United States in 1866. We are one of the few countries not now using the decimal system for all measurements. While others have enjoyed its simplicity and accuracy we have clung to unwieldy and inexact units based on the stride of a Roman soldier (foot), barleycorns (grain), and the distance from the tip of a king's nose to the end of his outstretched hand (yard).

The original metric system has not only been modified, refined, and extended, it also has changed its name. The modernized version of the seven basic units is now technically referred to as SI, for International System of Units (from the French Le Système International d'Unités).

Use of the metric system increases every year in the United States and it has already invaded the kitchen. Many containers of canned and packaged products carry the volume or weight in both the customary U.S. system (pounds, ounces; pints, quarts) and also the equivalent metric units.

Practice quickly indicates the convenience of metric measures in cooking. The relationship of all metric units is in multiples of ten. The system banishes common fractions, making it possible to expand or reduce a recipe without calling in the high school math teacher.

Here are the metric equivalents and conversion guides for volumes, weights and temperatures frequently used in home cooking. These are based on conversion guides recommended by the Bureau of Standards. More extensive information is available from the Bureau.

281

METRIC EQUIVALENTS FOR COMMON COOKING MEASURES

(close working approximations)

VOLUME

1 teaspoon	equals	5 milliliters
1 tablespoon	"	15 ml
1 ounce (fluid)	"	30 ml
1 cup (8 fluid ounces)	"	250 ml
1 pint	"	500 ml
1 quart	"	1000 ml

WEIGHT

1 ounce	"	28 grams
1 pound	"	450 grams
2.2 pounds	"	1 kilogram

TEMPERATURE

Metric temperatures are reckoned on the Celsius scale, named for Anders Celsius, Swedish astronomer of the 1700s, who invented the centigrade thermometer.

Freezing point (of water) is 32° F
" " " " 0° C
Boiling point (of water) is 212° F
" " " " 100° C

To convert Fahrenheit temperatures to Celsius:
1. Subtract 32 from the Fahrenheit temperature
2. Multiply the remainder by 5
3. Divide the product by 9

Example: oven temperature of 350° F
-32
$318 \times 5 = 1590 \div 9 = 176.6° C$

GLOSSARY

COOKERY TERMS

Bake: To cook, covered or uncovered, in an oven.

Barbecue: To roast or broil on a rack or revolving spit in front of, over, or under the heat source. The meat is usually basted with a sauce.

Baste: To moisten roasting meat or other food with juice from the pan or with another liquid.

Blend: To combine ingredients by stirring rather than beating.

Bouillon: A strong meat stock, strained and degreased.

Cube: To cut into small cubes.

Dice: To cut into very small cubes.

Deglaze: To use a hot liquid, usually stock or wine, to loosen bits of meat clinging to the cooking utensil for use as a basis for sauce or gravy.

Dredge: To coat completely with flour or sugar.

Drippings: The fat exuded while meat is being cooked.

En brochette: A French term describing food cooked and served on skewers.

Garnish: To decorate or to enhance the flavor or appearance of food by adding edibles, such as fruit or vegetables, to the dish just before serving.

Glaze: An edible glossy coating, cooked on.

Julienne: Long, narrow strips of meat or vegetables.

Kebab: Pieces of meat threaded on a skewer, usually alternated with vegetables.

Marinade: A seasoned liquid frequently having an acid base, in which meat (or other food) is soaked in order to tenderize and flavor it.

Mince: To cut into very fine pieces.

Mousse (in meat cookery): A combination of meat and vegetables, molded in gelatin.

283

Parboil: To partially cook by boiling before completely cooking by another method.

Pâté: A paste or spread made of lean and fat meat, served as a canapé or hors d'oeuvre.

Purée: To put solid food through a sieve, food mill, or blender to make into a mash of even consistency.

Ragoût: A thick and highly seasoned meat stew, with or without vegetables.

Reduce: To evaporate a liquid and to concentrate flavor by cooking without a cover.

Render: To draw fat from meat by heating slowly.

Roast: To cook, uncovered, by dry heat, in an oven or over coals.

Rotisserie: A device for cooking meat by rotating it over, under, or in front of the source of heat.

Roux: A thickening mixture made by blending fat and flour over low heat.

Sauté: To cook or to brown in a skillet using a small amount of hot fat.

Score: To make shallow, even cuts in the surface of meat.

Simmer: To cook in liquid just below the boiling point over low heat (bubbles breaking just below the surface of the liquid).

Skewer: A long thin metal pin to hold meat intact during cooking.

Spit: A metal rod on which to fasten meat for roasting or grilling.

Stock: Strained liquid in which meat, fish, or vegetables have been cooked.

HOG TERMS

Barrow: A male hog, castrated.

Boar: A male hog.

Farrow: A litter of pigs; to give birth to pigs.

Gilt: A young female hog.

Hogs: Domestic swine.

Lace fat (or caulfat): A thin membrane of white fat surrounding the hog's stomach.

Pig: A young hog.

Piglet: A baby pig.

Piggery: A place to keep or raise hogs.

Piggywidden: The runt of a litter.

Pork: The meat of the hog.
Porker: A young hog fattened for market.
Shoat (Shote): A young pig.
Sow: A fully grown female hog.
Stag: A castrated boar.
Swine: A collective term for hogs.
Swineherd: A tender or keeper of hogs.

INDEX

287